Photoshop® CS
QuickSteps

Photoshop® CS
QuickSteps

CAROLE MATTHEWS

MARK CLARKSON

DOUG SAHLIN

ERIK POULSEN

McGraw-Hill/Osborne

New York Chicago San Francisco
Lisbon London Madrid Mexico City
Milan New Delhi San Juan
Seoul Singapore Sydney Toronto

McGraw-Hill/Osborne
2100 Powell Street, 10th Floor
Emeryville, California 94608
U.S.A.

To arrange bulk purchase discounts for sales promotions, premiums, or fund-raisers, please contact McGraw-Hill/Osborne at the above address. For information on translations or book distributors outside the U.S.A., please see the International Contact Information page immediately following the index of this book.

234567890 WCK WCK 01987654

ISBN 0-07-223231-5

PUBLISHER / Brandon A. Nordin

VICE PRESIDENT AND ASSOCIATE PUBLISHER / Scott Rogers

ACQUISITIONS EDITOR / Roger Stewart

ACQUISITIONS COORDINATOR / Jessica Wilson

TECHNICAL EDITOR / Keith Eyer

COPY EDITOR / Harriet O'Neal

PROOFREADERS / Mike McGee, Kellen Diamanti

INDEXER / Deborah Fisher

LAYOUT ARTISTS / Keith Eyer, Bailey Cunningham

ILLUSTRATORS / Kathleen Edwards, Pattie Lee, Bruce Hopkins

SERIES DESIGN / Bailey Cunningham

COVER DESIGN / Patti Lee

Dedications:

Carole Matthews:

To Tank, Domino, and Tortise, my shadows and faithful companions. If they hadn't interrupted my computer work occasionally, I might have become permanently joined to the computer at the mouse!

Mark Clarkson:

To Joe, without whose diligent efforts this would have been much easier.

Doug Sahlin:

To the digital artist lurking in every Photoshop user.

Erik Poulsen

To Murphy and Ella, whose smiles say so much to us all.

About the Authors

Carole Boggs Matthews:

Carole Boggs Matthews has been around computers, as a programmer, systems analyst, technical consultant, and founder, co-owner, and Vice-President of a software company. She has been on all sides of computer software products, from designer and builder to an accomplished user of software in her business. Together with Marty Matthews, her husband, she has authored or co-authored over 40 books, including *Microsoft Office PowerPoint 2003 QuickSteps, Microsoft Office FrontPage 2003, The Complete Reference;* and *The Official Guide to CorelDraw! 6*.

Mark Clarkson

Mark Clarkson has been a professional writer since 1987, and a daily Photoshop user since that program first appeared under Windows in 1993. He is the author of four books, including *Photoshop Secrets of the Pros*, and a co-author and contributing author on three more. His books range in subject from Photoshop and cartooning to artificial life and robotics. A self-described dilettante, he lives with his wife and two children in Wichita, Kansas, and rarely leaves the basement.

Doug Sahlin:

Doug Sahlin is an author, photographer, graphic designer, and web site designer living in Central Florida. He uses Photoshop CS as his digital darkroom, and to edit and create images for client multimedia presentations and web sites. He is the author of 12 books on computer graphics and web animation including *How To Do Everything with Macromedia Contribute* and *How To Do Everything with Adobe Acrobat 6.0*, which was recently ranked 22nd in Amazon's top 50 computer books. He has authored online Flash courses, presented on-location seminars, and has co-authored a book on digital video.

Erik Poulsen:

Erik B. Poulsen is a Senior Web Developer with Sherman Software Solutions. Erik has more than 16 years of computer experience and works with corporations developing ASP.NET and database-driven web applications. He has also collaborated with the Matthews on a number of book projects, *including FrontPage 2003, The Complete Reference*.

Contents at a Glance

Chapter 1 **Stepping into Photoshop CS** 1
Get acquainted with Photoshop CS, use its tools and palettes, assign keyboard shortcuts, work with colors, and calibrate your monitor.

Chapter 2 **Creating, Importing, and Saving Images** 25
Learn about working with image types, using the File Browser to search and work with files, user scanners, and digital cameras

Chapter 3 **Making Selections** 47
Use Photoshop's selection tools, modify, crop, and manipulate selections, extract images from backgrounds, and use Quick Masks.

Chapter 4 **Using Layers** 65
Create layers, and then rearrange, copy, merge, and group layers. Work with layers masks, layer effects, and use blending modes.

Chapter 5 **Using Paths, Shapes and Painting** 89
Use the Pen and Shape tools to create shapes and paths. Paint with the Brush Tool. Personalize artwork with patterns and filters.

Chapter 6 **Color Correcting, Retouching, and Repairing Images** .. 109
Rotate, flip, straighten, crop, resize, and trim images. Color correct with curves and levels. Sharpen, blur, and retouch images.

Chapter 7 **Using Type and Type Effects** 137
Create and edit text, use text tasks, such as check spelling. Warp text, transform text, use paths, layer styles, and text masks.

Chapter 8 **Printing and Exporting Images** 151
Print all or part of an image. Create a contact sheet or a picture package, and save images, Add a digital copyright or metadata.

Chapter 9 **Preparing Your Art for the Web** 165
Optimize images for the web, use image maps, use ImageReady to slice images and use rollovers and states, animate your images.

Chapter 10 **Saving Time with Actions and Automations** 191
Automate images, work with the Actions palette to record actions, use the Automate Menu, and the Web Photo Gallery.

Index 217

1
2
3
4
5
6
7
8
9
10

Contents

Acknowledgments...xv

Introduction xvii

Chapter 1 **Stepping into Photoshop CS** 1

   Get Acquainted with Photoshop 1
     Start and Close Photoshop...2
     Set Photoshop Preferences 4
     Use the Photoshop Workspace 5
     Open and Create Images in Photoshop 6
     Creating a Preset 8
     Work with Photoshop's Interface 8
     Navigating within Your Document 10
     Use Photoshop's Online Help 11
     Work with Palettes 12
     Using the Palette Well 13
     Prepare and Save Your Workspace 13
     Turning a Text Box into a Slider 14
     Assign Keyboard Shortcuts 14
     Selecting Screen Modes 15
   Introducing Photoshop's Tools..16
     Work with Tool Options 18
     Set Foreground and Background Colors 19
     Undoing Actions..20
     Use the History Palette to Undo 20
     Work with the History Brush 21
     Work with Color and Calibration 22
     Work with Hue, Saturation and Luminance 23
     Calibrate Your Monitor 24

Chapter 2 **Creating, Importing, and Saving Images** 25

   Work with Image Types..25
     Understand Bitmaps..25
     Understand Vector Shapes...26
     Understanding Compression..27
     Work with Dimension vs. Resolution 27
     Understanding Bit Depth 29
     Use Grayscale 29
     Use RGB..29
     Use CMYK..30
     Use Indexed Color 30
   Use the File Browser..31
     View, Select, and Open files 31
     Sort, Flag, Rank, and Rearrange Files 33
     Customize the File Browser...34
     Saving and Loading a File Browser Workspace..................................36
     Search for Files..36

Rename, Move, Copy, and Delete Files..37
Importing from Adobe Illustrator..38
Save your Files...38
Use Scanners and Digital Cameras 40
Scan in Photoshop..40
Import Digital Photos...42
Work with Camera Raw Images...42

Chapter 3 **Making Selections** 47

Creating New Selections 47
Use the Marquee Tool...47
Use the Magic Wand Tool...48
Constraining Your Selections..49
Use the Lasso Tools...50
Select a Range of Colors..51
Exclude with Selections..52
Change, Save, and Load Selections..52
Modify a Selection..52
Anti-aliasing and Feathering...53
Crop to a Selection..54
Delete Using Selections..55
Expanding Selections..55
Remove Fringe Pixels..55
Save and Load Selections..56
Moving and Duplicating...56
Extract Images from Backgrounds...57
Copy to a New Layer...57
Copy to a New Document..57
Extract Background Elements...57
Use the Magic Eraser Tool..60
Use the Background Eraser Tool...60
Painting Selections with Quick Masks 62
Create a Quick Mask...62
Crop to a Selection..63
Use with the Pen Tool...63

Chapter 4 **Using Layers** 65

Work with Layers...65
Create New Layers...67
Hiding and Revealing Layers..67
Linking and Unlinking Layers..68
Work with the Background of a Layer...68
Copy Merged Layers...68
Rearrange Layer Order..69
Manipulating Layer Sets...70
Delete a Layer..70
Group Layers into Layer Sets...70
Flattening an Image...71
Merge Layers...71

Work with Layer Masks..72
    Create Layer Masks..72
    Editing a Mask 73
    Masking a Layer Set 74
Work with Layer Effects 76
    Add Layer Drop Shadows 77
    Create a Frame with Layer Effects...77
    Save and Load Layer Styles 79
Blend Modes and Transparency..80
    Work with Opacity and Fill 80
    Use Blend Modes..81
    Create an Adjustment Layer...83
    Creating a Quick Sepia Tone with a Color Layer.........................85
    Create a Collage 85

Chapter 5 **Using Paths, Shapes, and Painting**.............................89

Use the Pen Tool as a Drawing Tool...89
    Understand Bitmap and Vector Graphics.....................................90
    Use the Pen Tool 90
    Using the Freeform Pen Tool 92
    Use the Magnetic Pen Tool...92
    Use Paths to Create Artwork 93
    Stroke and Fill Paths 93
    Converting Selections...94
    Use the Shape Tools 94
    Editing Shapes 95
Work with Paint 95
    Use the Brush Tool 95
    Selecting Foreground and Background Colors 96
    Manage Brush Presets 98
    Using the Eraser Tool 99
    Erase Pixels...99
    Use the Gradient Tool 100
    Use the Paint Bucket Tool 102
    Create and Manage Patterns...102
    Use the Pattern Maker 102
    Use the Art History Brush...104
    Use the Preset Manager 105
Work with Filters 106
    Use the Filter Gallery 106
    Use the Liquify Filter 107

Chapter 6 **Color Correcting, Retouching, and Repairing Images** 109

Perform Simple Image Corrections 109
    Rotate and Flip the Images 110
    Straighten a Photo with Free Transform.....................................110
    Straightening a Photo with the Measure Tool + Rotate Canvas 111
    Resize and Trim Images 111

Using the Crop Command 114
Using the Eyedropper Tool 115
Color Correct with Curves and Levels 115
Use a Histogram to View the Tonal Range 115
Adjust Tonal Range with Levels 117
Use the Curves Command 119
Color Correct Images 123
Using Color Balance 124
Edit in 16-Bit Mode 129
Working with Adjustment Layers 130
Sharpen and Blur Images 130
Fine-tuning with the Sharpen, Blur, and Smudge Tools 131
Retouch and Repair Images 132
Changing Image Colors 134
Use the Dust & Scratches Filter 134
Creating a Sepia Tone from a Color or Grayscale Photo 136

Chapter 7 **Using Type and Type Effects** 137

Create and Edit Text 138
Create Text 138
Edit Type 140
Committing Type 140
Hyphenating and Justifying Type 141
Use Check Spelling 142
Transforming Type 143
Find and Replace Text 143
Warp Text 144
Create Text on a Path 144
Edit Text on a Path 145
Create Text within a Closed Path 145
Finding and Using Layer Styles 146
Add Special Type Effects with Layer Styles 146
Create Text Masks 150

Chapter 8 **Printing and Exporting Images** 151

Print Your Work 151
Preparing the Image for Printing 152
Print Images with a Desktop Printer 152
Printing a Single Copy of a Page 155
Print Vector Graphics 155
Printing Part of an Image 156
Use Color Management When Printing 156
Create a Contact Sheet 157
Create a Picture Package 159
Saving a Document 160
Save Images 160
Use the Save As Command 160
Save a Layered File 161

Add File Information and Metadata 162
Create a Digital Copyright..162
Import Document Metadata 163
Save Document Metadata as a Template 163
Create a PDF Presentation 163

Chapter 9 **Preparing Your Art for the Web** 165

Optimize Images for the Web...165
Optimize Using the Save For Web Dialog Box 166
Making Part of an Image Transparent...168
Creating Your Own Optimization Settings..169
Work with Image Maps..171
Work with Hexadecimal Values for Color...172
Using Layers to Create Image Maps 173
Set Output Options 173
Working with ImageReady..176
Slice an Image 176
Use Rollovers and States 179
Saving Sliced Images...180
Preview Images in a Browser 181
Export Layers as Files..182
Animate Your Images...183
Create an Animation..183

Chapter 10 **Saving Time with Actions and Automations** 191

Automate Your Images..191
Work with the Actions Palette...192
Record an Action to Automate a Multistep Task...193
Play and Undo Actions..194
Setting Playback Options 195
Edit Actions...195
Changing Action Options..197
Work with the Automate Menu 198
Use the Batch Command..198
Create a Droplet from an Action 199
Fitting an Image...201
Crop and Straighten Photos...201
Use Picture Package...202
Adding Copyright Information to an Image...206
Adding Digital Watermarks to an Image 207
Use Web Photo Gallery..208
Create a Panorama with Photomerge 213

Index...217

Acknowledgments

The people producing this book have been exceptionally talented and very hard working. They have been dedicated to making this book one to match their capabilities, which are substantial. And I think you'll find they succeeded. One wonderful by-product of the book has been the supportive and cohesive team that has been developed. Although many members of the team may never personally meet, they have interacted in a professional and caring way.

Harriet O'Neal, copy editor, worked tirelessly for long hours to bring four authors together, each with a distinctive voice, to make them readable and consistent. She gave us that secure feeling that comes from knowing that our mistakes and awkward wording would be discovered and corrected. Thank you Harriet, for your dedication and professionalism.

Keith Eyer, layout artist and prepress expert, worked long hours to lay out most of the book chapters with creative skill. The "look" of the pages belongs largely to Keith who took our writings and made them beautiful. Thanks, Keith, for your attention to detail.

Bailey Cunningham, series designer and layout artist, helped to lighten the load, laying out some of the chapters, and providing endless support to all of us. Thanks, Bailey, for your being there, for whomever needed it.

Mike McGee, proof reader, found those hidden and elusive errors that escaped all the other pairs of bleary eyes, and made the book better. Thanks, Mike, for those late hours.

Kellen Diamante, proofreader, stepped in to help out when the schedule was particularly demanding. Thanks, Kellen, for your skillful proofing and supportiveness.

Deborah Fisher, indexer, found the important words and ideas and at the last minute, placed them into a comprehensive and very usable index. Thanks, Deborah, for your planning and preparation to pull it all together at the last minute.

Russell Sparkman, consultant, worked with us early in the project to develop ideas and to aim us in the right direction. Thanks, Russell, for your time and willingness to work with us.

Roger Stewart, has been a believer in the QuickSteps idea, and in our abilities to pull it off. He has been at our side, supporting us with his good humor and good will. Thanks, Roger for your very-much appreciated support.

Introduction

QuickSteps books are recipe books for computer users. They answer the question "How do I…?" by providing quick sets of steps to accomplish the most common tasks in a particular program. The sets of steps are the central focus of the book. QuickSteps sidebars show you how to quickly do many small functions or tasks that support the primary functions. Notes, Tips, and Cautions augment the steps, yet they are presented in such a manner as to not interrupt the flow of the steps. The brief introductions are minimal rather than narrative, and numerous illustrations and figures, many with callouts, support the steps.

QuickSteps books are organized by function and the tasks needed to perform that function. Each function is a chapter. Each task, or "How To," contains the steps needed for accomplishing the function along with relevant Notes, Tips, Cautions, and screenshots. Tasks will be easy to find through:

- The Table of Contents, which lists the functional areas (chapters) and tasks in the order they are presented

- A How-To list of tasks on the opening page of each chapter

- The index with its alphabetical list of terms used in describing the functions and tasks

- Color-coded tabs for each chapter or functional area with an index to the tabs just before the Table of Contents

Conventions Used in this Book

Photoshop CS QuickSteps uses several conventions designed to make the book easier for you to follow. Among these are:

- A in the Table of Contents or the How To list in each chapter references a QuickSteps sidebar in a chapter.

- **Bold type** is used for words on the screen that you are to do something with, such as click **Save As** or open **File**.

- *Italic type* is used for a word or phrase that is being defined or otherwise deserves special emphasis.

- <u>Underlined type</u> is used for text that you are to type from the keyboard.

- SMALL CAPITAL LETTERS are used for keys on the keyboard such as **ENTER** and **SHIFT**.

- When you are expected to enter a command, you are told to press the key(s). If you are to enter text or numbers, you are told to type them. Specific letters or numbers to be entered will be underlined.

- When you are to click the mouse button on a screen command or menu, you will be told to "Click File | Open.", or sometimes, "Open **File** and click **Save** For Web."

How to...

- *Start and Close Photoshop*
- *Set Photoshop Preferences*
- *Use the Photoshop Workspace*
- *Open and Create Images in Photoshop*
- *Creating a Preset*
- *Work with Photoshop's Interface*
- *Navigating within Your Document*
- *Use Photoshop's Online Help*
- *Work with Palettes*
- *Using the Palette Well*
- *Prepare and Save Your Workspace*
- *Turning a Text Box into a Slider*
- *Assign Keyboard Shortcuts*
- *Selecting Screen Modes*
- *Work with Tool Options*
- *Set Foreground and Background Colors*
- *Undoing Actions*
- *Use the History Palette to Undo*
- *Work with the History Brush*
- *Work with Hue, Saturation, and Luminance*
- *Calibrate Your Monitor*

Chapter 1
Stepping into Photoshop

This chapter introduces you to some of Photoshop's basic capabilities and its user interface. You will learn to open and close Photoshop, to understand its screens and toolbars, and how to set up the program according to your personal needs. You will learn how to use Photoshop's Help and find additional help and tutorials online. You will get a glimpse into the tools that Photoshop offers and an introduction to working with color and calibration.

Get Acquainted with Photoshop

Getting acquainted with Photoshop involves starting and closing it; setting preferences, such as how to display the pointer; working with the Photoshop workspace and its menus, palettes, and other components; opening and creating images; and using Photoshop's interface, including navigating, zooming, and working with palettes.

I assume that you already know how to turn on the computer and load Windows and that Photoshop has been installed on your computer. Once

Photoshop is installed, you start it as you would any other program. The quickest way to start it is to simply double-click the Photoshop icon on your desktop. However, the most common way is to use the Start menu.

Start and Close Photoshop

You can start Photoshop with a menu, shortcut, or keyboard combination.

USE THE START MENU TO LOAD PHOTOSHOP

To load Photoshop using the Start menu on the Windows task pane:

1. Start your computer and log on to Windows, if necessary.
2. Click **Start**. The Start menu opens.
3. Select **All Programs** and click **Adobe Photoshop CS**.
4. The Photoshop window will open, as shown in Figure 1-1.

When Photoshop first starts, you are greeted by the Welcome Screen, which provides you with quick access to Tips, Tutorials, and tours of Photoshop's new features. If you don't want to see the Welcome screen every time Photoshop starts, deselect the check box labeled **Show This Dialog At Startup**.

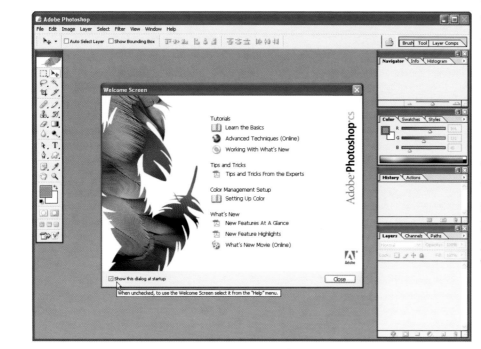

Figure 1-1: By default, the Welcome Screen appears every time you start up Photoshop.

START PHOTOSHOP FROM THE KEYBOARD

1. Press **CTRL+ESC**, or click the **Windows Flag** key on your keyboard to open the Start menu.
2. Press **P** to select the All Programs menu, and press **RIGHT ARROW** to open it.
3. Press **DOWN ARROW** until Adobe Photoshop CS is selected. Then press **ENTER** to start it.

CREATE AND USE A SHORTCUT TO START PHOTOSHOP

Another way to start Photoshop is to create and use a shortcut icon on your desktop.

1. Press **CTRL+ESC**, or click the **Windows Flag** key on your keyboard to open the Start menu.
2. Press **P** to select the All Programs menu, and press **RIGHT ARROW** to open it.
3. Press **DOWN ARROW** until Adobe Photoshop CS is selected.
4. Right-click and select **Send To**, and click **Desktop (Create Shortcut)**.
5. Double-click the shortcut icon on your desktop to start Photoshop.

CREATE AND USE A KEYBOARD SHORTCUT FOR PHOTOSHOP

Another way to start Photoshop is first to create a keyboard shortcut.

1. Press **CTRL+ESC**, or click the **Windows Flag** key on your keyboard to open the Start menu.
2. Press **P** to select the All Programs menu, and press **RIGHT ARROW** to open it.
3. Press **DOWN ARROW** until Adobe Photoshop CS is selected. Right-click; then select **Properties**.
4. Click within the **Shortcut Key** box, and type or press any letter, number, or function key. Windows then adds **ALT+CTRL** to these letters and numbers.
5. Click **OK** to create the keyboard shortcut.
6. From anywhere within Windows, press the key combination you defined (e.g., **ALT+CTRL+P**) to start Photoshop.

TIP

You can still resize a palette in the Palette Well by dragging its lower-right corner.

NOTE

If you ever encounter a problem in the layout of your workspace—for example, a palette gets pushed off screen where you can't reach it—click **Window | Workspace | Reset Palette Locations** to restore the workspace to its original layout.

Photoshop CS Properties

General | Shortcut | Compatibility

Photoshop CS

Target type: Application
Target location: Adobe CS
Target: "C:\Art\Programs\Adobe CS\Photoshop.exe"

Start in: "C:\Art\Programs\Adobe CS"
Shortcut key: CTRL + ALT + P
Run: Normal window
Comment:

Find Target...   Change Icon...   Advanced...

OK   Cancel   Apply

CLOSE PHOTOSHOP

1. Click **File** on the menu bar.

2. Click **Exit**. You will be prompted to save any unsaved work.

Set Photoshop Preferences

You can make changes in the way Photoshop works by setting its *Preferences*. You can change the look of the tool pointers, the color of guidelines, which units of measure you prefer to work in (e.g., inches, centimeters, or pixels) and much more. When you are first learning Photoshop, it is best to leave the default preferences intact. When you understand the implications, however, this is where you make changes.

Figure 1-2: The General page is the first of many pages of Photoshop preferences.

1. On the menu bar, click **Edit**, select **Preferences** and then **General Preferences**. The Photoshop Preferences dialog box appears, as shown in Figure 1-2.

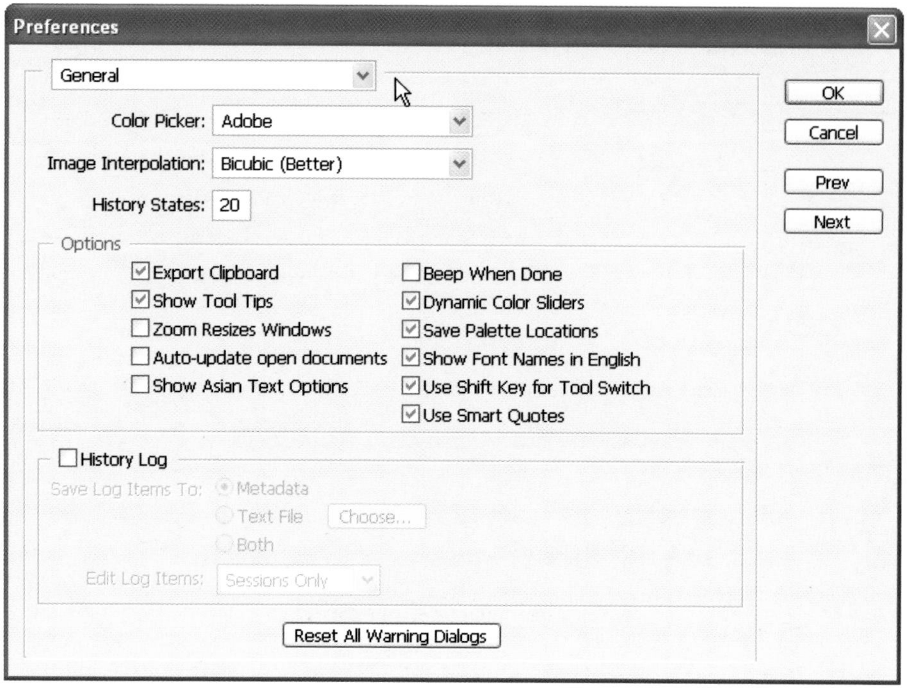

2. Click **Next** and **Previous** to cycle through Photoshop's nine pages of preferences. You will see these choices:

- General
- File Handling
- Display And Cursors
- Transparency And Gamut
- Units And Rulers
- Guides, Grid And Slices
- Plug-ins And Scratch disks
- Memory And Image Cache
- File Browser

All of the Preferences can be left at their defaults for now.

CHANGE CURSOR PREFERENCES

One preference that I *do* prefer to change is the display of the tool cursors. By default, Photoshop shows each tool cursor as an icon, indicating what tool is active. I prefer to use a cursor that shows the size and shape of the active tool.

1. From the menu, click **Edit** and select **Preferences** and then **Display And Cursors**.

2. Click **Next** until the Display And Cursors page appears.

3. Under Painting Cursors, click the **Brush Size** button. This shows an outline of the size and shape of the current brush.

4. Under Other Cursors, click the **Precise** button.

5. Click **OK** to close the dialog box.

Use the Photoshop Workspace

The Photoshop workspace appears in Figure 1-3. Yours will look slightly different, depending on what tools, documents, and windows you have open. Any of the items can be closed or moved about on the screen. In Windows, the empty workspace is filled with gray.

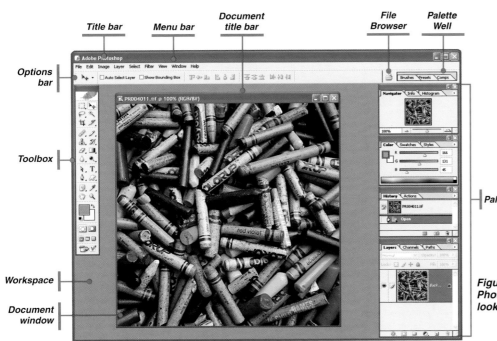

Title bar **Menu bar** **Document title bar** **File Browser** **Palette Well**

Options bar

Toolbox

Palettes

Workspace

Document window

Figure 1-3: The Photoshop workspace looks something like this.

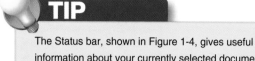

TIP

The Status bar, shown in Figure 1-4, gives useful information about your currently selected document and tool. If the Status Bar does not appear at the very bottom of your Photoshop workspace, turn it on by choosing **Window**, and then selecting **Status Bar**.

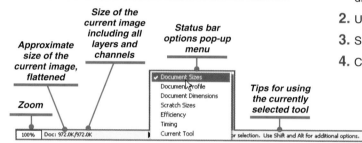

Figure 1-4: The Status bar gives useful information about the current document and tool.

Labels in figure: Approximate size of the current image, flattened; Size of the current image including all layers and channels; Status bar options pop-up menu; Zoom; Tips for using the currently selected tool; Document Sizes; Document Profile; Document Dimensions; Scratch Sizes; Efficiency; Timing; Current Tool; 100%; Doc: 972.0K/972.0K

TIP

If you hover the pointer over a file name in the Open dialog box, a Tool Tip will appear, giving that file's dimension, size, and type.

NOTE

Press **CTRL** while you click to select multiple files; or press **SHIFT** while you click to select a range of files; then click **Open** to open multiple files in Photoshop.

Open and Create Images in Photoshop

Opening a file in Photoshop works the same way as opening a file in almost any Windows program.

OPEN AN IMAGE FROM THE MENU BAR

To open a file in Photoshop from the Menu bar:

1. With Photoshop running and visible, click **File** and then **Open**. The Open dialog box is displayed, as shown in Figure 1-5.

2. Use standard Windows navigation techniques to find the folder containing your image.

3. Select the file name. A thumbnail of the image appears at the bottom of the dialog box.

4. Click **Open** or double-click the file's name to open the file in Photoshop.

Figure 1-5: The Open dialog box shows a thumbnail of selected files.

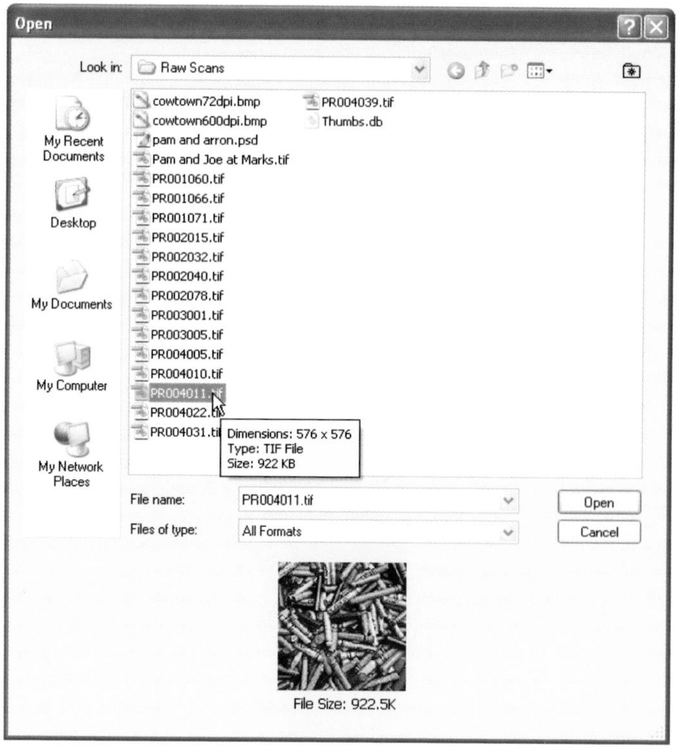

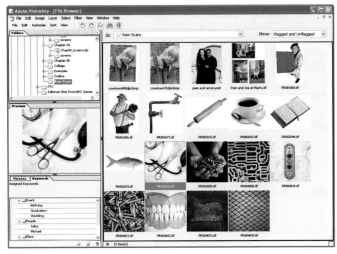

Figure 1-6: The Photoshop File Browser is a powerful tool in finding and opening files.

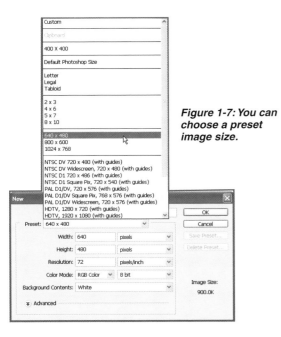

Figure 1-7: You can choose a preset image size.

OPEN AN IMAGE WITH THE FILE BROWSER

Photoshop's File Browser is a powerful way to browse, manage, and open your files. To open a file with the File Browser:

1. With Photoshop running and visible, click the **File Browser** button at the right of the Options bar next to the palette well. The File Browser window opens, as shown in Figure 1-6.

2. Use the Folders pane of the window to navigate to a folder containing images. Thumbnails of all images in the folder will appear in the thumbnails pane.

3. Click any thumbnail to select that file. A preview appears in the preview pane.

4. Double-click a thumbnail to open the file in Photoshop.

You'll see more about using the File Browser in Chapter 2.

CREATE A NEW IMAGE FROM A PRESET

Photoshop allows you to easily create an image from a list of preset sizes and resolutions. To create a new, blank image in Photoshop:

1. From the Menu bar, click **File** and then **New**. The New dialog is displayed.

2. Type in a name for the new blank image.

3. Click the Preset drop-down list box, and choose a preset image size, such as 640x480, as shown in Figure 1-7.

4. Click **OK** to create a new image.

Specify the Width and Height by typing the values in pixels, inches, centimeter, millimeters, point, picas, or columns.

Likewise, you can type in a resolution. The default for web images is 72 pixels/inch; 300 pixels/inch is the default for print images.

The background can be white, transparent, or set to the current background color.

Leave the color mode in either RGB (for color images) or Grayscale (for black and white images). We'll examine some of the other color modes in later chapters.

QUICKSTEPS

CREATING A PRESET

You can create a new preset image size for a frequently created image, such as a 120 pixel x 60 pixel web banner.

1. If the New file dialog box is not open, click **File** and then **New** on the Menu bar to open it.

2. Set the size, resolution, color mode, and background color; then click **Save Preset**.

3. Name the Preset and click **OK** to create it.

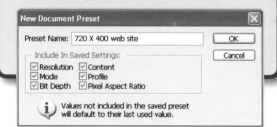

TIP

You can create a new file with the keyboard shortcut **CTRL+N**.

Work with Photoshop's Interface

Photoshop uses mostly standard interface conventions for opening and closing dialog boxes and windows, entering and changing values, and so forth, but it also offers some unique controls.

ZOOM IN AND OUT

Being able to work as close up, or as far away, as you desire is a big advantage. When working on images in Photoshop, you can zoom in until the image is displayed at 16 times its actual size (i.e., 1600 percent larger). At 1600 percent, each pixel in the image is 16 by 16 pixels on the screen. Similarly, you can zoom out until an entire image is only a few pixels wide.

ZOOM WITH THE ZOOM TOOL

1. With an image open and selected in Photoshop, click the **Zoom** tool in the Toolbox, or press **z**, to select the Zoom tool.

2. Click repeatedly within the image to zoom in.

3. Press and hold the **ALT** key. The Zoom tool changes from a + to a –.

4. Press **ALT** and click repeatedly within the image to zoom out.

ZOOM WITH THE KEYBOARD

1. With an image open and selected in Photoshop, press **CTRL++** repeatedly to zoom in.

2. Press **CTRL+-** repeatedly to zoom out.

3. Press **CTRL+0** to zoom the current image to fit on the screen. Press **ALT+CTRL+0** to zoom the current image to 100 percent.

4. Double-click the **Hand** tool in the Toolbox to zoom the current image to 100 percent.

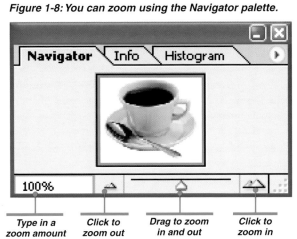

Figure 1-8: You can zoom using the Navigator palette.

Type in a zoom amount | Click to zoom out | Drag to zoom in and out | Click to zoom in

Zooming in and out does not in any way alter the image itself.

TIP

You can temporarily switch to the Hand Tool at any time by pressing the **SPACE BAR**.

ZOOM WITH THE NAVIGATOR PALETTE

1. Open and select an image in Photoshop. If the Navigator palette is not open, click **Window** and then **Navigator**. The Navigator palette is shown in Figure 1-8.

2. Drag the slider right to zoom in and left to zoom out.

-Or-

Click the large mountains at the right of the slider to zoom in, and click the small mountains at the left of the slider to zoom out.

-Or-

Type a zoom amount in the Navigator's text box. To display your image at twice its actual size, type <u>200</u>; for half the image's actual size, <u>50</u>.

ZOOM VIA THE STATUS BAR

1. To open the Status bar, if it is not shown, click **Window** and then **Status Bar**.

2. Type a zoom amount in the text box at the far left of the Status bar.

WORK WITH PHOTOSHOP CONTROLS

You use sliders, drop-down boxes and lists, drop-down controls, fly-out menus, and swatches as controls when working with Photoshop.

USE SLIDERS

Many Photoshop controls use sliders to change values. To use a slider control in Photoshop, click the triangle and hold down the pointer to drag the triangle left (to decrease the value) or right (to increase the value).

USE DROP-DOWN LISTS

Drop-down lists, or boxes, in Photoshop and ImageReady are indicated by this little downward-pointing button.

QUICKSTEPS

NAVIGATING WITHIN YOUR DOCUMENT

It is important to be able to move around within your image, especially when you are zoomed in for detail work.

MOVE AROUND WITH THE NAVIGATOR PALETTE

1. Open an image. If the Navigator palette is not open, open it by clicking **Window | Navigator**.

2. Drag the slider to the right until your image is much larger than the window it's displayed in.

3. Locate the red rectangle within the image thumbnail in the Navigator palette. This represents the visible area of your image.

4. Drag the rectangle to move around within your image, as shown in Figure 1-9.

MOVE AROUND WITH THE HAND TOOL

1. Open an image. Press CTRL++ several times until your image is larger than the window it's displayed in.

2. Click the Hand Tool in the Toolbox, or press H to select the Hand Tool.

3. Drag your image to move it around its window.

Figure 1-9: Drag the red rectangle in the Navigator to move around within your image.

To access a drop-down list:

1. Click the drop-down button.

2. Click your selection in the list.

   -Or-

1. Click within the displayed text of the drop-down list.

2. Use the **UP ARROW** and **DOWN ARROW** on the keyboard to scroll through the list.

USE DROP-DOWN CONTROLS

To access a drop-down control:

1. Click and hold the drop-down button.

2. Drag on the control.

USE FLY-OUT MENUS

Fly-out menus are indicated in Photoshop and ImageReady by this small arrow in a dialog box or by a small arrow at the corner of a tool in the Toolbox.

To access a fly-out menu:

1. Click the fly-out button.

2. Click your selection in the menu.

TIP

Most controls in Photoshop and ImageReady contain a text box which displays the current value. You can click within this text box and type values manually.

TIP

If you hover your pointer over a color swatch in the Swatches palette, the color's name will pop up on a Tool Tip.

USE CONTEXT MENUS

You access context menus, which display additional options, by right-clicking within the canvas, that is, right-clicking the image. To close the pop-up dialog box, either begin using the tool or click anywhere outside of the current canvas.

USE SWATCHES

Photoshop has several palettes and dialog boxes for picking colors. These include the Swatches palette and the Color palette. Simply click a color to select it.

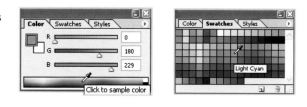

Use Photoshop's Online Help

Photoshop has a comprehensive online help system available from the menu. To access help:

- Press F1

  -Or-

- On the Menu bar, click **Help** and then **Photoshop Help**.

Photoshop's help opens in your default web browser, as shown in Figure 1-10. Navigate through the help from the left pane by searching for keywords or by browsing the alphabetical index, site map, or table of contents.

Figure 1-10: Photoshop's online help displays in your default web browser.

TIP

Click **Help** to find many great tutorials, such as "How to Create Web Images," or "How to Customize and Automate."

TIP

Press the **TAB** key to hide all palettes and give you an uncluttered workspace. Hit **TAB** again to bring them back, in the same positions as before. Press **ALT+TAB** to hide all palettes *except* the Toolbox.

TIP

To minimize or restore palettes, click **Minimize** or **Maximize** at the top of the palette, or double-click the palette's bar, at the top.

Work with Palettes

Photoshop has a number of small windows called palettes, which allow you to choose colors, set paragraph formatting options, sample the RGB values of pixels in an image, manage paths and layers, and so forth. To open a palette, click **Window** and select the name of the palette.

Palettes are grouped together with other related palettes. Each palette has a tab with its name extending from the top. To switch between palettes in a group, click the name tab as shown here:

QUICKSTEPS

USING THE PALETTE WELL

You can dock palettes with the Palette Well at the right of Photoshop's options bar. By default, you'll find the Brushes, Tool Presets, and Layer Comp palettes docked in the palette well, but you can replace any or all of these with the palettes you use most frequently.

USE A PALETTE

To use a palette in the palette well, click the tab and use the palette as you normally would.

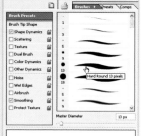

CLOSE A PALETTE

To close a palette, click outside the palette area.

REMOVE A PALETTE FROM THE PALETTE WELL

To remove a palette from the palette well, click the palette's tab, and drag the palette out of the well and into the workspace.

PLACE A NEW PALETTE IN THE PALETTE WELL

Open the palette you want to place in the palette well. Then:

1. Click the fly-out button near the top right of the palette.

2. Choose **Dock To Palette Well** from the fly-out menu.

   -Or-

1. Click and hold the palette's tab.

2. Drag the palette tab into the palette well.

3. Release the pointer.

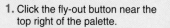

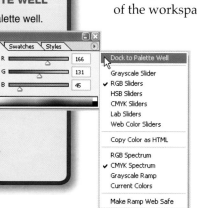

Prepare and Save Your Workspace

Photoshop allows you to customize your workspace–decide which palettes are open, what their positions are on the screen, and so forth–and then to save that workspace. You can create one workspace suitable for browsing through large folders or images and another suitable for retouching scanned photos.

1. Close any palettes you don't want open.

2. Open any additional palettes and windows you do want, and position them where you want them.

3. Click **Window | Workspace | Save Workspace**. The Save Workspace dialog box appears.

4. Type in a unique name, such as "Retouching," for your workspace.

5. Click **OK**.

To retrieve a custom workspace, click **Window** and then **Workspace**; then select the name of the workspace from the menu.

QUICKSTEPS

TURNING A TEXT BOX INTO A SLIDER

You can operate any text box which displays a numerical value, such as font size, like a slider.

1. Place the cursor over the text box.

2. Press and hold the **CTRL** key. The cursor changes to a hand with arrows.

3. Move the mouse left to decrease the displayed number; move the mouse right to increase it.

Assign Keyboard Shortcuts

Photoshop allows you to assign keyboard shortcuts for selecting tools, opening palettes, and selecting menu commands. Some keyboard shortcuts are assigned by default: **B** selects the Brush or Pencil Tool, for example; **F5** opens and closes the Brushes palette. However, you can change these defaults and create new shortcuts to suit the way you work.

ASSIGN A KEYBOARD SHORTCUT TO A MENU COMMAND

Use these steps to assign the keyboard shortcut **ALT+F10** to open and close the Navigator palette. The process is basically the same to create any shortcut.

1. Click **Edit**, choose **Keyboard Shortcuts**. The Keyboard Shortcuts dialog box appears, as shown in Figure 1-11.

2. Click the **Shortcuts For** drop-down button, and click **Application Menus** from the list.

3. Under Application Menu Command, double-click **Window** to expand the list of Window menu items.

4. Scroll down and click **Navigator** to select it. A text box appears to the right of the command name.

5. Press the key combination you want to assign to the Navigator palette, such as **ALT+F10**. Shortcuts must include either a CTRL key, a Function key, or both. Click **OK** to accept the change.

Pressing your select key combinations will now open and close the Navigator palette.

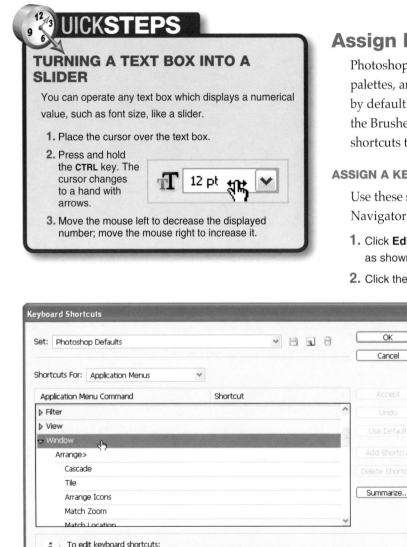

Figure 1-11: Use the Keyboard Shortcuts dialog box to assign new keyboard shortcuts.

QUICKSTEPS

SELECTING SCREEN MODES

Photoshop offers three different screen modes.

USE THE STANDARD SCREEN MODE

In Standard screen mode, your image is placed within a window. You can view multiple images at once in Standard screen mode, as shown in Figure 1-12. To select the Standard screen mode:

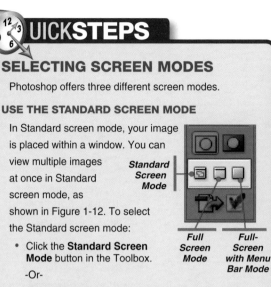

Standard Screen Mode

Full Screen Mode **Full-Screen with Menu Bar Mode**

- Click the **Standard Screen Mode** button in the Toolbox.

  -Or-

- Press **F** repeatedly to cycle through screen modes.

SELECT FULL-SCREEN MODE

In Full-screen mode, only your currently selected document is visible. All frames, scroll bars, title bars, menus, and so forth are hidden, as shown in Figure 1-13. To select Full-screen mode:

- Click the **Full Screen Mode** button in the Toolbox.

  -Or-

- Press **F** repeatedly to cycle through screen modes.

In Full-screen mode, the main menu is moved to the top of the Toolbox:

FULL-SCREEN MODE WITH MENU BAR

Full-screen mode with Menu bar is the same as Full-screen mode, but it retains the menu at the top of the workspace. To select Full-screen mode with Menu bar:

- Click the **Full Screen Mode With Menu Bar** button in the Toolbox.

  -Or-

- Press **F** repeatedly to cycle through screen modes.

Figure 1-12: Standard screen mode shows all open documents.

Figure 1-13: Full-screen mode hides all documents but the currently selected one.

Introducing Photoshop's Tools

Photoshop's primary tools are kept in a palette called the Toolbox. The Toolbox, shown in Figure 1-14, is open by default. If it is not visible, click **Window** on the Menu bar, and then select **Tools**.

At any time, no less than 33 buttons and controls are shown in the Toolbox, but actually more tools are there. Many of Photoshop's tools are hidden beneath other tools in the Toolbox. Whenever a tool icon has a small black triangle at the bottom, you can access a fly-out menu containing additional tools.

Some quick examples of the functions of many of the tools are shown in Figure 1-15.

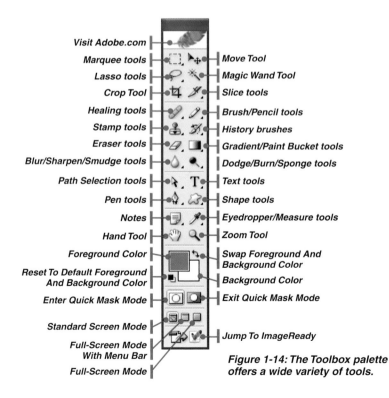

Figure 1-14: The Toolbox palette offers a wide variety of tools.

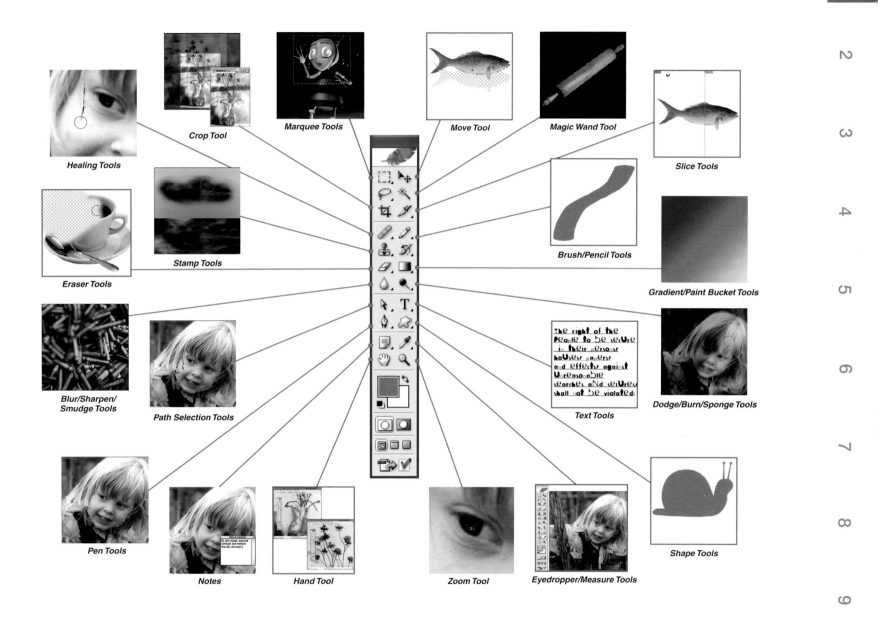

Healing Tools

Crop Tool

Marquee Tools

Move Tool

Magic Wand Tool

Slice Tools

Eraser Tools

Stamp Tools

Brush/Pencil Tools

Gradient/Paint Bucket Tools

Blur/Sharpen/
Smudge Tools

Path Selection Tools

The right of the
People to be secure
in their persons,
houses, papers,
and effects against
Unreasonable
searches and seizures
shall not be violated;

Text Tools

Dodge/Burn/Sponge Tools

Pen Tools

Notes

Hand Tool

Zoom Tool

Eyedropper/Measure Tools

Shape Tools

Figure 1-15: Photoshop's basic tools offer a wide variety options.

Work with Tool Options

All tools in Photoshop have options you can control: size, shape, color, and so forth. Let's take a close look at setting the options for a common tool.

CHANGE THE BRUSH TOOL OPTIONS

The Brush Tool serves as a good introduction to setting tool options in Photoshop; the same controls are available for many other tools, including the Smudge, Blur, Burn, Dodge, and Eraser tools. Here are some guidelines:

- Access basic options for most tools, including the Brush Tool, by right-clicking the image and changing settings from the context menu which appears as shown here.

- From this point, you can change the size of the brush as well as its hardness. The harder the brush, the harder and more distinct the brush strokes it creates, as shown here where the top brush stroke is set to 0% hardness and the bottom is set to 100%.

- Choose a brush tip from the Presets menu at the bottom of the Brush Options dialog box.

- Close the pop-up Options dialog box, either by starting to paint or by clicking somewhere outside the dialog box.

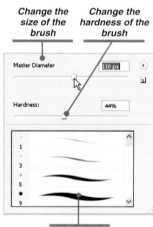

Change the size of the brush   *Change the hardness of the brush*

Choose a style from the presets

There are more options available from the Brush Tool options bar below the main menu, as shown in Figure 1-16. The one you'll be using most is Opacity, which controls the maximum paint opacity of the paintbrush.

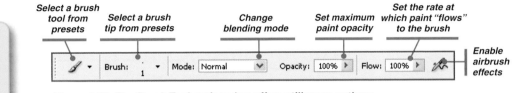

Figure 1-16: The Brush Tool options bar offers still more options.

To really get the most out of the paintbrush, you press **F5** or choose **Window,** then select **Brushes** to open the Brushes palette. You'll learn more about these advanced Brush options in Chapters 5 and 6.

Set Foreground and Background Colors

Painting, drawing, fills, type, and many Photoshop filters depend on the current foreground and background colors.

SAMPLE A NEW FOREGROUND COLOR FROM AN IMAGE

With an image file open in Photoshop:

1. Select the Eyedropper Tool from the Toolbox.

2. Click a color in the image to set the foreground color to that color.

SAMPLE A NEW BACKGROUND COLOR FROM AN IMAGE

With an image file open in Photoshop:

1. Select the Eyedropper Tool from the Toolbox.

2. Press **ALT** and click a color in the image to set the background color to that color.

NOTE

To load new sets of brushes from the context menu, click the **Palette Options** button at the top-right, and choose a new set of brushes from the pop-up.

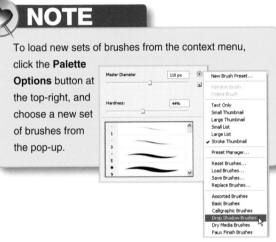

TIP

Selecting the Airbrush option on the Brush Tool options bar allows you to build up spray-painted effects with the Brush Tool.

QUICKSTEPS

UNDOING ACTIONS

USE UNDO

To undo your most recent action:

- Press **CTRL+Z**.

  -Or-

- Click **Edit** and then **Undo**.

REDO A CHANGE

To Redo the most recent change:

- Press **CTRL+Z**

  -Or-

- Click **Edit** and then **Redo [operation]**.

USE STEP BACKWARD

Undo only undoes the most recent operation. If you want to undo more than one operation, use Step Backward. To step backward through recent changes:

- Press **ALT+CTRL+Z**.

  -Or-

- Click **Edit** and select **Step Backward**.

USE STEP FORWARD

To step forward again through recent changes:

- Press **SHIFT+CTRL+Z**.

  -Or-

- Click **Edit** and select **Step Forward**.

NOTE

By default, Photoshop allows you to undo the last 20 changes to a document. To increase or decrease this number, press **CTRL+K** to edit General Preferences, and change the number of **History States**.

RESTORE DEFAULT FOREGROUND AND BACKGROUND COLORS (BLACK & WHITE)

To restore Photoshop to its default black-and-white foreground and background colors, do one of the following:

- Press **D**.

  -Or-

- Click the **Default Foreground And Background Color** button on the Toolbox.

Use the History Palette to Undo

Photoshop's History palette keeps track of recent changes and allows you to easily compare earlier states and to revert to an earlier state. To use the History palette:

1. Open an image in Photoshop and make at least three major changes to it. You might paint a circle with the Brush Tool, invert the colors (**CTRL+I**), or run a filter.
2. Choose Window and then select History to open the History palette.

The History palette contains a snapshot of the 20 most recent changes in your document. Every time you make a change to the image, Photoshop adds a new layer to the History palette. Each layer is named for the tool, filter, or other operation that created it—Brush Tool, Pencil Tool, Invert, and so forth. At the very top, unless you have made more than 20 changes, is the layer called Open. Click this layer to view the state of the image when it was first opened. Click any of the layers to view the state of the image after that operation.

To revert to a previous state, click that layer in the History palette and save the file, or begin working on it again. Any later changes to the document are discarded from the History palette.

MAKE A HISTORY PALETTE SNAPSHOT

Twenty Undos may seem like a lot, but you can use them up surprisingly quickly. Twenty quick strokes with the Brush Tool will do it, for example. The History palette can take a snapshot of an image at a particular point in time. This snapshot is available until you delete it or close the document.

To take a Snapshot of an image:

1. If the History palette is not open, open it by choosing **Window** and then selecting **History**.

2. If you want to take a snapshot of an earlier state, click that layer in the History palette. The image reverts to that state.

3. Click **Create New Snapshot** at the bottom of the palette.

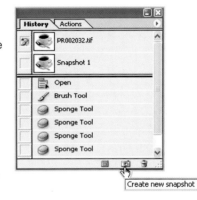

REVERT TO A SNAPSHOT

1. If the History palette is not open, open it by choosing **Window** and then selecting **History**.

2. In the History palette, click the snapshot. The image reverts to that state.

Work with the History Brush

The History Brush allows you to revert *parts* of your image to an earlier state while leaving changes intact across the rest of the image. You are essentially painting over the current image with the older image. You might, for example, open a photo of a person, remove the color from it, and then paint the color back in with the History Brush Tool.

1. Open a color photograph in Photoshop.

Figure 1-17: Click here to set the History Brush to paint from this layer of the History palette.

NOTE

History information is not saved with your files.

TIP

To revert to the last saved version of a file, choose **File** and then select **Revert**. The file is reloaded from disk and any changes made since the last save are discarded.

2. Press **CTRL+SHIFT+I** (Desaturate) to remove the color from the image.

3. If the History palette is not open, open it by clicking **Window** and then selecting **History**.

4. Find the layer just above the Desaturate layer, but do not click it.

5. Click the blank square to the left of the layer just above the Desaturate layer. The History Brush icon appears, as in Figure 1-17.

6. Paint on the image. Where you paint with the History Brush, the older, colored version of the photo replaces the newer black-and-white version.

For more about using the History Brush to create special effects, turn to Chapter 5.

Work with Color and Calibration

There are enumerable ways to describe particular colors. These are called color models, or color spaces. The computer primarily uses the RGB color space. RGB stands for Red, Green, and Blue. Every color on your computer monitor is created by mixing together different amounts of red, green, and blue light. Printers and photographs, on the other hand, generally exist in the CMYK color space. CMYK stands for Cyan, Magenta, Yellow, and blacK. Most color printing, whether on your desktop printer or a large commercial press, is done using these four colors of ink.

RGB and CMYK color spaces differ quite fundamentally. RGB is *additive*. It creates new colors by adding together red, green, and blue light. Red light plus green light plus blue light equals white light. The more light you add, the brighter the color gets.

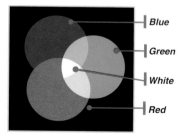

Blue

Green

White

Red

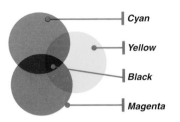

Cyan

Yellow

Black

Magenta

CMYK on the other hand is *subtractive*. It creates colors by *subtracting* colors from white. Cyan ink plus magenta ink plus yellow ink equals black. In printing, white is (usually) the complete absence of ink on the paper. The more ink you add, the darker the color gets.

On your computer monitor, a photo of a red ball is red because your monitor is actually emitting red light. However, a red ball, sitting in your driveway, is red because the ball absorbs every color of sunlight *except* red, which it reflects.

The problem of getting RGB images created on the computer to look the same when printed out in CMYK ink is a difficult one. We'll look at it in more detail in Chapter 8.

Work with Hue, Saturation, and Luminance

The other color model you will use most often in Photoshop is Hue, Saturation, and Luminance.

Hue is what most people think of as the basic color. Is it reddish or greenish? The difference between red and blue is a difference of *hue*.

Saturation is a measure of how intense a color is versus how much white is mixed with it. The difference between red and pink is a difference of *saturation*. White, gray, and black have no saturation at all.

Luminance is how bright a color is. The difference between white and black is a difference of *luminance*.

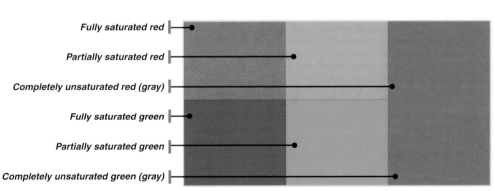

Fully saturated red

Partially saturated red

Completely unsaturated red (gray)

Fully saturated green

Partially saturated green

Completely unsaturated green (gray)

Calibrate Your Monitor

The first step in creating work that can be reproduced accurately either on a printer or on another monitor is to calibrate your own monitor.

The Adobe Gamma application is installed when you install Photoshop. Use the Adobe Gamma application to calibrate your monitor in Windows.

1. From the Windows desktop, click **Start**, select **Settings** and then **Control Panel**.
2. Double-click the **Adobe Gamma** icon to start Adobe Gamma.
3. Click **Step-by-Step (Wizard)**, and then click **Next**.
4. Follow the steps seen to calibrate your monitor and save a new monitor profile.

How to...

- *Understand Bitmaps*
- *Understand Vector Shapes*
- *Understanding Compression*
- *Work with Dimension vs. Resolution*
- *Understanding Bit Depth*
- *Use Grayscale*
- *Use RGB*
- *Use CMYK*
- *Use Indexed Color*
- *View, Select, and Open files*
- *Sort, Flag, Rank, and Rearrange Files*
- *Customize the File Browser*
- *Saving and Loading a File Browser Workspace*
- *Search for Files*
- *Rename, Move, Copy, and Delete Files*
- *Importing from Adobe Illustrator*
- *Save your Files*
- *Scan in Photoshop*
- *Import Digital Photos*
- *Work with Camera Raw Images*

Chapter 2
Creating, Importing, and Saving Images

Photoshop allows you to organize, sort, search for, preview, and open files on your hard drive or network, as well as to import images from digital scanners and cameras.

Work with Image Types

There are hundreds of different types of computer image files, employing different file formats, color models, and compression schemes. Fortunately, Photoshop will allow you to work with almost any image file in use today.

Understand Bitmaps

Bitmap images (sometimes called *raster images*) are composed of lots and lots of tiny square dots, called *pixels*. The larger the image, the more tiny dots it has. A typical piece of desktop wallpaper has a half million to three-quarters of a million pixels. If you open a color photograph in Photoshop and zoom all the way in by pressing CTRL++ ten times, you can clearly see the pixels that make up the photograph.

Most of the different image file formats you'll encounter—including BMP, PICT, GIF, JPG, TIF, and PNG—are bitmap formats.

Understand Vector Shapes

While bitmaps are made up of pixels, vector images are made up of points, lines, and curves. A vector image file doesn't record the position and color of every pixel; rather, it records the position and color of every curve. Where a bitmap image file is like a drawing or painting, a vector image file is like a *description* of that drawing or painting.

Because they are composed of shapes, rather than individual pixels, vectors can be scaled up or down as far as you'd like without losing image quality. These two images look identical:

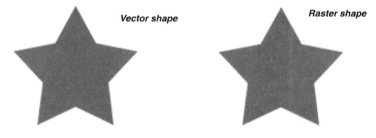

Vector shape

Raster shape

But when you scale them up, the difference becomes apparent:

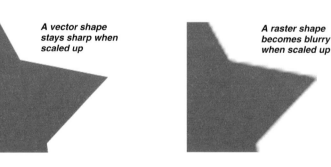

A vector shape stays sharp when scaled up

A raster shape becomes blurry when scaled up

NOTE

Photoshop supports a pure black-and-white color mode called Bitmap mode. It is not the same thing as a bitmap image.

NOTE

Your computer's monitor is a raster device, displaying one little dot of color for every pixel in an image. At a resolution of 800 × 600, your monitor will display 480,000 pixels at a time.

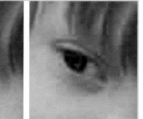

QUICKSTEPS

UNDERSTANDING COMPRESSION

To mitigate the size of bitmap images, you can *compress* them. Consider a red circle on a white background.

Imagine recording every pixel in that image, starting at the upper-left and reading from left to right and top to bottom, just as you read a page of text. You would go along writing, "pixel 1: white, pixel 2: white, pixel 3: white …" and so forth, until you finally reached a red pixel, around pixel 198 or so. But suppose, instead, that you wrote "pixel 1 is white and so are the next 197 pixels in this row." That's compression. Instead of 198 numbers—the color of each of the first 198 pixels, you have two numbers—the number of pixels of the same color and the color itself. GIFs, JPGs, and PICTs are all compressed file formats.

Compression is a good thing, but there's a catch. Compression can cause an image to lose information. Once image information is gone, you cannot get it back. JPG (or JPEG) compression is the worst offender. JPG uses what is called a *lossy* algorithm. It actually throws away information in order to squeeze the image down to a smaller size, and at higher compression settings the degradation becomes quite apparent.

The original image

Heavily compressed as a JPG

When creating JPGs, always keep a version of your image around in an uncompressed format, such as Photoshop PSD.

Vector files are generally much smaller than raster files. If a vector file of a red circle on a white background weighs in at, say, 2000 bytes (2K) in vector format, it will be about the same file size *regardless of the image size*. A ten-inch circle will be the same file size as a one-inch circle. In contrast, a bitmap of the same circle would grow larger as you increased the dimensions.

Vector files are best suited to graphics such as clip art and logos, bold graphics with relatively large, smooth areas filled with relatively simple colors. Common vector file formats include Adobe Illustrator (AI), Macromedia Flash (SWF), and Encapsulated PostScript (EPS).

Photoshop files can include both vector and raster components. A given Photoshop PSD file might be all vector, all raster, or some combination of the two. Photoshop files can include several forms of vector objects: text, shapes, and paths. You will learn more about these in Chapters 5 and 7.

Work with Dimension vs. Resolution

The difference between an image's *dimensions* and its *resolution* is the source of some confusion.

Resolution is generally measured in dots or pixels per inch—*dpi* or *ppi*. An image's resolution determines what size the image will be when printed. Consider an image, 300 × 300 pixels.

At a resolution of 72 dots per inch, it will print out a bit larger than four inches square. At a resolution of 150 dpi, it will print out at two inches square. At a resolution of 300 dpi, it will print out at an inch square. But the image *dimensions* remain unchanged at 300 × 300 pixels.

NOTE

The standard resolution for images to be displayed on a computer monitor is 72 dpi.

TIP

When you create a new image for printing in Photoshop, match the resolution of your image with the resolution at which you'll be printing it. Even though some new printers support resolutions of 1200 dpi or more, anything beyond 300-400 dpi is probably overkill.

TIP

To change the Width and Height of the image independently of each other, deselect **Constrain Proportions** in the Image Size dialog box.

TIP

When resizing an image upward (making it larger), choose **Resample Smoother** from the Resample drop-down list; when resizing an image downward (making it smaller), choose **Resample Sharper**.

You can examine and change an image's dimensions, resolution, and printed size by choosing **Image | Image Size** from the menu.

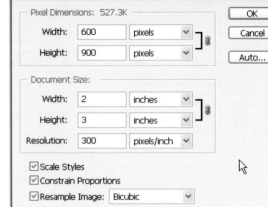

RESIZE AN IMAGE

To change the pixel dimensions of an image:

1. Choose **Image | Image Size**. The Image Size dialog box appears.

2. Under Pixel Dimensions, type in a new Width or Height for the image. The other dimensions automatically update.

   -Or-

   Under Document Size, type in a new Width or Height for the image. The other dimensions automatically update.

CHANGE IMAGE RESOLUTION

To change an image's resolution *without* changing its pixel dimensions:

1. Choose **Image | Image Size**. The Image Size dialog box appears.

2. Deselect **Resample Image**.

3. Type in a new Resolution, and click **OK**.

To change an image's resolution *and* its pixel dimensions:

1. Choose **Image | Image Size**. The Image Size dialog box appears.

2. Check **Resample Image**.

3. Type in a new Resolution. The Pixel Width and Height automatically update to reflect the new resolution.

4. Click **OK**.

Use Grayscale

Grayscale images have no color. In photography, *grayscale* is called black-and-white.

CREATE A NEW GRAYSCALE IMAGE

1. Choose **File | New**. The New dialog box appears.
2. Select a file size from the Preset drop-down list, or enter image dimensions and resolution.
3. Choose **Grayscale** from the Color Mode.
4. Click **OK** to create the file.

CONVERT A COLOR IMAGE TO GRAYSCALE

- Choose **Image | Adjustments | Desaturate**. This removes the color, but leaves the image in color mode. You can, for example, paint on it in color with the Brush tool.

  -Or-

1. Choose **Image | Image Mode | Grayscale**. Photoshop prompts you to confirm discarding the color information.
2. Click **OK** to convert the image to grayscale mode. You can now only paint on the image in shades of gray.

Use RGB

RGB (Red, Green, Blue) is the standard color space for images to be displayed on the computer. Images for web pages and other computer applications should almost always be RGB. Read more about color spaces in Chapter 1.

CREATE A NEW RGB IMAGE

1. From the menu, choose **File | New**. The New dialog box appears.
2. Choose a preset from the Preset drop-down list, or type in values for Width, Height, and Resolution.
3. Choose **RGB** from the Color Mode drop-down list.
4. Click **OK**.

Grayscale ⌄
Bitmap
Grayscale
RGB Color
CMYK Color
Lab Color

CONVERT AN IMAGE TO RGB

From the menu, choose **Image | Mode | RGB Color**.

Use CMYK

CMYK (Cyan, Magenta, Yellow, blacK) is the standard color space for printers. Images destined to be printed will be more accurately displayed in Photoshop if they are in CMYK mode. Read more about color spaces in Chapter 1.

CREATE A NEW CMYK IMAGE

1. From the menu, choose **File | New**. The New dialog box appears.
2. Choose a preset from the Preset drop-down list, or type in values for Width, Height, and Resolution.
3. Choose **CMYK** from the Color Mode drop-down list.
4. Click **OK**.

CONVERT AN IMAGE TO CMYK

From the menu, choose **Image | Mode | CMYK Color**.

Use Indexed Color

Indexed color mode is a unique animal. Every pixel in the image is in full RGB color, but there can be, at most, only 256 different colors. RGB images, in contrast, can include any and all of more than 16 million colors. The subset of colors used by an indexed color image is called its *palette*. Indexed color images can be much smaller than RGB images. GIF is the most common file type that uses indexed color.

You cannot create a new indexed color document in Photoshop or ImageReady, but you can convert an existing RGB image to indexed color, or you can save an RGB or CMYK file as an indexed color GIF via Photoshop's Save For Web command.

NOTE

You cannot convert a CMYK image directly to indexed color mode. To convert an image from CMYK color mode to indexed color mode, you must first convert it to RGB color mode; then convert it to indexed color.

CONVERT AN RGB IMAGE TO INDEXED COLOR MODE

1. From the menu, choose **Image | Image Mode | Indexed Color**. The Indexed Color dialog box appears.

2. In the Colors box, type in a number between 2 and 256 to set the number of colors to be used. Photoshop shows you a preview of the image converted to that number of colors.

3. Click **OK** to accept the conversion.

The other options, Palette, Dither, Transparency, and so forth, are explored in more depth in Chapter 9.

Use the File Browser

While you can browse, open, rename, and delete your files with the standard Windows interface, the Photoshop File Browser offers a much more powerful, customizable way to work with your files.

View, Select, and Open files

1. Click the **File Browser button** to the left of the palette well on the Options bar to open the File Browser, or choose **File | Browse**. The File Browser appears as shown in

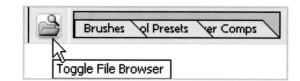

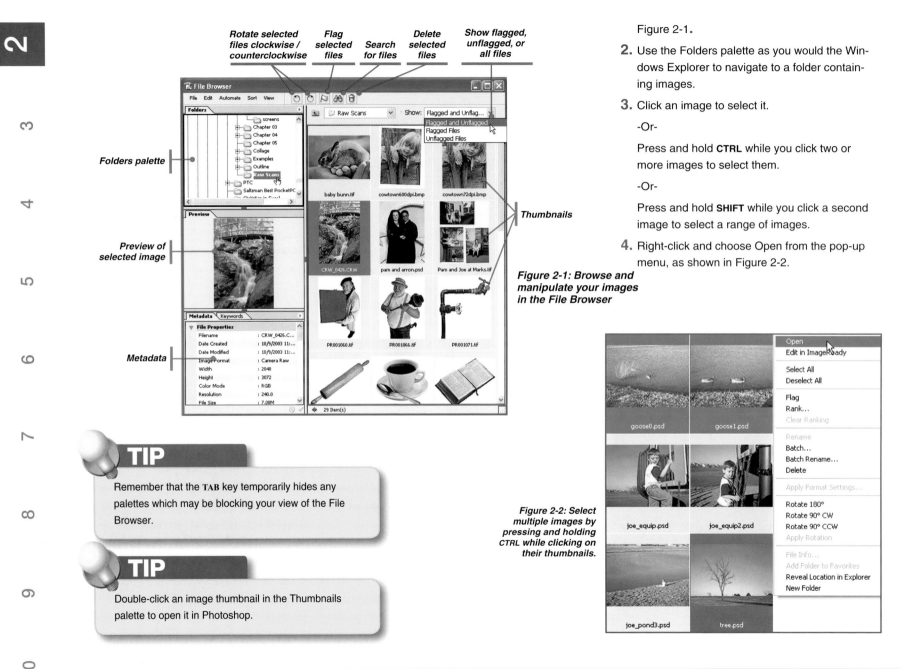

Rotate selected files clockwise / counterclockwise

Flag selected files

Search for files

Delete selected files

Show flagged, unflagged, or all files

Folders palette

Preview of selected image

Metadata

Thumbnails

Figure 2-1: Browse and manipulate your images in the File Browser

Figure 2-2: Select multiple images by pressing and holding CTRL while clicking on their thumbnails.

Figure 2-1.

2. Use the Folders palette as you would the Windows Explorer to navigate to a folder containing images.

3. Click an image to select it.

-Or-

Press and hold **CTRL** while you click two or more images to select them.

-Or-

Press and hold **SHIFT** while you click a second image to select a range of images.

4. Right-click and choose Open from the pop-up menu, as shown in Figure 2-2.

TIP

Remember that the TAB key temporarily hides any palettes which may be blocking your view of the File Browser.

TIP

Double-click an image thumbnail in the Thumbnails palette to open it in Photoshop.

Sort, Flag, Rank, and Rearrange Files

Within the File Browser, you can arrange your files to make them easier to find and manage.

SORT YOUR FILES

From the File Browser menu, choose **View | Sort**, and choose a sort order from the menu.

To sort in descending order (e.g., *Z* to *A*), choose **View | Sort**, and deselect **Ascending Order**.

FLAG YOUR FILES

You can *flag* files in the File Browser. The flag has no particular meaning. You can flag the best files, files to be deleted, files to be copied, and so on. To flag one or more files:

1. Click, hold **CTRL** while you click, or hold **SHIFT** while you click one or more image thumbnails in the File Browser to select them.

2. Press the **Flag File button** in the File Browser menu.

-Or-

Right-click a selected thumbnail, and choose **Flag** from the pop-up menu

| CRW_0426.CRW | baby bunn.tif | cowtown600dpi.bmp | cowtown72dpi.bmp |
| Rank: 01 | Rank: MARK01 | Rank: MARK02 | Rank: X |

RANK YOUR FILES

You can assign a rank to a file and then sort your files by rank. A rank can be a number, a letter, or any combination.

To rank one or more files,

1. Click, hold **CTRL** while you click, or hold **SHIFT** while you click one or more image thumbnails in the File Browser to select them.
2. Right-click a selected thumbnail, and choose Rank from the pop-up menu.
3. Type in a rank and click **OK**.

VIEW FILE RANKINGS

To view thumbnails with the rankings you have assigned to them:

From the File Browser menu, select **View | Show Rank**.

REARRANGE YOUR IMAGE THUMBNAILS

In addition to sorting your thumbnails in various ways, you can manually rearrange them within the thumbnail pane.

1. Click an image thumbnail, and hold down the mouse button.
2. Drag the thumbnail to a new position, and release the mouse button.

Drag on any palette's divider bar(s) to resize the palette

Customize the File Browser

You can alter the appearance of the File Browser to better suit your needs.

RESIZE THE PANES

You can change the relative size of the various panes—the thumbnails, the preview, and so forth.

Simply drag the frames between the panes.

OPEN AND CLOSE FILE BROWSER PALETTES

To open and close palettes in the File Browser:

- Double-click the name tab at the top of an open palette to close it.
- Double-click the name tab at the top of a closed palette to open it.

Choose thumbnail size

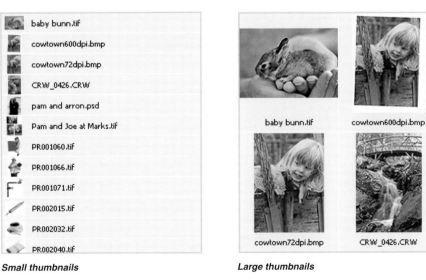

Small thumbnails

Large thumbnails

QUICKSTEPS

SAVING AND LOADING A FILE BROWSER WORKSPACE

You can save your File Browser configuration—thumbnail size, palette size, which palettes are open or closed—as a custom workspace, and recall it again at any time.

SAVE YOUR FILE BROWSER WORKSPACE

1. From the menu, choose **Window | Workspace | Save Workspace**.

2. Type in a name for the workspace, and click **Save**.

LOAD A FILE BROWSER WORKSPACE

From the menu, choose **Window | Workspace**, and select your named workspace from the submenu.

CHANGE THUMBNAIL SIZE

You can change the size of image thumbnails displayed in the File Browser.

1. Click **View** on the File Browser menu.

2. Select a Thumbnail size from the menu.

CREATE A NEW CUSTOM THUMBNAIL SIZE

To change the size of thumbnails displayed in the File Browser's Custom Thumbnail Size view:

1. Choose **Edit | Preferences** from the menu.

2. If necessary, click **Next** until File Browser preferences are displayed.

3. Type a new Custom Thumbnail Size, in pixels.

4. Click **OK**.

Search for Files

To search your computer or network for image files from within the File Browser:

1. Click the **Search button** in the File Browser menu. The Search dialog box, shown in Figure 2-3, appears.

2. Choose a criterion to search by, such as File Name or File Type.

3. To add another search criterion, click the **+** button to the right of the current criterion.

Rename, Move, Copy, and Delete Files

You can perform basic file operations—rename, move, copy, delete—from within the Photoshop File Browser.

RENAME A FILE

1. In the File Browser, click the file name beneath the thumbnail.
2. Type in a new name, and press **ENTER**.

MOVE A FILE

1. In the File Browser, click an image thumbnail and hold down the mouse button.
2. Drag the thumbnail to a new folder in the Folders pane. Release to move the file to that folder.

COPY A FILE

1. In the File Browser, click an image thumbnail and hold down the mouse button.
2. Press and hold the **CTRL** key. A **+** appears next to the cursor to indicate copying.
3. Press **CTRL** while you drag the thumbnail to a new folder in the Folders pane. Release to copy the file to that folder.

DELETE A FILE

1. In the File Browser, click an image thumbnail.
2. Press **DELETE**. Photoshop asks for confirmation of the deletion.
3. Click **OK** to delete the file.

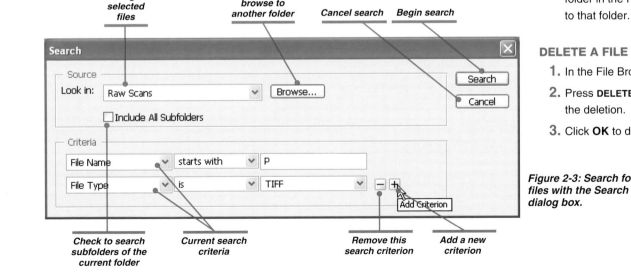

Figure 2-3: Search for files with the Search dialog box.

QUICKSTEPS

IMPORTING FROM ADOBE ILLUSTRATOR

You can copy and paste vector artwork directly from Adobe Illustrator into Photoshop. Choose one of the three options: Paste As Pixels, Paste As Path, or Paste As Shape Layer.

Paste dialog box:

> **Paste**
>
> Paste As:
> ◉ Pixels
> ○ Path
> ○ Shape Layer
>
> [OK]
> [Cancel]

PASTE AS PIXELS

1. In Adobe Illustrator, select your object(s) and choose **Edit | Copy**.
2. Switch to Photoshop, and with your document selected, choose **Edit | Paste**. The Paste dialog box appears.
3. Select **Pixels** in the Paste dialog box, and click **OK**. Sizing handles appear.
4. Drag the handles to resize the objects, if necessary.
5. Press **ENTER** to paste the shapes as pixels to a new layer.

PASTE AS PATH

1. In Adobe Illustrator, select your object(s) and choose **Edit | Copy**.
2. Switch to Photoshop, and with your document selected, choose **Edit | Paste**. The Paste dialog box appears.
3. Select **Path** in the Paste dialog box, and click **OK**.
4. Photoshop creates a new work path from the vector shapes.

You'll learn more about paths in Chapter 5.

Continued...

Save Your Files

Photoshop allows you to save your work in the original format, as a new file type, or optimized for the Web.

SAVE CHANGES TO A FILE

Choose **File | Save**, or press **CTRL+S**.

SAVE A NEW FILE

1. If the file is new and has not been saved before, choose **File | Save As**. The Save As dialog box appears.
2. Type a file name in the File Name field.
3. Choose a file format from the Format drop-down list.
4. Click **OK** to save the file.

Format drop-down list:

> Photoshop (*.PSD;*.PDD)
> Photoshop (*.PSD;*.PDD)
> BMP (*.BMP;*.RLE;*.DIB)
> CompuServe GIF (*.GIF)
> Photoshop EPS (*.EPS)
> Photoshop DCS 1.0 (*.EPS)
> Photoshop DCS 2.0 (*.EPS)
> GIF (RD) (*.GIF)
> IFF Format (*.IFF;*.TDI)
> JPEG (*.JPG;*.JPEG;*.JPE)
> PCX (*.PCX)
> Photoshop PDF (*.PDF;*.PDP)
> Photoshop Raw (*.RAW)
> PICT File (*.PCT;*.PICT)
> Pixar (*.PXR)
> PNG (*.PNG)
> Scitex CT (*.SCT)
> Targa (*.TGA;*.VDA;*.ICB;*.VST)
> TIFF (*.TIF;*.TIFF)

SAVE A FILE WITH A NEW NAME

1. From the menu, choose **File | Save As.** The Save As dialog box appears.
2. Type a new name in the File Name field. Photoshop will automatically fill in the extension. (e.g., BMP).

SAVE A FILE IN A NEW FILE FORMAT

To save a file in a new format (e.g., to save a JPG as a BMP):

1. Choose **File | Save As**. The Save As dialog box appears.
2. Type a file name in the File Name field.
3. Choose a new file format from the Format drop-down list.
4. Click **OK** to save the file.

IMPORTING FROM ADOBE ILLUSTRATOR *(Continued)*

PASTE AS SHAPE LAYER

1. In Adobe Illustrator, select your object(s) and choose **Edit | Copy**.

2. Switch to Photoshop, and with your document selected, choose **Edit | Paste**. The Paste dialog box appears.

3. Select **Shape Layer** in the Paste dialog box, and click **OK**.

4. Photoshop creates a new shape layer from the vector shapes.

You'll learn more about shapes in Chapter 5.

OPEN AN ILLUSTRATOR FILE IN PHOTOSHOP

You can open Adobe Illustrator files in Photoshop, but they will be converted to bitmap images.

1. Use the File Browser to locate an Adobe Illustrator (AI) file.

2. Double-click the image thumbnail to open it. The Rasterize Generic PDF Format dialog box appears.

3. Photoshop can open a vector file at any size. Change the **Width**, **Height**, **Resolution** or **Color Mode** if necessary.

4. Click **OK** to open the file as a bitmap image in Photoshop.

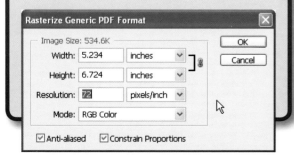

SAVE A FILE CONTAINING LAYERS AND TRANSPARENCY

To save a file containing multiple layers, or transparency, your best option is to save it as a Photoshop file.

1. From the menu, choose **File | Save As.** The Save As dialog box appears.

2. Type a new name in the File Name field.

3. Choose a file format from the Format drop-down list. Photoshop will only display those file types capable of storing layers and transparency.

4. Click **OK**.

SAVE A FILE FOR THE WEB

To save an image in a web format, such as PNG, JPG or GIF:

1. From the menu, choose **File | Save For Web**. The Save For Web dialog box appears.

2. Click one of the preview panes to select it.

3. Choose a preset from the Preset drop-down list at the right of the dialog box.

4. Repeat steps 2 and 3 with different preview panes and presets to compare the various settings. Photoshop shows the file size beneath each preview thumbnail for comparison.

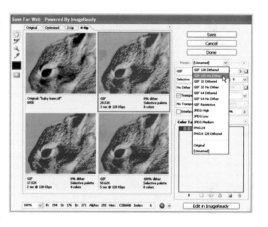

5. Click **OK** to save the selected version of the image. The Save Optimized As dialog box appears.

6. Type in a name for your new file, and click **Save**.

You'll learn more about the Save For Web option in Chapter 9.

Use Scanners and Digital Cameras

Photoshop allows you to import images directly from scanners and digital cameras connected to your computer.

Scan in Photoshop

To scan an image from within Photoshop:

1. From the menu, choose **File | Import**. A submenu appears, listing devices from which Photoshop can import.

2. Click to select your scanner from the list. The scan software will start. The exact appearance and operation will depend on your scanner.

3. Use your scanner software to perform the scan. The scanned image will open in Photoshop.

SCAN A COLOR PHOTOGRAPH

1. From the menu, choose **File | Import**. A submenu appears, listing devices from which Photoshop can import.

2. Click to select your scanner from the list. The scan software will start.

3. Choose color photograph settings. The details will depend on your scanner.

4. Perform the scan. The scanned image will open in Photoshop.

SCAN A BLACK-AND-WHITE PHOTOGRAPH

Although most scanning software has a setting for scanning grayscale (black-and-white) photographs, you will often get better results by scanning the photo as a *color photograph*, and then converting it within Photoshop. When you convert from color to grayscale, you throw away image data. If you make the conversion within Photoshop, you can at least control the process.

1. Scan the photo into Photoshop as a color photograph.
2. To convert to grayscale, select **Image | Adjustments | Desaturate** to remove color from the photo.

You'll learn about retouching and color-correcting photos in Chapter 6.

SCAN LINE ART

Although most scanning software has a setting for scanning line art, you will get better results by scanning the image as a grayscale photograph.

1. Scan the photo into Photoshop as a grayscale (black-and-white) photograph.
2. Press **ALT+CTRL+0**, or double-click the **Zoom** tool to zoom to 100 percent.
3. Select **Image | Adjustments | Threshold.** The Threshold dialog box appears.
4. Threshold will render your image pure black and white. Drag the threshold slider to the left to make lines lighter; drag it to the right to make lines heavier.

5. Click **OK** to accept the threshold adjustment.
6. Use the **Eraser** and **Brush Tools** to clean up any extra spots and specks.

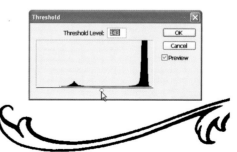

You'll learn more about converting and retouching images in Chapter 6.

Import Digital Photos

1. From the menu, choose **File | Import**. A submenu appears, listing devices from which Photoshop can import.

2. Click to select your camera from the list. The camera's software will start.

3. Select one or more photos, and click the appropriate button (**OK**, **Get Pictures**, etc.) to import the photos into Photoshop. The exact appearance and operation will depend on your camera.

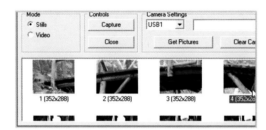

Work with Camera Raw Images

Some cameras will save photos as camera raw files. A camera raw file contains the original, *raw*, data captured by the hardware of a digital camera; it hasn't been compressed or modified in any way. Camera raw format bypasses any in-camera sharpening, contrast, color correction, and so forth. Think of a camera raw file as the digital equivalent of a film negative. By working with camera raw files, *you* get to decide how deep the shadows are, or how bright the sky is, rather than leaving it up to your camera's on-board computer.

Not every camera allows you to save raw image files. You may not want to bother with camera raw files, even if the feature is available for your camera. For snapshots and the like, JPGs or TIFs are smaller and more convenient. Few programs outside of Photoshop can open camera raw files.

NOTE

Photoshop does not support every camera raw file format. Supported cameras are listed in Table 2-1. If your camera is not supported, check the Adobe web site for updates.

NOTE

Unlike JPG or GIF, raw is not an acronym. Each camera manufacturer has its own proprietary file format and extension for its camera raw files, including RAW, RAF, CRF, NEF, RAF, ORF, MRW, and THM.

NOTE

Refer to your camera manual for advanced information on your camera's settings.

The camera raw file contains more data than a JPG or TIF, making it possible to compensate for a wider range of problems: underexposed or overexposed images, bad lighting, incorrect camera settings, and so forth.

OPEN AND CORRECT A CAMERA RAW FILE

Open a camera raw file from the File Browser, or choose **File | Open**. The Camera Raw interface opens, as shown in Figure 2-4.

Make any needed adjustments in the Adjustment panel:

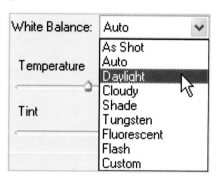

- **White Balance** – Choose a white balance from the White Balance menu to reflect the lighting conditions under which the photo was taken. White balance alters the Temperature and Tint settings.

- **Temperature** – Adjust the color temperature of the photo by dragging the Temperature slider left for cooler, bluer light or right for warmer, more yellow light.

- **Tint** – Adjust the tint by dragging the Tint slider left to add more green or right to add more magenta.

- **Exposure** – Adjust the exposure by dragging the Exposure slider left to darken or right to lighten. A setting of 1.0 is equivalent to setting the camera aperture one F-stop wider. A setting of –1.0 is equivalent to setting the camera aperture one F-stop narrower. The Exposure slider will clip off light areas, forcing them to white.

- **Shadows** – Drag the Shadows slider right to darken the shadows in the photo or left to lighten them. The Shadows slider will clip off dark areas, forcing them to black.

- **Brightness** – Adjust the overall brightness of the photo by dragging the Brightness slider left to darken it or right to lighten it. Unlike Exposure and Shadows, the Brightness slider will not clip off dark and light areas.

- **Contrast** – Adjust the overall contrast of the photo by dragging the Contrast slider left to decrease contrast or right to increase contrast.

- **Saturation** – Adjust the overall saturation (color brightness) of the photo by dragging the Saturation slider left to decrease saturation or right to increase saturation.

You can also make these changes to your photo:

- **Image Rotation** - Rotate the image clockwise or counterclockwise by clicking the rotate image buttons beneath the image.

- **Resolution** - Change the photo's resolution by typing a new value in the Resolution field at the bottom of the Camera Raw window.

- **Size** - Change the photo's dimensions by choosing a new size from the Size drop-down list at the bottom of the Camera Raw window.

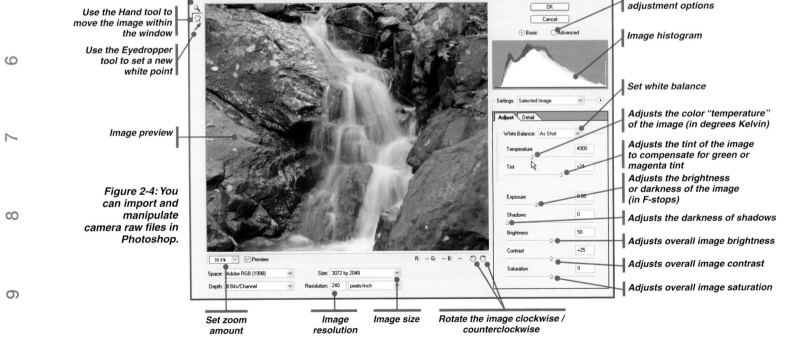

Camera, file name, ISO speed, shutter speed, F-stop, and lens (these may vary)

Use the Zoom tool to zoom in and out

Use the Hand tool to move the image within the window

Use the Eyedropper tool to set a new white point

Image preview

Figure 2-4: You can import and manipulate camera raw files in Photoshop.

Enable advanced adjustment options

Image histogram

Set white balance

Adjusts the color "temperature" of the image (in degrees Kelvin)

Adjusts the tint of the image to compensate for green or magenta tint

Adjusts the brightness or darkness of the image (in F-stops)

Adjusts the darkness of shadows

Adjusts overall image brightness

Adjusts overall image contrast

Adjusts overall image saturation

Set zoom amount

Image resolution

Image size

Rotate the image clockwise / counterclockwise

When you are done:

- Click **OK** to accept your adjustments and open the photo in Photoshop.

  -Or-

- Click **Cancel** to abandon your adjustments. The photo will not open in Photoshop.

TABLE 2-1: CAMERA RAW FILES SUPPORTED BY PHOTOSHOP

CANON	FUJIFILM	LEAF	KONICA MINOLTA	NIKON	OLYMPUS
EOS-1D(s)	3. FinePix S2 Pro	Valeo 6	DiMAGE A1	D1	E-10
EOS-10D		Valeo 11	DiMAGE 5	D1H	E-20
EOS-D30, D60			DiMAGE 7	D1X	C-5050 Zoom
EOS 300D				Coolpix 5700	
PowerShot 600				Coolpix 5000	
PowerShot A5, A50					
PowerShot S30, S40, S45, S50					
PowerShot G1, G2, G3, G5					
PowerShot Pro70					
PowerShot Pro90 IS					

How to...

- Use the Marquee Tool
- Use the Magic Wand Tool
- 🔍 Constraining Your Selections
- Use the Lasso tools
- Select a Range of Colors
- Exclude with Selections
- Modify a Selection
- 🔍 Anti-aliasing and Feathering
- Crop to a Selection
- Delete Using Selections
- 🔍 Expanding Selections
- Remove Fringe Pixels
- Save and Load Selections
- 🔍 Moving and Duplicating
- Copy to a New Layer
- Copy to a New Document
- Extract Background Elements
- Use the Magic Eraser Tool
- Use the Background Eraser Tool
- Create a Quick Mask
- Crop to a Selection
- Use the Pen Tool

Chapter 3

Making Selections

Selections are key to using Photoshop to its fullest. Selections allow you to operate on just part of an image. Any operations you perform on the image will only affect these pixels, as shown in Figure 3-1. You can perform almost any Photoshop operation—applying filters, adjusting colors, painting, erasing, and so forth—on the pixels within a selection; any unselected pixels are entirely unaffected. You can also copy the selected pixels to a layer within your document or to a new document altogether.

Creating New Selections

There are a number of ways to create new selections in Photoshop.

Use the Marquee Tool

You use the Marquee Tool to select a rectangular or elliptically shaped area. In addition, you also have options for a single-pixel-wide row or column.

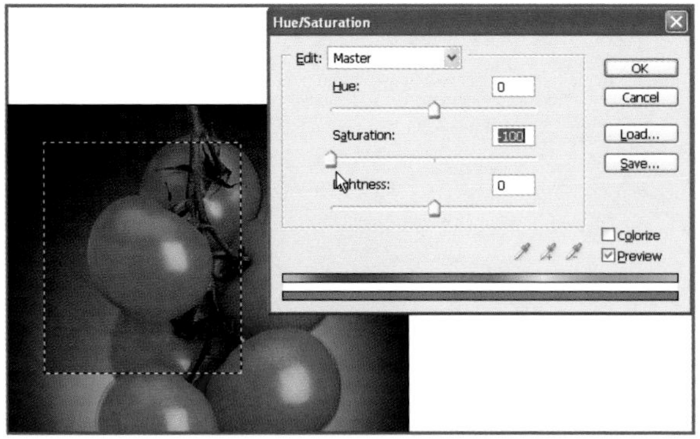

Figure 3-1: Filters and adjustments are only applied to the active selection, if any.

NOTE

Only the pixels *inside* of the marquee are selected.

NOTE

To place a marquee selection around the entire image, press **CTRL+A** (select all).

NOTE

You can select the Marquee Tool and switch between the Rectangular and Elliptical Marquee Tools by pressing the **M** key on your keyboard.

MAKE A RECTANGULAR SELECTION

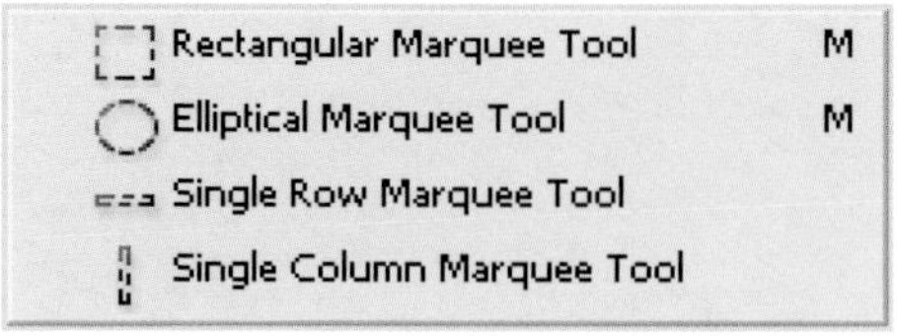

You can make a rectangular selection with the Rectangular Marquee Tool.

1. To select the Rectangular Marquee Tool from the Toolbox palette, click the current **Marquee tool icon** in the Toolbox palette, and hold the mouse button down. The Marquee Tool pop-up menu appears.

2. Click the **Rectangular Marquee Tool** to select it.

3. Drag within the image to create the marquee selection.

   –Or–

   Hold down **SHIFT** while dragging to constrain the selection to a square.

MAKE AN ELLIPTICAL SELECTION

To make a circular or elliptical selection with the Elliptical Marquee Tool:

1. To select the Elliptical Marquee Tool, click the current **Marquee tool icon** in the Toolbox palette, and hold the mouse button down. The Marquee Tool pop-up menu appears.

2. Click the **Elliptical Marquee Tool** to select it.

3. Click within the image, then drag to create the selection.

   –Or–

   Hold down the **SHIFT** while dragging to constrain the selection to a circle.

Use the Magic Wand Tool

Marquee selections are great for selecting circles and squares and rectangles, but sometimes you need to select all the pixels of the same *color*, regardless of the shape. Then it's time for the Magic Wand Tool.

SELECT AN AREA WITH THE MAGIC WAND

1. Select the **Magic Wand Tool** from the Toolbox.

2. Set the **Tolerance** on the Magic Wand options bar. This tells Photoshop how similar in color pixels must be to be included in the selection. The larger the tolerance, the more colors will be selected. A tolerance of 32 is a good place to start.

QUICKSTEPS

CONSTRAINING YOUR SELECTIONS

MAKE A REGULAR SELECTION OF A FIXED SIZE

You can tell Photoshop in advance exactly what size you want your rectangular or elliptical selection to be. With the Rectangular Marquee or Elliptical Marquee Tool selected,

1. Open the **Style** drop-down list in the Options bar, and click **Fixed Size**.

2. Type in the **Width** and **Height** in pixels (px), inches (in), centimeters (cm), or millimeters (mm).

3. Click to establish the upper-left corner of the selection, and drag to position it.

MAKE A SELECTION OF A FIXED-ASPECT RATIO

You can constrain the aspect ratio of a selection so that, for example, it is twice as tall as it is wide no matter the actual size of the area selected.

With the Rectangular Marquee or Elliptical Marquee Tool selected,

1. Open the **Style** drop-down list in the Options bar.

2. Click **Fixed Aspect Ratio**.

3. Type in the **Width** and **Height**.

4. Click on the image, and drag to create the selection.

3. Check **Anti-alias** to soften the edges of the selection.

4. Check **Contiguous** in the options bar.

5. Click within the area you want to select.

6. If too many pixels are selected, reduce the tolerance. If too few pixels are selected, increase the tolerance. Click twice within the selection to reselect the area using the new tolerance.

The Magic Wand Tool's option bar, shown in Figure 3-2, gives you more control over the tool's selections.

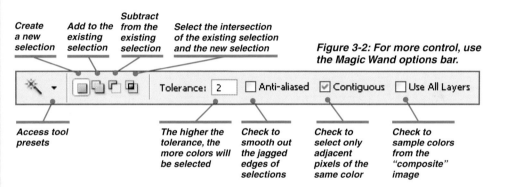

Figure 3-2: For more control, use the Magic Wand options bar.

Create a new selection

Add to the existing selection

Subtract from the existing selection

Select the intersection of the existing selection and the new selection

Access tool presets

The higher the tolerance, the more colors will be selected

Check to smooth out the jagged edges of selections

Check to select only adjacent pixels of the same color

Check to sample colors from the "composite" image

MAKE CONTIGUOUS AND NONCONTIGUOUS SELECTIONS WITH THE MAGIC WAND TOOL

- If you select **Contiguous** on the Magic Wand options bar, the tool will only select a single contiguous area. Pixels of the same color elsewhere in the image will not be selected.

- If you deselect **Contiguous** on the Magic Wand options bar, the tool will select all pixels of the same color, regardless of their location within the image.

Use the Lasso Tools

Photoshop has three different Lasso tools: the Lasso Tool, the Polygonal Lasso Tool, and the Magnetic Lasso Tool.

SKETCH A FREEHAND SELECTION

You can sketch, freehand, the outline of your selection:

1. To select the Lasso Tool, click the current **Lasso tool icon** in the Toolbox palette, and hold the mouse button down. The Lasso Tool pop-up menu appears.

2. Click the **Lasso Tool** to select it.

3. Click within the image, and drag to sketch a selection.

4. Release the mouse button to close the selection

You can fine-tune the way the Lasso Tool works by changing its options, shown in Figure 3-3.

TIP

While using the Lasso Tool, hold down the **ALT** key to temporarily switch to the Polygonal Lasso Tool.

SELECT AN AREA WITH THE POLYGONAL LASSO TOOL

You can create a selection made up of a number of straight segments:

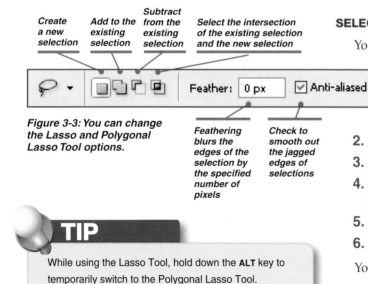

Create a new selection · Add to the existing selection · **Subtract from the** existing selection · Select the intersection of the existing selection and the new selection

Feather: 0 px · ☑ Anti-aliased

Figure 3-3: You can change the Lasso and Polygonal Lasso Tool options.

Feathering blurs the edges of the selection by the specified number of pixels

Check to smooth out the jagged edges of selections

1. To select the Polygonal Lasso Tool, click the current **Lasso tool icon** in the Toolbox palette, and hold the mouse button down. The Lasso Tool pop-up menu appears.

2. Click the **Polygonal Lasso Tool** to select it.

3. Click your image once.

4. Move the mouse to a new position. A line segment follows the cursor.

5. Click the image repeatedly to create your selection.

6. Double-click to finish the selection.

You can fine-tune the way the Polygonal Lasso Tool works by changing its options, shown in Figure 3-3.

TIP

While using the Lasso Tool, hold down the **ALT** key to temporarily switch to the Polygonal Lasso Tool.

SELECT AN AREA WITH THE MAGNETIC LASSO TOOL

Use the Magnetic Lasso Tool to select areas with sharp contrast. The Magnetic Lasso Tool will attempt to automatically follow and "snap to" edges. You can fine-tune the way the Magnetic Lasso Tool works by changing its options, shown in Figure 3-4.

1. To select the Magnetic Lasso Tool, click the current **Lasso tool icon** in the Toolbox palette, and hold the mouse button down. The Lasso Tool pop-up menu appears.

2. Click the **Magnetic Lasso Tool** to select it.

3. Click your image once to begin creating a selection.

4. Move the mouse to a new position. A line segment follows the cursor. Photoshop places small, square "anchors" as it goes.

5. Press **BACKSPACE** at any time to delete the last anchor.

6. Click the image at any time to force the Magnetic Lasso Tool to place an anchor at the cursor location.

7. Double-click to finish the selection.

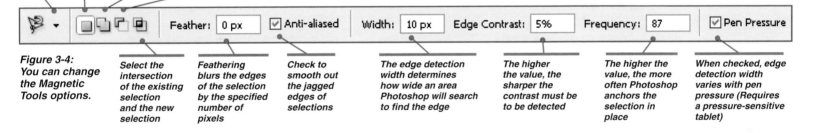

Access tool presets	Create a new selection	Add to the existing selection	Subtract from the existing selection

Feather: 0 px ☑ Anti-aliased Width: 10 px Edge Contrast: 5% Frequency: 87 ☑ Pen Pressure

Figure 3-4:
You can change the Magnetic Tools options.

	Select the intersection of the existing selection and the new selection	Feathering blurs the edges of the selection by the specified number of pixels	Check to smooth out the jagged edges of selections	The edge detection width determines how wide an area Photoshop will search to find the edge	The higher the value, the sharper the contrast must be to be detected	The higher the value, the more often Photoshop anchors the selection in place	When checked, edge detection width varies with pen pressure (Requires a pressure-sensitive tablet)

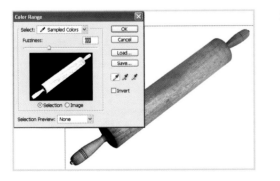

Select a Range of Colors

To select all pixels within a range of colors:

1. From the menu, choose **Select | Color Range**. The Color Range dialog box appears.

2. Click within the image to sample the color you want to select. The Color Range dialog box displays a thumbnail of the selection: white areas in the preview will be selected; black areas will not; gray areas will be partially selected

3. Use the **Fuzziness slider** to adjust the range of colors selected. The greater the fuzziness, the more colors will be selected.

4. To select additional colors, hold down the **SHIFT** key while clicking the image.

5. To subtract colors from the selection, hold down the **ALT** key while clicking the image.

6. When you are happy with the selection, click **OK**.

Exclude with Selections

Sometimes, the elements you *don't* want to work with are easier to select than the elements you *do* want, as in the case of an object on a simple background. In that case, select the background elements first and then invert the selection.

1. Use any combination of selection tools to select the background elements you do *not* ultimately want selected.

2. Choose **Select | Invert,** or press **SHIFT+CTRL+I** to invert the selection. Now everything that was selected is deselected, and everything that was deselected is selected.

Change, Save, and Load Selections

Once you have created a selection, you can change it.

Modify a Selection

You can modify a selection in a number of ways: repositioning, resizing, expanding or contracting, adding to it, or subtracting from it.

MOVE A SELECTION BORDER

To move a selection border:

1. With any Selection tool, click inside the active selection border.

2. Hold down the mouse button, and drag the border to a new position.

TRANSFORM A SELECTION

You can transform a selection—making it larger or smaller, moving it, or even rotating it.

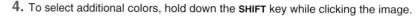

White background selected with Magic Wand Tool

Selection inverted to select just the rolling pin.

UICKSTEPS

ANTI-ALIASING AND FEATHERING

Anti-aliasing and Feathering smooth the edges of your selections. Feathering softens a selection by blurring the selection's edges. The pixels at the edge of the selection are only *partially* selected. When they are copied, they will be partially transparent. If an effect or filter is applied to them, that filter or effect is rendered partially transparent.

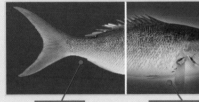

Without feathering.   **With feathering of 20 pixels.**

FEATHER AN EXISTING SELECTION

1. From the menu, choose **Select | Feather**.
2. Enter a Feather Radius value between 0.2 and 250 pixels. The larger the number, the more the edges of the selection will be blurred.

CREATE A FEATHERED SELECTION WITH A SELECTION TOOL

1. Select any of the Lasso or Marquee tools.
2. In the tool's option bar, enter a Feather value between 0.2 and 250 pixels. The larger the number, the more the edges of the selection will be blurred.

Continued...

To transform an existing selection:

1. From the menu, choose **Select | Transform Selection**.
2. Handles appear at the sides and corners of the selection. Drag these handles or the lines that connect them to resize the selection.
3. Click within the selection and drag to move it to another position within your image.
4. Click outside of the selection and drag to rotate the selection.

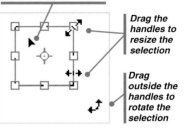

Drag inside the handles to move the selection

Drag the handles to resize the selection

Drag outside the handles to rotate the selection

ADD TO A SELECTION

To add to an existing selection:

1. Choose any selection tool from the Toolbox palette.
2. Hold down the **SHIFT** key and make another selection.
3. Change tools at any time, and hold down the **SHIFT** key to continue adding to the current selection.

SUBTRACT FROM A SELECTION

To subtract from an existing selection:

1. Choose any selection tool from the Toolbox palette.
2. Hold down the **ALT** key and select part of the active selection to subtract from it.
3. Change tools at any time, and hold down the **ALT** key to continue subtracting from the current selection.

CONVERT A SELECTION TO A BORDER

To convert the active selection into a border:

1. From the menu, choose **Select | Modify | Border**.
2. Type in the size of the border in pixels, and click **OK**. Photoshop creates a new border selection, centered on the original selection.

ANTI-ALIASING AND FEATHERING (*Continued*)

ANTI-ALIASING

Anti-Aliasing smoothes out the jagged edges of a selection. It works by blending the color of the pixels at the very edge of the selection with the background pixels. An element selected and copied without anti-aliasing, then pasted in front of a different colored background will display an unsightly, ragged edge.

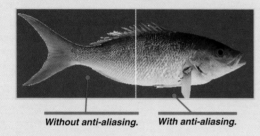

Without anti-aliasing.   **With anti-aliasing.**

Anti-aliasing helps minimize this problem. You'll usually want to enable anti-aliasing on the option bar of whatever selection tool you're using: Lasso, Marquee, or Magic Wand.

ENABLE ANTI-ALIASING

Check **Anti-aliased** on the selection tool's options bar.

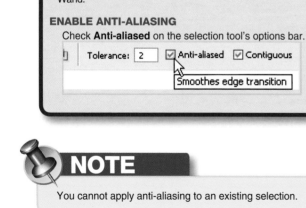

NOTE

You cannot apply anti-aliasing to an existing selection.

EXPAND OR CONTRACT A SELECTION

To expand a selection:

1. Choose **Select | Expand**.
2. Type in the number of pixels to expand the selection by.
3. Click **OK**.

To contract a selection:

1. Choose **Select | Contract**.
2. Type in the number of pixels to contract the selection by.
3. Click **OK**.

MAKE MULTIPLE SELECTIONS

To make multiple selections with any combination of selection tools:

1. Choose a selection tool, such as the Marquee Tool, from the Toolbox palette.
2. Make your first selection.
3. Hold down the **SHIFT** key and make another selection.
4. Change tools at any time, and hold down the **SHIFT** key to continue adding to the current selection.

Crop to a Selection

Cropping cuts off unwanted areas on the outside of an image. Photoshop has a Crop Tool, but it is often convenient to crop an image to fit a selection.

1. Select the Rectangular Marquee Tool from the Toolbox.
2. Click a point and drag to select a rectangle on screen.
3. If necessary, move, resize, or rotate the selection by choosing **Select | Transform Selection** from the menu.

UICKSTEPS

EXPANDING SELECTIONS

The Grow and Similar commands expand the current selection, adding pixels of similar color to those already selected.

GROW A SELECTION

Grow expands the selection to include any adjacent pixels that fall within the Tolerance range specified in the Magic Wand tool options. With a selection active:

Original selection

> From the menu, choose **Select | Grow**. Similarly colored adjacent pixels are selected.

EXPAND A SELECTION WITH SIMILAR

Selection expanded with the Grow command.

Similar expands the selection to include *any* pixels, throughout the image, that fall within the Magic Wand's Tolerance range, whether those pixels are adjacent to the current selection or not.

With a selection active:

> From the menu, choose **Select | Similar**. Similarly colored pixels are selected throughout the image.

Selection expanded with the Similar command.

Delete Using Selections

If a selection is active, the delete key only deletes pixels within the selection. You can use selections to quickly and safely erase large parts of an image.

1. Use one or more selection tools to select the areas you want to delete.

2. Press **DELETE** to delete the selected area.

3. Use the Eraser Tool to clean up the image.

 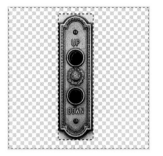

Remove Fringe Pixels

When you copy the contents of an anti-aliased selection to a new layer or document, they will often retain a fringe of the original background color. The timer below has a green fringe.

Defringe replaces the color of edge pixels with the color of nearby pixels further away from the edge. To remove the fringe:

1. Choose **Layer | Matting | Defringe**. The Defringe dialog box appears.

2. Enter the width in pixels of the colored halo to be replaced.

3. Press **OK**. The colored halo disappears.

If Defringe replaces the color on too many, or too few pixels, press **CTRL+Z** to undo the Defringe command and try again, specifying a different Defringe width.

3

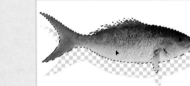

NOTE

If you delete selected pixels while working on the background layer, they are replaced with the current background layer.

QUICKSTEPS

MOVING AND DUPLICATING

MOVE THE CONTENTS OF A SELECTION

With a selection active:

1. Select the **Move Tool** from the Toolbox.
2. Drag within the selection to move the contents.

DUPLICATE THE CONTENTS OF A SELECTION

With a selection active:

1. Select the **Move Tool** from the Toolbox.
2. Hold down the **ALT** key, and drag within the selection to duplicate the contents.

Save and Load Selections

You can save selections and then load them again later, easily reselecting the same area. It is important to note that saved selections will not be saved with your image in all image formats. If you want to be able to load a selection the next time you open an image, save the document in Photoshop (PSD) format.

SAVE A SELECTION

With a selection active:

1. Choose **Select | Save Selection**. The Save Selection dialog box opens.
2. Type in a name for your selection.
3. Leave the other settings alone, and click **OK** to save your selection.

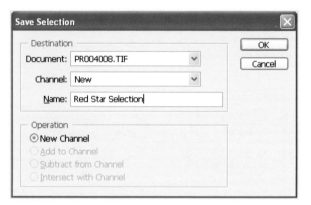

LOAD A SELECTION

To reselect a previously saved selection:

1. Choose **Select | Load Selection**. The Load Selection dialog box opens.
2. Open the **Channel** drop-down list, and click your named selection.
3. Leave the other settings alone, and click **OK** to load your selection.

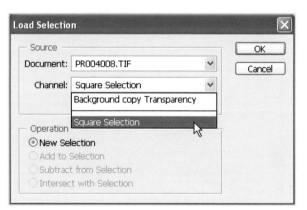

Selections are saved in your Photoshop document as new channels. You'll learn more about channels in Chapter 6.

Extract Images from Backgrounds

Copy to a New Layer

1. Use any combination of selection tools to select the elements you want to extract from the background.

2. Press **CTRL+J** to copy the contents of the selection to a new, blank layer.

Since the copy will be positioned on a new layer, directly above the original, the results of this process will not be apparent at first. To see the copy by itself:

1. Open the Layers palette by choosing **Window | Layers**. The Layers palette appears.

2. In the Layers palette, click the **Eyeball icon** at the left of the background layer to hide the background layer. The new copy, without background, becomes apparent.

You'll learn more about layers in Chapter 4.

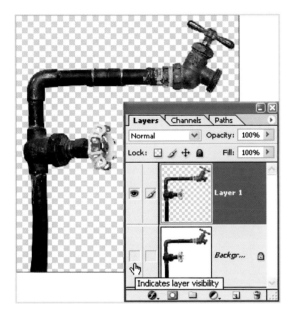

Copy to a New Document

1. Use any combination of selection tools to select the elements you want to extract from the background.

2. Press **CTRL+C** to copy the contents of the selection to the clipboard.

3. Choose **File | New** to create a new document. By default, Photoshop sizes the new document to fit the contents of the clipboard.

4. Press **CTRL+V** to paste the clipboard into the new document.

Extract Background Elements

While not exactly a selection tool, Photoshop's Extract filter automates the task of removing the background from around foreground elements in your image. To extract an element from its background with the Extract filter:

1. Choose **Filter | Extract**. The Extract dialog box opens, as seen in Figure 3-5.

2. Click the **Highlight Tool** at the top-left of the Extract dialog box to select it.

3. Drag with the Highlight Tool to highlight the edge of the element you want to extract. This highlight shows Photoshop where to look for the edges of your elements.

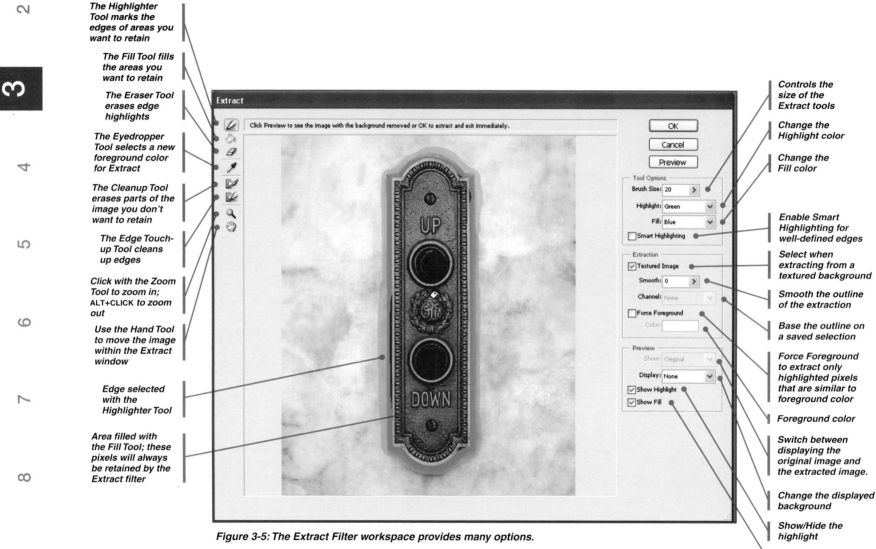

The Highlighter Tool marks the edges of areas you want to retain

The Fill Tool fills the areas you want to retain

The Eraser Tool erases edge highlights

The Eyedropper Tool selects a new foreground color for Extract

The Cleanup Tool erases parts of the image you don't want to retain

The Edge Touch-up Tool cleans up edges

Click with the Zoom Tool to zoom in; ALT+CLICK to zoom out

Use the Hand Tool to move the image within the Extract window

Edge selected with the Highlighter Tool

Area filled with the Fill Tool; these pixels will always be retained by the Extract filter

Controls the size of the Extract tools

Change the Highlight color

Change the Fill color

Enable Smart Highlighting for well-defined edges

Select when extracting from a textured background

Smooth the outline of the extraction

Base the outline on a saved selection

Force Foreground to extract only highlighted pixels that are similar to foreground color

Foreground color

Switch between displaying the original image and the extracted image.

Change the displayed background

Show/Hide the highlight

Show/Hide the fill

Extract

Click Preview to see the image with the background removed or OK to extract and exit immediately.

UP

DOWN

OK
Cancel
Preview

Tool Options
Brush Size: 20
Highlight: Green
Fill: Blue
Smart Highlighting

Extraction
Textured Image
Smooth: 0
Channel: None
Force Foreground
Color:

Preview
Show: Original
Display: None
Show Highlight
Show Fill

Figure 3-5: The Extract Filter workspace provides many options.

1
2
3
4
5
6
7
8
9
10

3

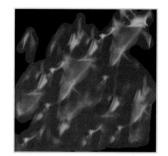

4. If necessary, adjust the **Brush Size**. The smaller the brush, the better job Photoshop will usually do of finding the edges in your picture.

5. If your element has a clearly defined border, such as this one, make sure the highlight goes all the way around it.

6. If your element has no clearly defined border, cover it completely with the Highlighter.

7. If your element has a clearly defined border, select the **Fill Tool** at the top left of the Extract dialog box, and click inside the area outlined by the Highlight Tool to fill it. Pixels within the filled area will always be retained by the Extract filter.

8. Click **Preview** to preview the extraction.

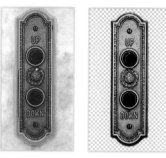

If you don't like the results, change the settings and try again. To reset the Extract filter:

1. In the Preview section of the Extract dialog box, check **Show Highlight** and **Show Fill**, to redisplay your highlight and fill.

2. Open the **Show** drop-down list, and click **Original**.

Make changes in your settings:

- Use a smaller Highlighter brush to make it easier for Photoshop to detect edges.

- Increase the Smooth setting to even out jagged edges. Too much Smoothing will blur outlines.

- If your element is against a textured background, check Textured Image to improve the extraction results.

- Change the Highlight and Fill colors to make them easier to see against your image.

- Preview and change the results as many times as you want. When you are happy, click **OK** to accept.

If no amount of tweaking produces good results in Extract filter, you can manually touch up areas.

Smart Highlighting

CLEAN UP AN EXTRACTION WITH THE CLEANUP TOOL

The Cleanup Tool paints with transparency. To clean up problem areas:

1. With your preview visible in the Extract filter, select the **Cleanup Tool**.
2. Paint with the Cleanup Tool to erase any remaining extra pixels from the background.
3. Hold down **ALT** while painting with the Cleanup Tool to restore areas you want to extract.

CLEAN UP AN EXTRACTION WITH THE EDGE TOUCHUP TOOL

The Edge Touchup Tool cleans up ragged areas around the edges of extracted elements.

1. With your preview visible in the Extract filter, select the **Edge Touchup Tool**.
2. Drag the tool along the edges of your preview to clean them up.
3. When you are happy with the results displayed in Extract's preview, click **OK** to perform the extraction and return to your document.

Use the Cleanup Tool to erase extra bits of the background

Use the Magic Eraser Tool

The Magic Eraser Tool works like a combination of the Magic Wand Tool and the **DELETE** key. It selects an area of similar color and deletes it.

1. To select the Magic Eraser Tool, click the current **Eraser tool icon** in the Toolbox palette, and hold the mouse button down. The Eraser Tool pop-up menu appears.
2. Click the **Magic Eraser Tool** to select it.
3. Set the **Tolerance** in the options bar. The higher the Tolerance, the wider the range of colors that will be deleted. A good starting Tolerance is 32.
4. Click a background area in your image to delete it.

Use the Background Eraser Tool

The Background Eraser Tool erases areas of similar color. Use the Background Eraser Tool to erase the background from around a foreground element.

When you first click with the Background Eraser Tool, it samples the background color.

1. To select the Background Eraser Tool, click the current **Eraser tool icon** in the Toolbox palette, and hold the mouse button down. The Eraser Tool pop-up menu appears.

2. Click the **Background Eraser Tool** to select it.

3. Open the **Limits** drop-down list, and click **Contiguous**.

4. Open the Sampling drop-down list, and click **Once**. This samples the background color each time you click with the tool.

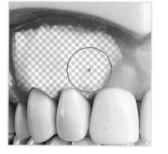

5. Click in an area you want to erase, to sample the background color.

6. Without releasing the mouse button, drag the tool over the background to erase pixels of similar color.

7. To erase multiple areas or multiple colors, repeat Steps 5 and 6.

The Background Eraser Tool has a number of options which you can adjust for better results, as shown in Figure 3-6.

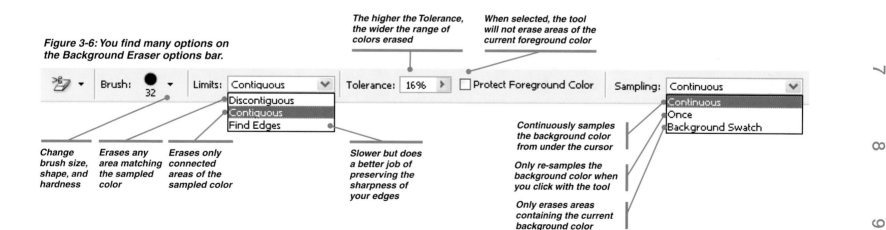

Figure 3-6: You find many options on the Background Eraser options bar.

The higher the Tolerance, the wider the range of colors erased

When selected, the tool will not erase areas of the current foreground color

Brush: 32 Limits: Contiguous Discontiguous Contiguous Find Edges Tolerance: 16% Protect Foreground Color Sampling: Continuous Continuous Once Background Swatch

Change brush size, shape, and hardness

Erases any area matching the sampled color

Erases only connected areas of the sampled color

Slower but does a better job of preserving the sharpness of your edges

Continuously samples the background color from under the cursor

Only re-samples the background color when you click with the tool

Only erases areas containing the current background color

Painting Selections with Quick Masks

A Quick Mask is a selection that you paint on, usually with the Brush Tool.

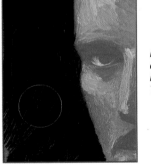

Create a Quick Mask

To select an area with a Quick Mask:

1. Click the **Quick Mask button** in the Toolbox, or press **Q** to enter Quick Mask mode.

2. Click the **Brush Tool** in the Toolbox.

3. Press **D** to set the foreground and background colors to black and white.

4. With the Brush Tool, paint over the areas you do *not* want selected.

Figure 7a: Clean with Quick Mask: A selection made with the Magic Wand Tool.

Figure 7b: Switching to Quick Mask mode …

Figure 7c: … to clean up unselected bits with the Brush Tool.

TOUCH UP A SELECTION WITH QUICK MASK

You can use Quick Mask mode in combination with other selection tools to make your selections more easily.

1. Use a selection tool, such as the Magic Wand Tool, to create a rough selection

2. Click the **Quick Mask button** in the Toolbox, or press **Q** to enter Quick Mask mode.

3. Press **D** to set the foreground and background colors to black and white.

4. Select the **Brush Tool** from the Toolbox.

5. Right-click the image, and adjust the brush's size and shape.

6. Paint with the Brush Tool to touch up the mask, as shown in Figure 3-7c.

7. Press **X** to switch the foreground color between black and white. Black adds to the mask; white subtracts from the mask.

8. When the mask is complete, press **Q** again to leave Quick Mask mode and view your selection.

NOTE

Remember that the tinted parts of the image are the parts which are *not* selected.

Crop to a Selection

To crop away parts of an image outside the current selection:

1. Use the **Rectangular Marquee Tool** (or other selection tool) to select part of the image.
2. From the menu, select **Image | Crop**.

Use the Pen Tool

You can create a selection by drawing with the Pen Tool.

1. Select the **Pen Tool** from the Toolbox palette.
2. In the Pen Tool options bar, select the **Paths icon**.

3. Click repeatedly around the area you wish to select to create a Pen path. Every time you click, the Pen creates a new anchor.
4. To close the path, click once in the anchor at the beginning of the path.
5. Press **CTRL+ENTER** to select the area within the path.

You'll learn more about the Pen Tool in Chapter 5.

How to...

- Create New Layers
- Hiding and Revealing Layers
- Linking and Unlinking Layers
- Work with Layer Backgrounds
- Copy Merged Layers
- Rearrange Layer Order
- Manipulating Layer Sets
- Delete a Layer
- Group Layers into Layer Sets
- Flattening an Image
- Merge Layers
- Create Layer Masks
- Editing a Mask
- Masking a Layer Set
- Add Layer Drop Shadows
- Create a Frame with Layer Effects
- Save and Load Layer Styles
- Work with Opacity and Fill
- Use Blend Modes
- Create an Adjustment Layer
- Creating a Quick Sepia Tone
- Create a Collage

Chapter 4

Using Layers

Layers and layer masks are absolutely key to achieving advanced effects, such as collages, with Photoshop. They allow you to build very complex compositions while still maintaining control of the individual elements. Better yet, they allow you to keep all your assets intact so you can change how you use them later. Think of layers as a combination of photographs and overhead transparencies that can be stacked up, one on top of the other, almost indefinitely. You can hide all or part of a layer and vary a layer's transparency. Layers can cast shadows and create other effects.

Work with Layers

Photoshop's Layers palette allows you to create, copy, delete, rearrange, and add special effects to your layers. You'll do most of your manipulation of layers via the Layers palette, shown in Figure 4-1.

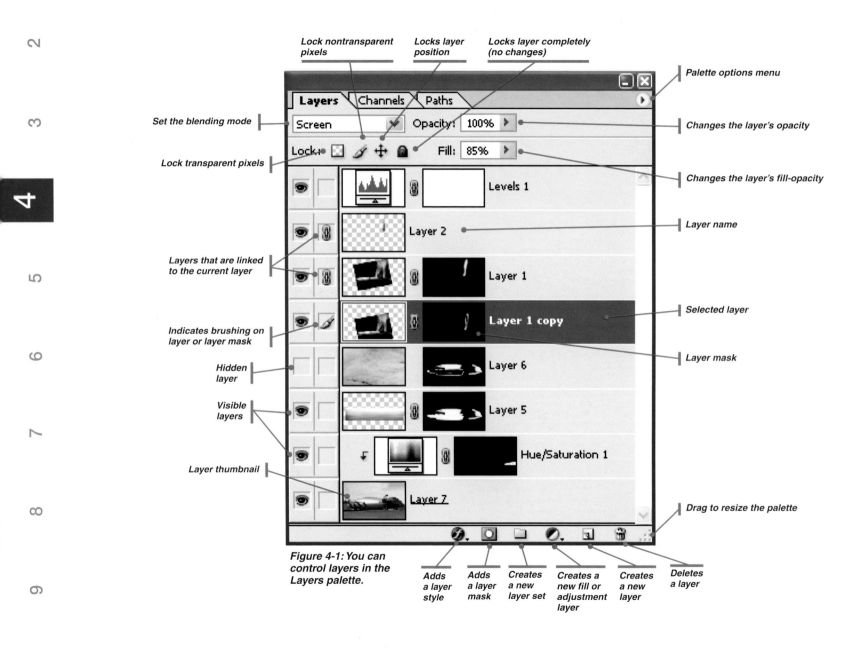

Lock nontransparent pixels

Locks layer position

Locks layer completely (no changes)

Palette options menu

Set the blending mode

Changes the layer's opacity

Lock transparent pixels

Changes the layer's fill-opacity

Layer name

Layers that are linked to the current layer

Selected layer

Indicates brushing on layer or layer mask

Layer mask

Hidden layer

Visible layers

Layer thumbnail

Drag to resize the palette

Layers Channels Paths

Screen   Opacity: 100%

Lock: Fill: 85%

Levels 1

Layer 2

Layer 1

Layer 1 copy

Layer 6

Layer 5

Hue/Saturation 1

Layer 7

Figure 4-1: You can control layers in the Layers palette.

Adds a layer style

Adds a layer mask

Creates a new layer set

Creates a new fill or adjustment layer

Creates a new layer

Deletes a layer

TIP

To rename a layer, double-click the layer's name in the Layers palette, and type a new name.

UICKSTEPS

HIDING AND REVEALING LAYERS

In documents with multiple layers, you often want to temporarily hide individual layers.

TEMPORARILY HIDE A LAYER

Click the Eye icon at the far left of the layer thumbnail in the Layers palette. The Eye disappears and the layer is hidden.

REVEAL A HIDDEN LAYER

Click the empty button at the far left of the layer thumbnail in the Layers palette. The Eye reappears and the layer is revealed.

Create New Layers

You can create layers in a variety of ways.

CREATE NEW BLANK LAYER

To create a new blank layer:

- Click the **Create New Layer** button at the bottom of the Layers palette

  –Or–

- Click **Layer | New | New Layer**.

  –Or–

- Press **SHIFT+CTRL+N**.

COPY AN EXISTING LAYER

You also can create a new layer by copying an existing layer.

- In the Layers palette, click the source layer. The cursor changes to a fist. Drag the layer to the **Create A New Layer** button at the bottom of the Layers palette, then release the mouse button.

  –Or–

- Click **Layer | New | Layer Via Copy**.

  –Or–

- Press **CTRL+J**.

Photoshop creates a new layer that is an exact copy of the original. The new layer appears immediately above the source layer in the Layers palette.

CREATE A NEW LAYER FROM A SELECTION

You can create a new layer by copying only the selected portions of an existing layer. This is a useful way to separate a selected element or elements from the background while leaving your original image intact.

Select the portions of a layer which you wish to copy.

- Click **Layer | New | Layer Via Copy**.

  –Or–

- Press **CTRL+J**.

LINKING AND UNLINKING LAYERS

Layers that are linked move, rotate, and transform together. If you move the contents of a layer 50 pixels left, the contents of all layers linked to that layer will also move 50 pixels left.

LINK LAYERS

To link another layer to the currently selected layer:

On a layer other than the currently selected layer, click the blank button immediately to the left of the layer thumbnail. A chain appears.

UNLINK LAYERS

Click on the chain icon to the left of the thumbnail in the Layers palette to break the link with the currently selected layer.

NOTE

Hidden layers cannot be modified or copied.

Work with Layer Backgrounds

The background layer in a Photoshop document is locked. You cannot erase it (other than painting over it with the background color). You cannot move or rotate or resize it, nor can you create a mask for it. To make these kinds of changes on the background, you must first turn it into a layer. To do this:

● Click **Layer | New | Layer From Background**. The background becomes a normal layer.

COPY AND DELETE THE BACKGROUND

1. In the Layers palette, drag the background to the **New Layer button**, and release. The background is copied to a new layer.

2. Drag the background to the **Delete Layer** button, and release. The original background is deleted.

Copy Merged Layers

You will often want to copy a merged version of a layered document—a version that looks the same but does not contain multiple layers—to the clipboard.

1. Select the entire document by choosing **Edit | Select All**, or by pressing **CTRL+A**.

2. Click **Edit | Copy Merged**, or press **SHIFT+CTRL+C**.

When you paste the contents of the clipboard into a new document, it contains only a single layer. See Figure 4-2a and Figure 4-2b.

Figure 4-2a: Before Copy Merged, this document is made up of many interacting layers.

Figure 4-2b: When the merged document is copied to the clipboard, it can be pasted to a new document or to another program as a single layer.

Figure 4-3a: If the text is above the other layer, it is visible.

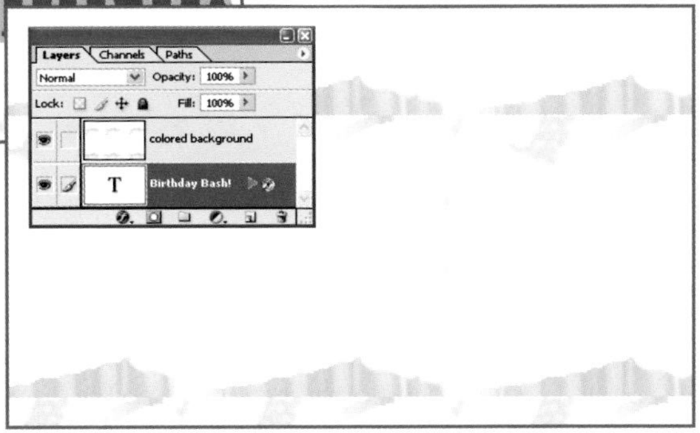

Figure 4-3b: If it is beneath the other layer, it is hidden.

PASTE FROM ANOTHER APPLICATION TO A NEW LAYER IN PHOTOSHOP

1. Open an image in Photoshop.
2. Switch to another application, such as a web browser, and select and copy an image.
3. Return to Photoshop and click **Edit | Paste**. The new image is pasted into the Photoshop document on a new layer.

PASTE A NEW LAYER FROM ANOTHER PHOTOSHOP DOCUMENT

1. Open two images in Photoshop.
2. Click **Window | Arrange | Tile** to display both images at once.
3. Select the **Move Tool** from the Toolbox.
4. Click within the first document to select it.
5. Click **Edit | Select All**, or press **CTRL+A** to select the entire image.
6. Click within the second document to select it.
7. Click **Edit | Paste**, or press **CTRL+V** to paste the first image into a new layer in the second document.

COPY A LAYER USING DRAG

You can drag layers directly from one Photoshop document to another.

1. With two documents and the Layers palette open in Photoshop, click the title bar of the first document to select it.
2. In the Layers palette, drag the layer you want to copy and place it anywhere in the second document. A copy of that layer appears in the second document.

Rearrange Layer Order

The order of layers in the Layers palette usually determines the final result, as shown in Figures 4-3a and 4-3b.

To change the order of layers:

1. Click a layer's name in the Layers palette.
2. Hold down the mouse button, and drag the layer up or down to a new position.

MANIPULATING LAYER SETS

MOVE THE CONTENTS OF A LAYER SET

1. Select the **Move** tool from the Toolbox palette.

2. Click a layer set in the Layers palette.

3. Drag the image with the Move tool to move the entire layer set.

RESIZE A LAYER SET

1. In the Layers palette, click the layer set to be resized.

2. Press **CTRL+T** to enter Free Transform mode, or select **Edit | Free Transform**.

3. Drag the handles to resize every layer in the layer set.

4. Press **ENTER**, or double-click the image to accept the changes.

DELETE A LAYER SET

1. Click a layer set thumbnail in the Layers palette.

2. Drag the layer set to the **Delete Layer** button at the bottom of the palette.
   –Or–

1. Right-click the layer set's name in the Layers.

2. Choose **Delete Layer Set** from the pop-up menu.

3. Photoshop asks you to confirm the deletion. Click **Yes**.

DUPLICATE A LAYER SET

1. Click a layer set thumbnail in the Layers palette.

2. Drag the layer set to the **Create A New Layer** button at the bottom of the palette.
   –Or–

1. Right-click the layer set's name in the Layers.

2. Choose **Duplicate Layer Set** from the pop-up menu.

TIP

Before making changes, copy your work to a new layer. Make changes on the new layer, and if you don't like them, simply delete the layer.

Delete a Layer

1. Click a layer's thumbnail in the Layers palette.

2. Drag the layer to the **Delete Layer** button at the bottom of the palette.
   –Or–

1. Right-click the layer's name in the Layers palette.

2. Choose **Delete Layer** from the pop-up menu.

3. Photoshop asks you to confirm the deletion. Click **Yes**.

Group Layers into Layer Sets

Layers can be grouped together into folders called layer sets. Sets help you keep multilayer documents organized.

Although you cannot paint on a layer set, in most ways they act the same way as individual layers. You can reposition, resize, mask, and hide all the layers in a layer set at the same time.

CREATE A LAYER SET

To create a new layer set:

Click the **Create A New Set** button at the bottom of the Layers palette.

MOVE A LAYER INTO A LAYER SET

1. In the Layers palette, click an existing layer.

2. Drag it onto the Layer set, and release.

REMOVE A LAYER FROM A LAYER SET

1. In the Layers palette, click a layer within the layer set.

2. Drag it to a position outside of the Layer set, and release.

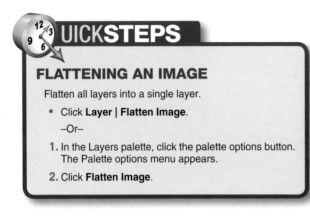

QUICKSTEPS

FLATTENING AN IMAGE

Flatten all layers into a single layer.

- Click **Layer | Flatten Image**.

  –Or–

1. In the Layers palette, click the palette options button. The Palette options menu appears.

2. Click **Flatten Image**.

NOTE

The original background layer cannot be moved.

NOTE

Merge Down will not be available if the bottom layer is a Text or Shape layer.

Merge Layers

You can combine two or more layers into a single layer.

MERGE A LAYER WITH THE LAYER BENEATH IT

1. In the Layers palette, select the topmost of the two layers you want to merge.

2. Click the **menu** button at the top right of the Layers palette, and choose **Merge Down** from the fly-out menu.

   –Or–

   Press **CTRL+E**.

MERGE LINKED LAYERS

To merge all linked layers into a single layer:

1. In the Layers palette, click one of the linked layers to select it.

2. Click **Layer | Merge Linked**.

   –Or–

1. Click the **palette options** button. The palette options menu appears.

2. Click **Merge Linked**.

MERGE VISIBLE LAYERS

Merge all visible layers into a single layer.

1. In the Layers palette, click one of the linked layers to select it.

2. Click **Layer | Merge Linked**.

   –Or–

1. Click the palette options button. The Palette options menu appears.

2. Click **Merge Linked**.

TIP

Mask, don't erase. When you erase a pixel, it's gone forever; but you can always change a mask if you change your mind later, nothing is ever lost.

Work with Layer Masks

A layer mask hides, or *masks*, part of a layer. Layer masks are black, white, and shades of gray. Where the layer mask is black, the masked layer doesn't show.

Create Layer Masks

You can create layer masks by painting them with the Brush Tool, from a Quick Mask, or from a selected area of the image.

PAINT A LAYER MASK

The most common way to create a layer mask is to paint one with the Brush Tool.

1. In the Layers palette, select the layer to be masked.
2. Click the **Add Layer Mask** button at the bottom of the Layers palette to create a new blank mask for the selected layer. The icon to the immediate left of the layer thumbnail changes to a mask to show that you are editing a layer mask.

   Add layer mask

3. Choose the **Brush Tool** or other painting tool from the Toolbox.
4. Photoshop has set the foreground color to black. Paint with black to mask out parts of the image, as shown in Figure 4-4.

Figure 4-4: Paint with the Brush Tool to create a new mask.

CREATE A LAYER MASK FROM A QUICK MASK

1. Press **Q** to switch to Quick Mask mode.
2. Select a painting or drawing tool from the Toolbox, and paint a Quick Mask.
3. Press **Q** again to leave Quick Mask mode.
4. In the Layers palette, click the layer to be masked to select it.
5. Click **Add Layer Mask** at the bottom of the Layers palette. Photoshop creates a new layer mask from the selection.

TIP

Masks don't have to be only black and white. You can paint in shades of gray, as well, to partially mask an area. The darker the gray the less the underlying image will show through.

CREATE A LAYER MASK FROM A SELECTED AREA

1. In the Layers palette, click the layer to be masked to select it.
2. Use one or more of Photoshop's selection tools (e.g., the Magic Wand tool) to select part of the image to be masked.

EDITING A MASK

The best thing about masks is that they aren't permanent. You can edit them at any time, hiding or revealing the underlying image.

EDIT A MASK WITH THE BRUSH TOOL

1. In the Layers palette, click the layer mask you want to edit.
2. Select the **Brush Tool** or other painting tool from the Toolbox.
3. Select a foreground color: black to mask, white to reveal, or gray to partially reveal.
4. Paint to alter the mask.

Click the Layer Thumbnail to edit the layer. The paintbrush icon appears here.

Click the Mask Thumbnail to edit the layer mask. The mask icon appears here.

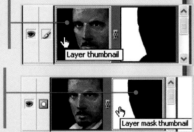

ADD A SELECTION TO A MASK

You can expand a layer mask by selecting additional pixels to be masked and adding them to the layer mask.

1. In the Layers palette, click the layer mask you want to modify.
2. Use any selection tool to select an area you want to mask.
3. Press **D** to set the foreground and background colors to black and white.
4. Press **CTRL+DELETE** to fill the selected area of the mask with black.

CREATE A NEW SELECTION FROM A MASK

In the Layers palette, press **CTRL** while you click the mask thumbnail. All unmasked pixels are selected.

3. Press the **Add Layer Mask** button at the bottom of the Layers palette. Photoshop creates a new layer mask from the selection. Only pixels that were within the selection will now be visible in this layer.

CREATE A NEW BLANK LAYER MASK

- Press the **Add Layer Mask** button at the bottom of the Layers palette.

–Or–

- Click **Layer | Add Layer Mask | Reveal All**.

You can now paint in the layer mask with black or shades of gray to hide parts of the image.

HIDE A LAYER WITH A NEW LAYER MASK

- Click **Layer | Add Layer Mask | Hide All**.

You can now paint in the layer mask with white or shades of gray to reveal parts of the image.

CREATE A GRADIENT MASK

1. In the Layers palette, click the layer to be masked to select it.
2. Click **Add Layer Mask** at the bottom of the Layers palette to create a new blank layer mask.
3. Select the **Gradient Tool** from the Toolbox.
4. Right-click within the image to bring up the Gradient context menu.
5. If you hover the pointer over a gradient, a tool tip appears showing you that gradient's name. Choose **Foreground To Background** from the presets.

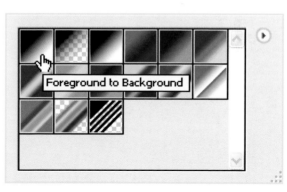

6. Drag from one edge of the image to the other to create the background gradient, as shown in Figure 4-5.

MASKING A LAYER SET

Layer Sets can be masked in the same way as can individual layers.

CREATE A LAYER SET MASK

1. In the Layers palette, click a layer set thumbnail to select it.
2. Click **Add Layer Mask** at the bottom of the palette to create a new mask for the layer set.
3. Use the **Brush** or **Gradient** tools to paint a new mask.

NOTE

It's not necessary for the gradient to run completely across the image. You can create gradient masks that shade from white to black over a smaller area to smooth edge transitions. You can also create masks with radial gradients, angle gradients, and so forth.

TIP

To see a mask full screen while you edit it, press **ALT** while you click the layer's mask thumbnail in the Layers palette, as shown in Figure 4-7. Click the layer thumbnail to return to layer view.

NOTE

You cannot mask the original background layer.

In the same way, you can use any of Photoshop's other gradient settings—radial, angle, reflected, or diamond—to create different effects, as shown in Figure 4-6.

Figure 4-5: The gradient mask causes the top layer to fade in, from left to right.

Figure 4-6: A radial gradient creates a different effect, in this case radiating out from the eye.

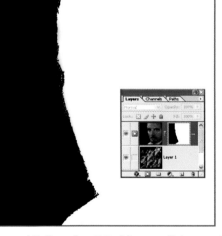

Figure 4-7: Pressing ALT while you click a mask thumbnail displays the mask full screen.

TURN MASKS OFF AND ON

To temporarily disable a layer mask:

In the Layers palette, right-click a layer mask, and choose **Disable Layer Mask** from the pop-up menu. A red *X* appears across the layer mask.

Disabling a mask does not delete it. To turn the mask on again:

In the Layers palette, right-click a layer mask, and choose **Enable Layer Mask** from the pop-up menu. A red *X* appears across the layer mask.

DELETE A LAYER MASK

In the Layers palette, right-click a layer mask, and choose **Discard Layer Mask** from the pop-up menu.

APPLY A MASK

When you apply a mask, masked pixels are permanently deleted from the layer, and the layer mask is discarded. Visually, the image will look the same, but you will no longer be able to make changes to the mask.

In the Layers palette, right-click a layer mask, and choose **Apply Layer Mask** from the pop-up menu.

Work with Layer Effects

Most layer effects happen around the edges of things, so if you apply them to layers
that are full, you may not see any effect at all, as shown in Figures 4-8a and 4-8b.
Layer effects are usually, though not always, applied to layers that contain at least
some areas of transparency. Figure 4-9 shows some common layer effects.

Photoshop layer effects are almost infinitely malleable, and you can use them to
create a wider variety of effects than would at first seem possible. Drop shadows are
usually dark, but they can be colorful and lighter than the surroundings. The Stroke
effect is usually used to create a simple line around the outside of a shape, but you
can use it to create a realistic 3-D picture frame, as we will see later in the chapter.

*Figure 4-8a: Applying a drop shadow to the layer
containing this photo has no discernable effect.*

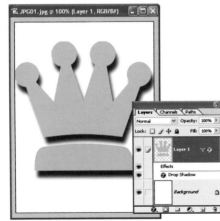

*Figure 4-8b: The same drop shadow to a layer
with a smaller shape is perfectly visible.*

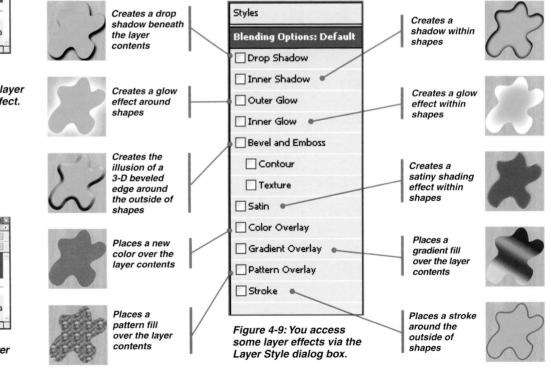

Creates a drop
shadow beneath
the layer
contents

Creates a
shadow within
shapes

Creates a glow
effect around
shapes

Creates a glow
effect within
shapes

Creates the
illusion of a
3-D beveled
edge around
the outside of
shapes

Creates a
satiny shading
effect within
shapes

Places a new
color over the
layer contents

Places a
gradient fill
over the layer
contents

Places a
pattern fill
over the layer
contents

*Figure 4-9: You access
some layer effects via the
Layer Style dialog box.*

Places a stroke
around the
outside of
shapes

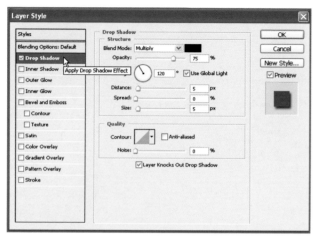

Figure 4-10: Add Drop Shadows and other effects from the Layer Style dialog box.

Figure 4-11: You can create a drop shadow with layer effects.

TIP

To create a new Type layer, select one of the Type tools from the Toolbox, and click anywhere on the image to begin typing. (See Chapter 7 for additional details on how to use the Type tool.)

Add Layer Drop Shadows

Drop Shadow is probably the most commonly used of all layer effects.

CREATE A SIMPLE DROP SHADOW

1. Create a Photoshop document with at least two layers. The top layer should not fill the entire canvas. A text layer or shape layer works well.

2. In the Layers palette, right-click the layer that will cast the shadow, and choose **Blending Options** from the pop-up menu. The Layer Style dialog box appears, as shown in Figure 4-10.

3. In the Blending Options dialog, click **Drop Shadow**.

4. Drag the **Size** slider until the shadow is the desired size. Size controls the fuzziness of the shadow.

5. Drag the **Distance** slider until the shadow falls the desired distance from the layer. Distance controls how high the layer appears to be above the background.

6. Drag within the **Angle** circle control to change the apparent direction of the light source and the direction the shadows fall. The results should be something like Figure 4-11.

Create a Frame with Layer Effects

You can combine any number of layer effects on a given layer. You are not limited to just a drop shadow or just a stroke. Let's look at an example which creates a realistic picture frame from a simple rectangle using nothing but layer effects.

DEFINE THE FRAME AREA

1. Load a photo which you'd like to put a frame around.

2. In the Layers palette, click the **Add New Layer** button to create a new blank layer above the photo.

3. Select the **Rectangular Marquee Tool** from the Toolbox.

4. Click in the photo and drag to create a marquee outline of your frame, as shown in Figure 4-12.

Figure 4-12: Create a rectangular marquee where you want the frame to go.

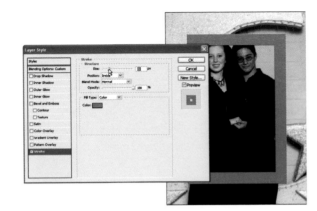

Figure 4-13: This simple outline is the basis for the picture frame.

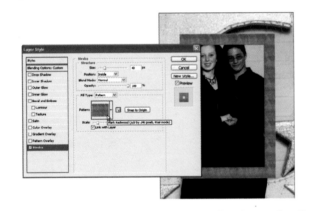

Figure 4-14: Changing the fill to a wood pattern makes it look much more like a picture frame.

NOTE

You can edit existing layer effects at any time by right-clicking a layer in the Layers palette and choosing Blending Options from the pop-up menu.

If you don't like your first outline:

- Click and drag again with the Marquee tool to define a new outline.

  –Or–

- Click **Select | Transform Selection** and resize and reposition your outline.

Don't worry about getting it perfect, it will be easy to change things later.

CREATE THE FRAME

1. Press **CTRL+DELETE** to fill the selection with the foreground color; it doesn't matter what color that is.

2. Press **CTRL+D** to deselect the selection. This gets rid of the distracting marquee around the edge of your rectangle.

3. In the Layers palette, set the Fill—not the Opacity—to **0**. This causes the rectangle, the fill, to disappear, but all layer effects will still be visible.

4. In the Layers palette, right-click the new layer, and choose **Blending Options** from the pop-up menu. The Blending Options dialog box appears.

5. Under Blending Options at the left, click **Stroke**. Don't worry about the color.

6. Set **Position** to **Inside**, **Blend Mode** to **Normal**, and leave **Opacity** at **100%**.

7. Drag the **Size** slider until the stroke is the desired size for your frame. Your frame will look something like Figure 4-13.

8. Under Fill Type, select **Pattern** and choose a pattern for your frame. A wood pattern works well, as show in Figure 4-14.

9. Drag the **Scale** slider beneath the pattern thumbnail to adjust the fit of the pattern in the frame.

BEVEL THE FRAME

The frame doesn't look very three-dimensional yet. Adding a bevel will fix that.

1. Under Blending Options at left, click **Bevel And Emboss**.

2. Set **Style** to **Inner Bevel**, **Technique** to **Chisel Hard**, and **Direction** to **Up**.

3. Experiment with different settings for **Size** and **Depth** to find a combination you like.

4. Under Shading, click and drag in the circle control to adjust the height and angle of the light, as shown in Figure 4-15.

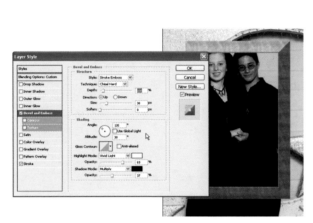

Figure 4-15: Adding a bevel effect gives the frame a 3-D look.

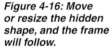

Figure 4-16: Move or resize the hidden shape, and the frame will follow.

5. Under Shading, set the **Highlight** and **Shadow** modes. Multiply usually works best for shadows, but experiment with different modes such as Vivid Light and Color Dodge for the highlights.

6. You can change the **Opacity** of the shadows and highlights as well to change the look of the simulated lighting. The higher the opacity is set, the brighter the simulated lighting will appear.

7. When you are happy with the results, press **OK** to accept the effects.

POSITION THE FRAME AND CROP

You can resize, move, and transform the layer contents to your heart's content; any layer effects will follow along.

With the frame layer still selected, press **CTRL+T** to enter Free Transform mode, as shown in Figure 4-16.

1. Drag on the handles to resize the frame.

2. Drag within the frame to move the frame within the canvas.

3. Press **ENTER** to accept the changes.

Crop the image to fit the new frame.

1. Press **CTRL** while you click the frame layer's thumbnail in the Layers palette to select all visible pixels.

2. Click **Edit | Crop** to crop the image to fit.

Save and Load Layer Styles

You needn't recreate a layer style every time you want to use it. You can save layer styles and recall them easily at any time.

1. If the Layer Style dialog box is not open, right-click the layer with the style you want to save, and select **Blending Options** from the pop-up menu.

2. In the Blending Options dialog box, click **New Style**.

3. Give your style a name, and click **OK** to save it.

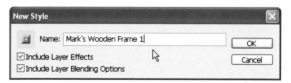

LOAD A STYLE

To load a saved style:

1. In the Layers palette, right-click the thumbnail of the layer you want to add layer effects to, and select **Blending Options** from the pop-up menu.

2. Click the **Styles** button at the top left of the Layer Style dialog box. Thumbnails of the currently available styles are displayed at right.

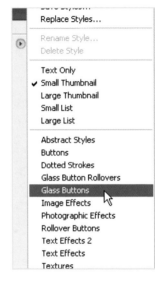

LOAD A COLLECTION OF PRESET STYLES

Photoshop ships with several collections of preset styles for creating photographic effects, buttons, and so forth. Load a collection of presets.

1. In the Layer Style dialog box, click **Styles** at the top left.

2. Click the **blue triangular button** at the top right of the style thumbnails.

3. Choose the collection of styles from the pop-up menu.

4. Either replace the current styles with the new styles, or append the new styles to the bottom of the list of available styles.

Blending Modes and Transparency

Simply placing one layer on top of another layer covers up the bottom layer. Sometimes this is just what you want, but Photoshop's layers allow you much more control than that. You can control the opacity (or transparency) of any layer. You can also change a layer's blending mode, which changes the way that layer interacts with any layers beneath it.

Work with Opacity and Fill

Each layer has two settings which control its transparency or lack thereof: Opacity and Fill.

The difference between Opacity and Fill is not initially very clear. A layer containing a photograph looks the same at 50 percent Opacity as it does at 50 percent Fill, as

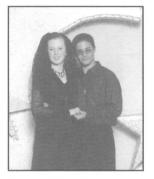

Figure 4-17a: Here is a photo layer at 50 percent Opacity.

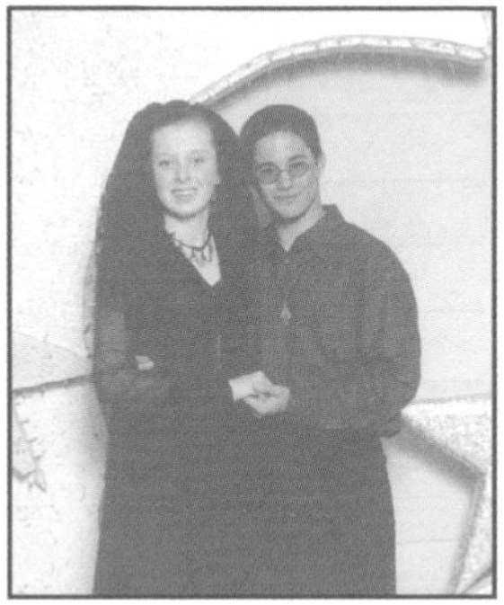

Figure 4-17b: Here is a photo layer at 50 percent Fill.

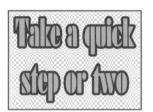

Figure 4-18a: Here you see text with a blue Stroke effect applied.

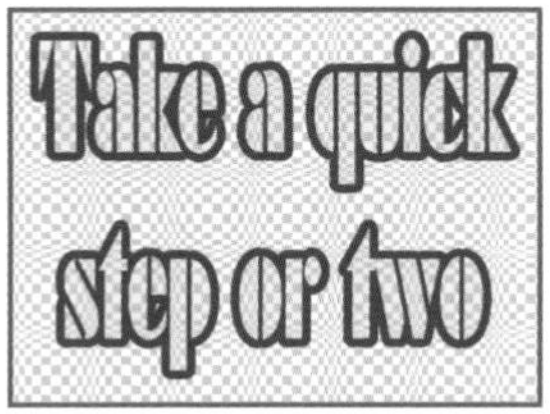

Figure 4-18b: Reducing the Fill leaves layer effects intact.

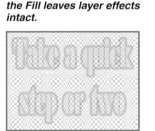

Figure 4-18c: Reducing the Opacity affects the entire layer.

NOTE

By reducing a layer's Fill to 0 percent, you can create layer effects such as drop shadows, without showing the shapes that create them.

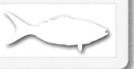

you can see in Figures 4-17a and 4-17b. The difference is that Fill affects the pixels in the layer; it does *not* affect any layer effects such as drop shadows. Opacity, on the other hand, affects the pixels in the layer *and* any layer effects. Look at Figures 4-18a and 4-18b. These show a text layer with a Stroke effect applied. As you can see, reducing the Fill to 50 percent makes the actual text partially transparent while leaving the Stroke effect entirely intact. On the other hand, reducing the Opacity to 50 percent renders the entire layer, including the Stroke effect, partially transparent.

ADJUST LAYER OPACITY

1. With an image open in Photoshop, create a second layer using any of the methods given above.
2. In the Layers palette, click the thumbnail of the top layer to select it.
3. Locate the **Opacity** control at the top of the Layers palette.
4. Click the **arrow** to the right of the current value, and use the drop-down slider to reduce the layer's **Opacity**. The lower layer shows through, as shown in Figure 4-19.

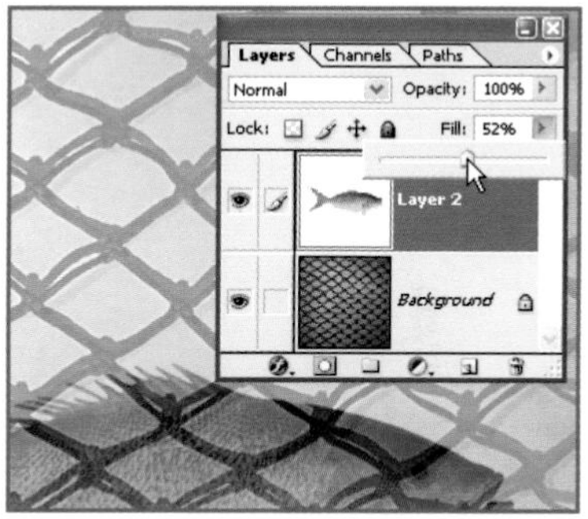

Figure 4-19: Set a layer's transparency in the Layers palette.

Use Blend Modes

So far, we have only explored layers using the Normal blending mode. But Photoshop has no less than 22 additional blend modes. Blend modes control the way Photoshop blends layers together. You can see many of them in Figure 4-20.

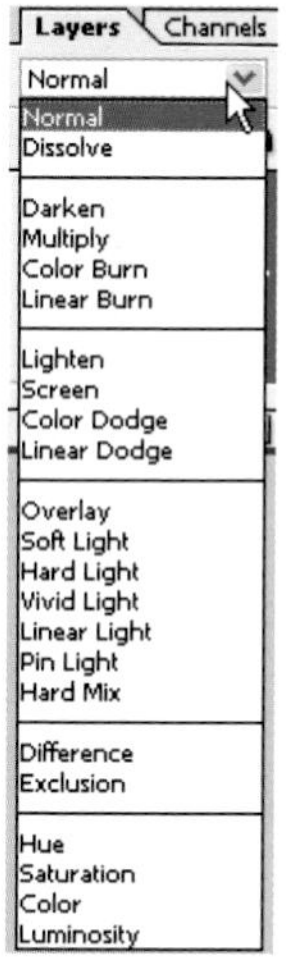

CHANGE A LAYER'S BLEND MODE

You can change a layer's blend mode at any time.

1. In the Layers palette, locate the **Blending** mode drop-down list at the top. It probably shows the word Normal.
2. Click the **Blending mode**. A menu of blending modes drops down.
3. Click a new blending mode, such as **Vivid Light**, to observe the effect.

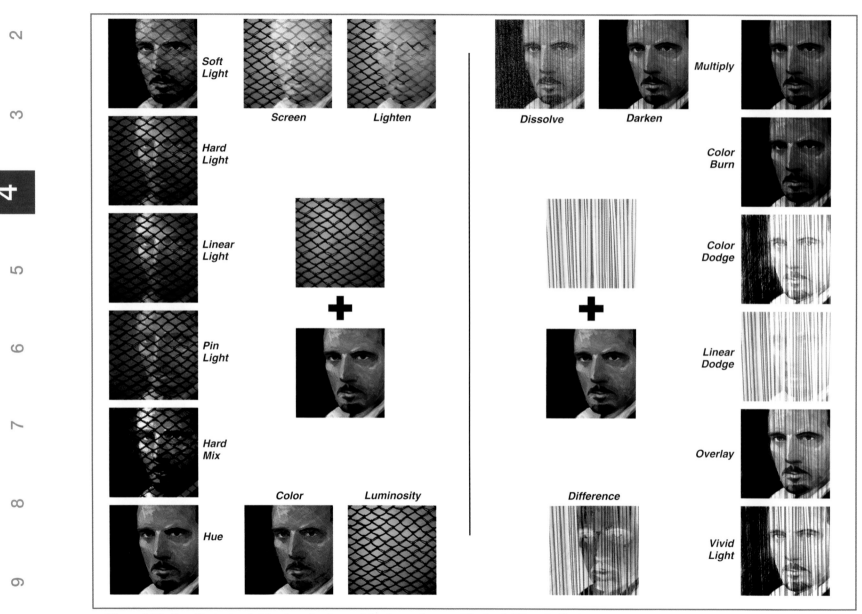

Figure 4-20: Use Photoshop's blend modes to combine layers for a multitude of different effects.

Figure 4-21: This is the original Mask photograph.

USE COMMON BLENDING MODES

Although you can choose from more than 20 layer blend modes, a few of them are especially handy.

USE MULTIPLY MODE

A layer in Multiply mode *always* darkens the image (except where the layer is pure white or transparent in which case Multiply has no effect). Placing a copy of the mask in Figure 4-21 on a new layer in Multiply mode darkens the original everywhere except in areas of pure white. The lighter a pixel in the Multiply layer, the less it darkens the overall image.

USE SCREEN MODE

Screen mode is the opposite of Multiply mode. A layer in Screen mode *always* lightens the image (except where the layer is pure black or transparent in which case it has no effect). Placing a copy of the mask in Figure 4-21 on a new layer in Screen mode lightens the original everywhere except in areas of pure black. The lighter a pixel in the Multiply layer, the more it lightens the overall image.

Create an Adjustment Layer

Layers don't always contain images or fills; they can also be adjustment layers. Adjustment layers allow you to make adjustments to an image without making any permanent changes to it. Your original image is preserved and you can tweak the adjustment further at any time.

Layer Select Filter View Window Help

New   ▶
Duplicate Layer...
Delete   ▶

Layer Properties...
Layer Style   ▶

New Fill Layer   ▶
New Adjustment Layer   ▶   Levels...
Change Layer Content   ▶   Curves...
Layer Content Options...   Color Balance...
Type   ▶   Brightness/Contrast...
Rasterize   ▶
                                    Hue/Saturation...
New Layer Based Slice   Selective Color...
                                    Channel Mixer...
Add Layer Mask   ▶   Gradient Map...
Enable Layer Mask   Photo Filter...

Add Vector Mask   ▶   Invert
Enable Vector Mask   Threshold...
                                    Posterize...
Create Clipping Mask   Ctrl+G

Figure 4-22: You can create a new adjustment layer via the Layer menu.

Figure 4-23: Hiding the adjustment layer shows that the original scan is untouched.

NOTE

If you select Use Previous Layer To Create Clipping Mask when creating an adjustment layer, the new adjustment layer will only affect the layer directly beneath it.

To create an adjustment layer:

1. Open a photograph in Photoshop.

2. Click **Layer | New Adjustment Layer**. You are presented with a submenu of adjustments you can make to your image, as shown in Figure 4-22.

3. For now, choose **Levels** (although you could choose any of the adjustments from the menu.) The New Layer dialog box appears. Click **OK**.

Click here to limit the new adjustment layer's effects to the layer directly beneath it.

New Layer

Name: Levels 1

☐ Use Previous Layer to Create Clipping Mask

Color: ☐ None

Mode: Normal   Opacity: 100 ▶ %

OK   Cancel

4. The Levels dialog box appears. Drag on the center of the three sliders beneath the image thumbnail. Drag far enough to one side to make the image significantly darker or lighter.

5. Click **OK**.

Levels

Channel: RGB

Input Levels: 0   3.23   255

Output Levels: 0   255

☑ Preview

OK
Cancel
Load...
Save...
Auto
Options...

The image looks very different, but the original photo layer is actually untouched. To see this:

In the Layers palette, click the Eye at the left of the adjustment layer to temporarily hide it. The photo returns to normal, as shown in Figure 4-23.

MAKE CHANGES TO AN ADJUSTMENT LAYER

In the Layers palette, double-click the layer thumbnail to reopen the appropriate dialog box (e.g., Levels).

DELETE AN ADJUSTMENT LAYER

In the Layers palette, click the **Adjustment** layer you want to delete, and drag it to the **Trashcan** icon at the bottom of the palette.

CREATING A QUICK SEPIA TONE

Blending modes make it easy to tint an image in Photoshop.

1. Open any color or black-and-white photograph in Photoshop, such as the one in Figure 4-24.

2. Click the **Create A New Layer** button at the bottom of the Layers palette, or click **Layer | New | Layer** to create a new blank layer.

3. Click the **foreground color** in the Toolbox, and use the **Color Picker** to choose a dark orange or brown. RGB 166, 131, 45 works well.

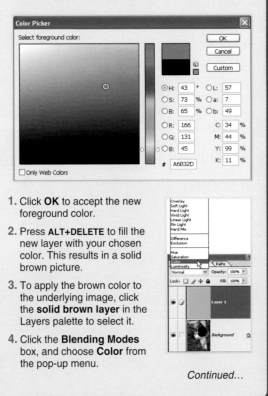

1. Click **OK** to accept the new foreground color.

2. Press **ALT+DELETE** to fill the new layer with your chosen color. This results in a solid brown picture.

3. To apply the brown color to the underlying image, click the **solid brown layer** in the Layers palette to select it.

4. Click the **Blending Modes** box, and choose **Color** from the pop-up menu.

Continued...

Create a Collage

The combination of layer blend modes, masking, and layer effects makes Photoshop a powerful tool for creating collages and multi-element compositions of all sorts. Here is an exercise that goes through the whole process, demonstrating the potential steps you might take.

CHOOSE YOUR IMAGES

Perhaps you have been given the task of designing the cover of a fictional novel called "Dust in my Teeth."

1. First, browse your collection of stock photographs, and find a few that seem to fit the title, including a photo of some false teeth and a photo of some worn leather.

2. Create a new Photoshop document the size of the book cover, say, 5 inches by 8, and drag both images into it on new layers. Now comes the fun part: combining the layers in different ways to see what comes up.

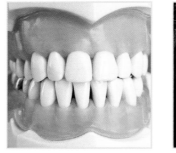 

BLEND THE LAYERS

1. Placing the teeth over the leather at 50 percent opacity, as shown in Figure 4-27, shows that the teeth line up nicely with the seams in the leather, but the effect isn't very pleasing.

2. Placing the teeth over the leather in Multiply mode produces an intriguing blend, as shown in Figure 4-28. The dark cracks in the leather make the teeth look dirty, but the result is too dark. Remember that Multiply mode darkens underlying layers; the dark leather completely overpowers the lighter teeth.

3. Placing the teeth over the leather in Screen mode, as shown in Figure 4-29, doesn't work. Screen mode always lightens, and the lighter tooth layer completely washes out the darker underlying leather layer.

QUICKSTEPS

CREATING A QUICK SEPIA TONE *(Continued)*

The results are seen in Figure 4-25. The color of every pixel in the underlying photo is replaced by the sepia color from the top layer. Luminance (the darkness or lightness of the pixels) is unaffected. This technique could be used to add any amount of any tint to an image. It works on black-and-white photos as well, as seen in Figure 4-26.

To fine-tune the effect:

● **Fill** the color layer with a different color.

–Or–

● Adjust the **Opacity** of the color layer.

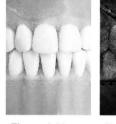

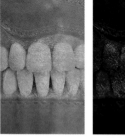

Figure 4-27: With the teeth layer at 50 percent Opacity, the leather shows through.

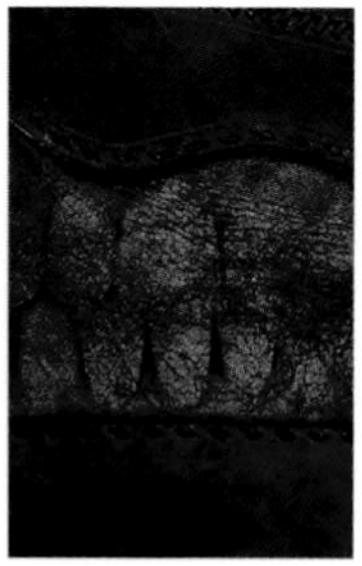

Figure 4-28: The teeth layer in Multiply mode makes things too dark.

Figure 4-29: Placing the teeth in Screen mode washes everything out.

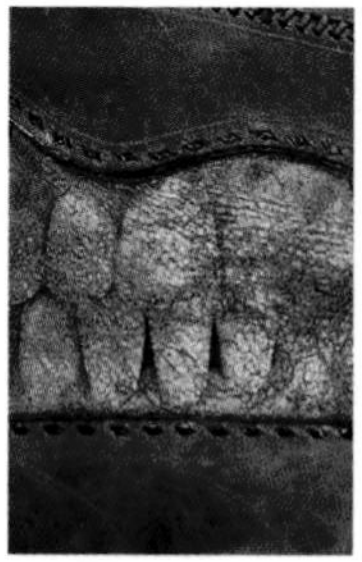

Figure 4-30: Overlay mode is the best so far.

Figure 4-31: Placing two copies of the teeth layer in Overlay mode heightens the effect.

Figure 4-24: Here is a scanned photograph.

Figure 4-25: The original photo is sepia toned, thanks to Color blend mode.

Figure 4-26: The original black-and-white scan is on the left; the sepia-toned version is on the right.

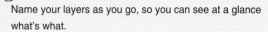

TIP

Name your layers as you go, so you can see at a glance what's what.

4. Trying different blend modes eventually leads you to Overlay mode, as show in Figure 4-30. This is pretty good. It has the same "dirty teeth" effect as Multiply mode produced, but the image is much brighter and easier to "read." (Overlay tends to preserve the highlights and shadows of the base layer while mixing in the colors of the top—Overlay—layer.) To heighten the effect, you could duplicate the tooth layer, leaving the new layer in Overlay mode, as well. The results are shown in Figure 4-31.

5. You might decide the image is a little too bright. To darken things up a bit, you could duplicate the leather layer, placing the new duplicate above the teeth layers in Multiply mode. (Nothing darkens like Multiply.) You can control the strength of the effect by reducing the Opacity of the Multiply layer, as shown in Figure 4-32.

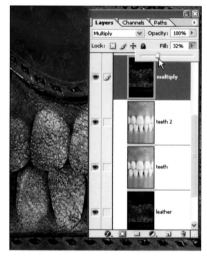

Figure 4-32: A copy of the leather layer, on top in Multiply mode, darkens the image up again.

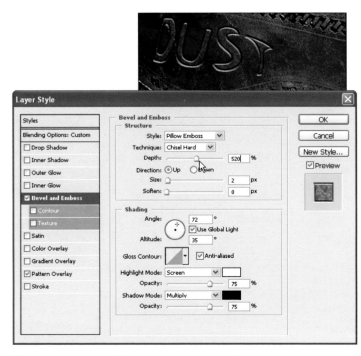

Figure 4-33: Layer effects make the text look hand carved into the leather.

ADD SOME TEXT

You might want to add some text.

Find a suitable font and begin to create the look of letters carved into the leather; for example, you could add a Bevel layer effect, using the Pillow Emboss style, as shown in Figure 4-33.

The final results might look like this:

Pretty nifty, and created with two stock photos and a few words ... plus, of course, plenty of blending modes, transparency, and layer effects.

How to...

- *Understand Bitmap and Vector Graphics*
- *Use the Pen Tool*
- *Using the Freeform Pen Tool*
- *Use the Magnetic Pen Tool*
- *Use Paths to Create Artwork*
- *Stroke and Fill Paths*
- *Converting Selections*
- *Use the Shape Tools*
- *Use the Brush Tool*
- *Editing Shapes*
- *Selecting Foreground and Background Colors*
- *Manage Brush Presets*
- *Using the Eraser Tool*
- *Erase Pixels*
- *Use the Gradient Tool*
- *Use the Paint Bucket Tool*
- *Create and Manage Patterns*
- *Use the Pattern Maker*
- *Use the Art History Brush*
- *Use the Preset Manager*
- *Use the Filter Gallery*
- *Use the Liquify Filter*

Chapter 5
Using Paths, Shapes and Painting

In addition to being one of the best image-editing applications on the planet, Photoshop also has a robust set of drawing tools. The drawing tools enable you to add vector-based graphics to your documents. With Photoshop, you can easily marry vector-based graphics with your bitmap images to create compelling illustrations, for commercial use or to spice up your holiday photos, by using shapes as borders for text captions.

Use the Pen Tool as a Drawing Tool

The pen may be mightier than the sword, but the Pen Tool is not mightier than the bitmap. The Pen Tool can, however, be used to add shapes to your documents as well as paths. You can align text to a work path. You can also use the Pen Tool to create intricate shapes with pinpoint accuracy. You can use the Pen Tool to trace a shape from a bitmap on another layer and use the shape as artwork for the illustration after deleting the bitmap.

Understand Bitmap and Vector Graphics

Bitmap images, also known as *raster* images, are comprised of individual dots of color that combine to create recognizable images. Bitmaps contain a given number of pixels and are resolution dependent. When a bitmap image is greatly enlarged, the individual pixels are readily apparent.

On the other hand, vector graphics are comprised of curves and lines that are mathematically created. Therefore, you can move and resize vector graphics without losing fidelity. Vector graphics are well suited for large areas of solid color. The lines and curves used to create a vector graphic remain crisp no matter how much they are enlarged. Use vector shapes to create graphics such as logos.

Use the Pen Tool

The Pen Tool enables you to create complex shapes and paths. You begin by clicking within the document where you want the shape or path to begin, and then you click to add additional points to define the shape. You use a combination of straight points and curve points to define the shape or path. After creating the shape or path, you can edit it point to point until you achieve the look you're after.

1. Select the **Pen Tool**.

2. In the Options bar, click the **Shape Layers** button to create a shape with a fill, or click the **Paths** button to create a path.

3. Click the **Color swatch** to open the Color Picker. This option determines the fill of a shape layer you create with the Pen Tool.

4. Select a color.

5. Click inside the document to define the first point of the shape or path.

6. Click to add additional points to the shape or path.

Pen Tool   P
Freeform Pen Tool   P
Add Anchor Point Tool
Delete Anchor Point Tool
Convert Point Tool

*Shape
Layers   Paths*

☑ Auto Add/Delete   Style: Color:

DRAW A STRAIGHT PATH

The straightest distance between two points is a straight line, something you can easily create with the Pen Tool.

1. Select the **Pen Tool**.

2. Click inside the document to define the first point of the shape or path.

3. Click elsewhere inside the document to create an anchor point for a straight-line segment.

DRAW A CURVED PATH

To create a complex shape or path, you combine straight-line segments with curves.

1. Select the **Pen Tool**.

2. Click and drag to create a curve point.

3. Click at the desired position to create a second curve point and drag. As you drag, two Bézier handles emanate from the point.

4. Continue adding points to define the shape or path.

5. Click the first point to close the shape or path.

EDIT ANCHOR POINTS

You can fine-tune a shape or path by moving, adding, deleting or converting points.

1. Select the **Direct Selection Tool**.

2. Click the **layer shape** or **path** whose points you want to edit. When you click a shape or path, the individual points that comprise the shape or path are displayed.

3. Select a **point** with the Direct Selection Tool, and drag it to a new location.

4. Select a **curve point** with the Direct Selection tool to display the curve's Bézier handles.

5. Drag a **Bézier handle** with the Direct Selection tool to reshape a curved segment.

6. Select the **Add Anchor Point Tool**, and click a location on the path where you want to add a point.

7. Select the **Delete Anchor Point Tool**, and click a point to delete it.

8. Select the **Convert Point Tool**, and click a curve point to convert it to a straight point.

9. Select the **Convert Point Tool**, and click and drag a straight point to convert it to a curve point. As you drag, two Bézier handles appear.

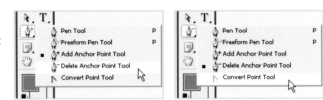

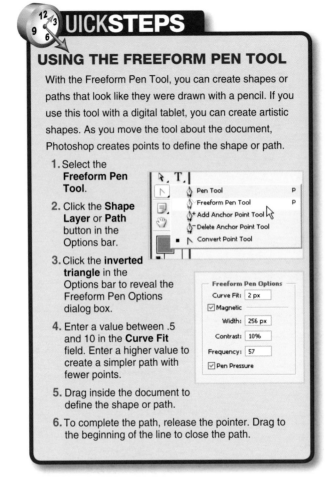

QUICKSTEPS

USING THE FREEFORM PEN TOOL

With the Freeform Pen Tool, you can create shapes or paths that look like they were drawn with a pencil. If you use this tool with a digital tablet, you can create artistic shapes. As you move the tool about the document, Photoshop creates points to define the shape or path.

1. Select the **Freeform Pen Tool**.

2. Click the **Shape Layer** or **Path** button in the Options bar.

3. Click the **inverted triangle** in the Options bar to reveal the Freeform Pen Options dialog box.

4. Enter a value between .5 and 10 in the **Curve Fit** field. Enter a higher value to create a simpler path with fewer points.

5. Drag inside the document to define the shape or path.

6. To complete the path, release the pointer. Drag to the beginning of the line to close the path.

Use the Magnetic Pen Tool

The Magnetic Pen Tool is a derivative of the Freeform Pen Tool. This tool develops a magnetic attraction to object edges in your document. You can define the range and sensitivity of the tool's snapping behavior as well as the complexity of the resulting path.

1. Select the **Freeform Pen Tool**.

2. In the Options bar, click the **down-pointing triangle** beneath the Help menu group to reveal the Freeform Pen Options dialog box and set the following parameters:

   ● **Width** determines how far an edge must be from the pointer before the tool detects it. Enter a value between 1 and 256.

   ● **Contrast** determines how much the contrast between pixels must differ before they are considered an edge. Enter a value between 1 and 100. Use a higher value when you are using the tool to trace objects in a low contrast image.

   ● **Frequency** determines how quickly the tool creates points. Enter a higher value and the tool snaps the path to edges more quickly.

   ● **Pen Pressure** varies the width of the path depending on the amount of pressure you apply when using a digital stylus and tablet. Deselect this option when using the tool with a mouse.

3. In the Options bar, click the **Magnetic** check box.

4. Drag the tool along the edges you want to trace.

Use Paths to Create Artwork

You can use paths to create vector artwork. You can create logos, or stylized versions of bitmap images. This process can be rather tedious if you are attempting to create vector artwork from a complex bitmap image.

1. Open the bitmap image you want to use as the basis for your vector artwork.
2. In the Layers palette, click the **Create A New Layer** button.
3. Select the **Pen Tool**.
4. Create the desired shapes, generating points as needed to create a reasonable facsimile of the shapes on the bitmap layer.
5. Fill the shapes as needed.
6. Delete the background layer.

TIP

The Magnetic Pen Tool will detect edges on a different layer.

Stroke and Fill Paths

If you use the Pen Tool to create a path and not a shape layer, the path has no stroke nor fill until you add it. You add a stroke (outline) and/or fill (solid color or pattern) to a path by selecting the path and then using options in the Paths palette.

FILL A PATH

1. Select one of the **Pen** tools.
2. In the Options bar, click the **Paths** button.
3. Create a path as outlined previously.
4. Select the **Path Selection Tool**.
5. Select the **Path**.
6. Select **Window | Paths** to open the Paths palette.
7. Click the **right-pointing triangle** in the upper-right corner of the palette, and from the drop-down menu select **Fill Path** to open the Fill Path dialog box.
8. Open the **Use** drop-down list, and select an option.
9. Click **OK** to fill the path.

Fill Path dialog box:

Contents
Use: Pattern
Custom Pattern:

Blending
Mode: Normal
Opacity: 100 %
Preserve Transparency

Rendering
Feather Radius: 0 pixels
Anti-aliased

OK
Cancel

TIP

Open the **Use** drop-down list, and choose an option to create a stroke using the current settings for a different tool.

QUICKSTEPS

CONVERTING SELECTIONS TO PATHS

If you create an intricate selection using the techniques outlined in Chapter 3, you can convert the selection to a path. After converting the selection to a path, you can add a stroke and fill as outlined previously, and use it as the basis for vector artwork.

1. Create a selection using any of the techniques outlined in Chapter 3.

2. Select **Windows | Paths** to display the Paths palette.

3. Click the **right-pointing triangle** in the upper-right corner of the palette, and select **Make Work Path** from the menu to open the Work Path dialog box.

Make Work Path

Tolerance: 10.0 pixels   OK   Cancel

4. Type a value in the **Tolerance** field, or accept the default value of 2.0 pixels. You can type a value between .50 and 10.0. This value determines the number of points that are used to create the path. Specify a high value for a smooth path with fewer points.

5. Click **OK** to convert the selection to a path.

ADD A STROKE TO A PATH

1. Select one of the **Pen** tools.

2. In the Options bar, click the **Paths** button.

3. Create a path as outlined previously.

4. Click the **Foreground** color swatch, and select a color for the stroke from the Color Picker.

5. Select the **Brush Tool**.

6. Define the size and shape of the brush. This determines the look of the stroke. You can choose a wide brush that feathers gradually to blend with surrounding pixels or a hard-edged brush to create a high-contrast outline for the path.

7. Click the **right-pointing triangle** in the upper-right corner of the palette, and from the drop-down menu select Stroke Path to reveal the **Stroke Path** dialog box.

Stroke Path

Tool: Brush   OK
☑ Simulate Pressure   Cancel

8. Accept the default **Pressure** option to simulate a stroke that was created with a digital stylus and tablet. Click the **Pressure** check box to deselect the option, and the stroke will be of uniform thickness.

9. Click **OK** to apply the stroke to the path.

Use the Shape Tools

You can use the Shape tools to add vector shapes to a document. You have six shape tools from which to choose: Rectangle Tool, Rounded Rectangle Tool, Ellipse Tool, Polygon Tool, Line Tool, and Custom Shape Tool. You specify the settings for each tool in the Options bar. For example, when you create a shape using the Rounded Rectangle Tool, you can specify the radius of the rectangle's corners. When you select the Custom Tool, you can select a preset shape.

1. Select one of the **Shape** tools.

2. In the Options bar, click one of the following buttons to define the type of shape you create:

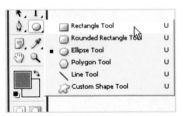

- **Shape Layers** creates a shape with a vector mask.

- **Paths** creates a working path.

- **Fill Pixels** creates a rasterized (bitmap) shape.

EDITING SHAPES

If you create a shape using the Shape Layers or Paths option, you can edit the shape. You can edit the shape by adding, converting, moving, or deleting points as outlined earlier in this chapter.

1. Select the **Direct Selection Tool**.

2. Select the shape you want to edit to reveal the points used to create the shape.

3. Select the applicable tool to edit the points as needed.

NOTE

Mode, Opacity, and Anti-aliased options are only available for a shape you create with the Fill Pixels option.

NOTE

The options vary for each shape. For the Rounded Rectangle Tool, you specify the corner radius; for the Polygon Tool you specify the number of sides; for the Line Tool, you specify the weight (thickness) of the line; and for the Custom Tool, you select a preset shape from the Shape menu.

TIP

Hold down the **SHIFT** key while dragging to create a rectangle or polygon of equal width and height or to create a circle.

3. Specify the Mode and Opacity for the shape you are about to create.

4. Accept the Anti-aliased option to blend pixels at the border of the shape with the pixels surrounding the shape. The Anti-aliased option prevents jagged edges at the border of the shape.

5. Specify other options for the shape.

6. Click the **inverted triangle** to reveal a menu that enables you to specify geometry options for the tool. The following image shows the geometry options for the Rounded Rectangle. Note that you can specify the exact size of the shape.

Rounded Rectangle Options		
○ Unconstrained		
○ Square		
◉ Fixed Size	W:	H:
○ Proportional	W:	H:
☐ From Center		☐ Snap to Pixels

7. Drag diagonally inside the document to create the shape. If you've specified the size of the shape, click inside the document.

Work with Paint

If you have a digital stylus or are adept at drawing with a mouse, you can use the Photoshop brushes to paint inside a document and add artistic splashes of color or perhaps to create a stylized work of art by painting on a separate layer with an underlying image as a template. You can also add color to a document in the form of a gradient (a blend of two or more colors) or a pattern.

Use the Brush Tool

You use brushes in Photoshop for many things: creating selections, specifying the stroke for a path, and so on. You also use the Brush Tool when you want to create an artistic daub of color in a document or to paint stylized strokes of color in a document.

1. Set the **Foreground color** as outlined previously.

2. Select the **Brush Tool** shown next.

3. In the Options bar, click the **triangle** to the right of the current brush tip to reveal the Brush Options menu.

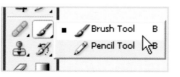

SELECTING FOREGROUND AND BACKGROUND COLORS

At the bottom of the toolbox are two color swatches. These are the Foreground and Background colors. When you use the Brush Tool or other tools that require color, you can set the Foreground and Background colors to the two colors you'll use most. Any tool requiring color will use the Foreground color. You can easily switch between the Foreground and Background colors by clicking an icon or pressing a keyboard shortcut.

1. Click the **Foreground swatch** to reveal the Color Picker.

2. Select the desired color and click **OK** to close the Color Picker.

3. Click the **Background color swatch** to reveal the Color Picker.

4. Select the desired color and click **OK** to close the Color Picker.

TIP

When you click either color swatch, an Eyedropper appears. Click the Eyedropper anywhere in the workspace to replace the current color in the Color Picker with the sampled color. Click OK to exit the Color Picker and apply the sampled color to the selected color swatch.

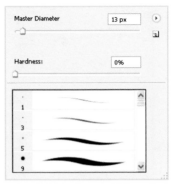

4. Drag the **scrollbar** to reveal thumbnail images of available brush types. The thumbnail gives you an idea of the type of stroke you can expect to paint with the brush tip.

5. Click a **brush tip thumbnail** to replace the current tip.

6. Drag the **Master Diameter slider** to specify the size of the brush tip in pixels.

7. Drag the **Hardness slider** to specify a value. Choose a low value for a soft-edged brush, a high value for a hard-edged brush.

8. Specify the **Mode, Opacity, and Flow**.

9. Click the **Airbrush Capabilities** button to enable airbrush capabilities. Use this option if you're using a digital airbrush with a tablet.

10. Drag inside the document to create the desired brush strokes. Alternatively, use your digital stylus and tablet to paint the desired brush strokes.

CHANGE BRUSH GROUPS

Photoshop has a wide variety of brushes you can use to create calligraphic brush strokes, watercolor brush strokes, and realistic facsimiles of objects like grass. The default brush group is powerful, but if you want more, you need look no further than the Brush Tip Options menu or the Preset Manager.

1. Select the **Brush Tool**.

2. Click the **triangle** to the right of the current brush tip to reveal the Brush menu.

3. Click the **right-pointing triangle** icon in the upper-right corner of the menu, and select a Brush group from the menu.

CREATE A CUSTOM BRUSH

If you like diversity (and who doesn't?), you can modify a brush preset. You can also create a brush from an image or a portion of an image. After doing either, you can save the brush preset for future use.

New Brush Preset...
Rename Brush...
Delete Brush

Text Only
Small Thumbnail
Large Thumbnail
Small List
Large List
✓ Stroke Thumbnail

Preset Manager...

Reset Brushes...
Load Brushes...
Save Brushes...
Replace Brushes...

Assorted Brushes
Basic Brushes
Calligraphic Brushes
Drop Shadow Brushes
Dry Media Brushes
Faux Finish Brushes
My Brushes
Natural Brushes 2
Natural Brushes
Special Effect Brushes
Square Brushes
Thick Heavy Brushes
Wet Media Brushes

TIP

You can switch between Foreground and Background colors by clicking the curve-with-two-arrows icon, or by pressing **X**.

TIP

You can restore the default Foreground and Background colors (black and white) by clicking the small icon at the left of the color swatches or by pressing **D**.

1. Open an image that contains an area you want to use for a brush preset.

2. Using one of the Selection tools, select the area of the image you want to define as the brush tip.

3. Select **Edit | Define Brush Preset** to display the Brush Name dialog box.

4. Type a name for the preset.

5. Click **OK** to add the preset to the Brushes palette using the selection area as the tip size.

CREATE A NEW DYNAMIC BRUSH

A brush with dynamic elements changes its tip as you paint with it. When you create a dynamic brush, you work with two elements: Jitter and Control. Jitter determines how much an element will vary as you paint with the brush. For example, you can vary the Hue, Saturation, and Opacity of a brush tip. Control options are available if you have a digital tablet, such as one manufactured by Wacom, attached to your system.

1. Create a new document with a white background. This blank canvas will be where you test your new brush.

2. Select the **Brush Tool**.

3. Select a brush preset.

4. Select **Window | Brushes** to open the Brushes palette.

5. Click the desired option check box to select an option, and then click the option title to reveal the parameters for that option. This image shows the parameters for the Scattering option.

6. Adjust the parameters as desired.

7. Click the **button** to the right of the **Control field** if you're using a digital tablet, and select one of the options from the drop-down list.

Create New Brush

8. Test your new brush by painting on the canvas.
9. Click the **Create New Brush** button to open the Brush Name dialog box.
10. Type a **Name** for the brush, and click **OK**.

Manage Brush Presets

When you add several custom brushes to a library, the sheer volume of brushes may make finding a specific brush a difficult task. You can save a brush library as a custom library and manage the new library by deleting the presets that are duplicates of another library.

SAVE A BRUSH LIBRARY

1. Select the **Brush Tool**.
2. Click the **inverted triangle** to the right of the current Brush tip to reveal the Brush menu.
3. Click the **right-pointing triangle** in the upper-right corner of the menu, and select **Save Brushes** to open the Save dialog box.
4. Type a **File Name** for the new brush library.
5. Click **OK**.

LOAD A BRUSH LIBRARY

1. Select the **Brush Tool**.
2. Click the **inverted triangle** to the right of the current Brush tip to reveal the Brush menu.
3. Click the **right-pointing triangle** in the upper-right corner of the menu, and select **Load Brushes** to open the Load dialog box.
4. Select the brush library you want to install, and then click **Load**.

DELETE A BRUSH

1. Select the **Brush Tool**.
2. Select the thumbnail of the brush you want to delete.
3. Click the **right-pointing triangle** in the upper-right corner of the menu, and select **Delete Brush**. The Delete Brush dialog box appears.
4. Click **OK** to delete the brush.

QUICKSTEPS

USING THE ERASER TOOL

1. Select the **Eraser Tool**.

2. In the Options bar, click the **button** to the right of the **Mode field**, and select **Block**, **Brush**, or **Pencil**. Block mode has no options

3. Specify brush size and tip if you've selected Brush or Pencil mode.

4. Specify **Opacity** if you've selected Brush or Pencil mode.

5. Specify **Flow** if you've selected Brush mode.

6. Click the **Enable Airbrush Capacities** button if you're using a digital airbrush stylus in Brush mode.

7. Drag inside the document to erase pixels.

TIP

To prevent erasing an area such as a silhouette of a building or a line of trees, click the **Foreground** color swatch, and use the Eyedropper to sample the color you want to protect. Select the **Protect Foreground Color** option for the Background Eraser Tool prior to dragging the tool along the border of the area you want to preserve.

Erase Pixels

To err is human, which is why every graphics application has an erase tool. Photoshop designers have hedged all bets by giving you a choice of three erase tools: the Eraser Tool to erase unwanted pixels of color; the Background Eraser Tool to erase parts of a layer to transparency while preserving the edges of an object in the foreground; the Magic Eraser Tool to erase pixels similar in color to the background color.

USE THE BACKGROUND ERASER TOOL

1. Select the **Background Eraser Tool.**

2. In the Options bar, click the **inverted triangle** to reveal the Background Eraser settings dialog box.

3. Specify settings for **Diameter**, **Hardness**, **Spacing**, **Angle**, and **Roundness**.

4. If you're using a digital stylus, click the **button** to the right of the **Size Tolerance** fields, and select **Pen Pressure** or **Stylus Wheel** depending on the type of digital stylus you are using. Select **Off** if you're not using a digital stylus.

5. Open the **Limits** drop-down list, and select one of the following options:

   - **Discontiguous** erases pixels of the sampled color wherever they occur under the brush.

   - **Contiguous** erases pixels of the sampled color that are connected to each other.

   - **Find Edges** erases pixels of the sampled color that are connected to each other while preserving the integrity of edges.

6. Type a **value** in the **Tolerance** field. Specify a low value to erase areas similar to the sampled color; a high value to erase a broader range of colors.

7. Select the **Protect Foreground Color** option to prevent the tool from erasing pixels of the Foreground color.

8. Open the **Sampling** drop-down list, and choose one of the following options:

- **Once** erases only areas of the sampled color that you first click.

- **Continuous** samples colors under the Eraser continuously as you drag the tool across the document.

- **Background Swatch** erases only pixels of the current Background color.

9. Drag the tool across the area you want to erase.

USE THE MAGIC ERASER TOOL

1. Select the **Magic Eraser Tool**.

2. In the Options bar, type a **value** in the **Tolerance** field. Specify a low tolerance to erase pixels similar in color to the first pixels you click with the tool, a high tolerance to erase a wider range of colors.

3. Select the **Anti-Aliased** option (the default) and Photoshop smoothes the edges of areas you erase.

4. Select the **Contiguous** option (the default) to erase only areas of contiguous pixels containing the sampled color. Deselect the option to erase all areas of pixels of similar color as you erase.

5. Select the **Use All Layers** option to erase similar colors on all visible layers in the document.

6. Type a **value** in the **Opacity** field. The default value of 100 percent erases pixels completely. Specify a lower value to partially erase pixels.

7. Drag the tool over the area you want to erase.

Use the Gradient Tool

The Gradient Tool enables you to apply a blend of two or more colors to a background layer or to a selection.

APPLY A GRADIENT FILL

1. Select the **layer** to which you want to apply the gradient fill. Alternatively, use one of the Selection tools to select the area to which you want to apply the fill.

2. Select the **Gradient Tool**.

> **NOTE**
>
> If you are going to save a document as a GIF file, refrain from using the Gradient Tool as gradients in GIF images have a tendency to show bands due to the limited color palette.

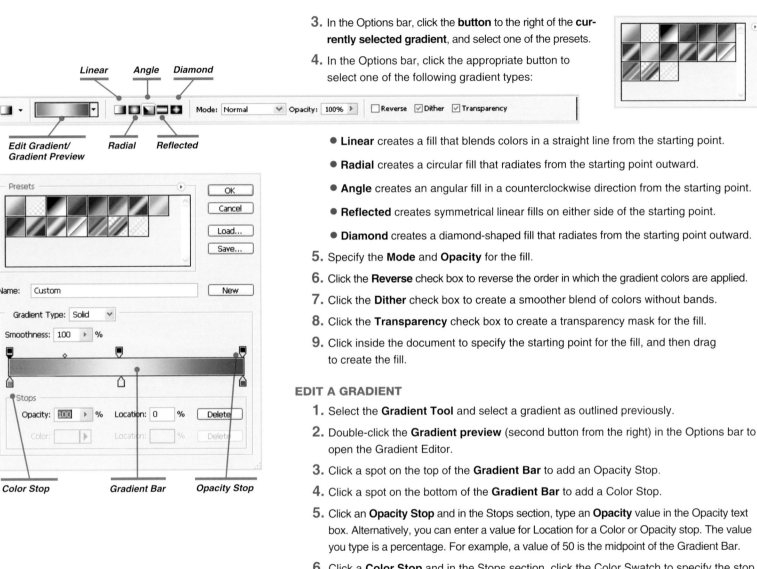

3. In the Options bar, click the **button** to the right of the **currently selected gradient**, and select one of the presets.

4. In the Options bar, click the appropriate button to select one of the following gradient types:

- **Linear** creates a fill that blends colors in a straight line from the starting point.
- **Radial** creates a circular fill that radiates from the starting point outward.
- **Angle** creates an angular fill in a counterclockwise direction from the starting point.
- **Reflected** creates symmetrical linear fills on either side of the starting point.
- **Diamond** creates a diamond-shaped fill that radiates from the starting point outward.

5. Specify the **Mode** and **Opacity** for the fill.

6. Click the **Reverse** check box to reverse the order in which the gradient colors are applied.

7. Click the **Dither** check box to create a smoother blend of colors without bands.

8. Click the **Transparency** check box to create a transparency mask for the fill.

9. Click inside the document to specify the starting point for the fill, and then drag to create the fill.

EDIT A GRADIENT

1. Select the **Gradient Tool** and select a gradient as outlined previously.

2. Double-click the **Gradient preview** (second button from the right) in the Options bar to open the Gradient Editor.

3. Click a spot on the top of the **Gradient Bar** to add an Opacity Stop.

4. Click a spot on the bottom of the **Gradient Bar** to add a Color Stop.

5. Click an **Opacity Stop** and in the Stops section, type an **Opacity** value in the Opacity text box. Alternatively, you can enter a value for Location for a Color or Opacity stop. The value you type is a percentage. For example, a value of 50 is the midpoint of the Gradient Bar.

6. Click a **Color Stop** and in the Stops section, click the Color Swatch to specify the stop color from the Color Picker stop. Alternatively, you can double-click the **Color Stop** to open the Color Picker.

7. Click **OK** to apply the changes.

Use the Paint Bucket Tool

Use the Paint Bucket Tool to replace areas of color with a different color. You can determine the extent of the color replacement by specifying a Tolerance value.

1. Select a **Foreground color**.

2. Select the **Paint Bucket Tool**.

3. In the Options bar, click the **button** to the right of the **Fill** field, and select **Foreground**, to fill the tool with the Foreground color, or **Pattern**. If you select **Pattern**, the Pattern field becomes available.

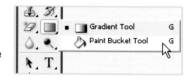

4. Click the **inverted triangle** to the right of the current pattern preview, and select a **preset**.

5. Specify **Mode** and **Opacity** for the tool.

6. Type a **value** in the **Tolerance** field. This value determines how closely pixels must match before they are filled. You can specify a value between 0 and 255. Enter a low value to fill pixels that are similar in color, a high value to fill pixels with a wider color range.

7. Click the **Anti-Aliased** check box (the default) to ensure smooth blending of adjacent pixels.

8. Click the **Contiguous** check box (the default) to fill contiguous pixels of similar color. Deselect the option to fill all similar pixels within the image.

9. Click the **All Layers** check box to apply the fill to pixels of similar color in all layers.

10. Click inside the area you want to fill.

Create and Manage Patterns

You can create patterns by sampling an area from within an image. After creating a pattern, you can apply it as a fill using the Paint Bucket Tool.

Use the Pattern Maker

The Pattern Maker enables you to create your own patterns by sampling selected areas of an image. You can use the tool to add patterns to the Pattern library. The Pattern Maker is capable of generating up to twenty patterns from a selection. You select the patterns you want to add to the Pattern library and delete the rest.

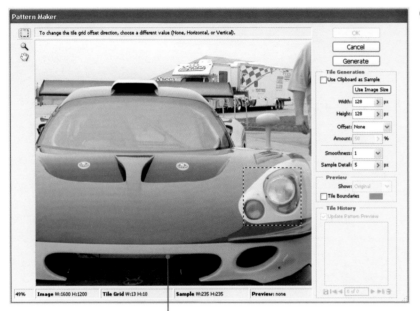

Original image in Pattern
Maker dialog box

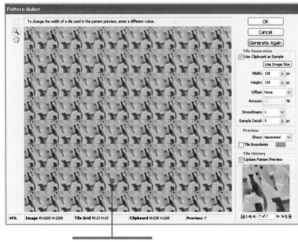

Generated pattern

CREATE A PATTERN

1. Open the desired image.

2. Select the **Rectangular Marquee Tool**, and select the pixels you want to use as the basis for your pattern. Hold down the **SHIFT** key while making the selection to constrain the selection bounding box to a square.

3. Select **Edit | Copy** to copy the selection to the clipboard.

4. Select **Filter | Pattern Maker** to open the Pattern Maker dialog box.

5. Click the **Use Clipboard As Sample** check box.

6. Type equal values in the **Width** and **Height** fields to create a square pattern. Alternatively, you can click the button to the right of each field, and drag the sliders to set Width and Height.

7. To offset the tiles, click the **button** to the right of the **Offset** field, and select **Vertical** or **Horizontal**. After you select an offset option, the Amount field becomes available. Type the **amount** by which you want the tiles offset. This value is a percentage of the dimension in the specified direction.

8. Click the **button** to the right of the **Smoothness** field, and choose a value from the drop-down list. Alternatively, you can type a value from 1 to 3 in the field. A higher value produces a more complex pattern, and the pixel transitions are not as smooth.

9. Click the **button** to the right of the **Sample** field, and drag the slider to specify the sample size from within the selected area. Small values work better and create more interesting patterns.

10. Click **Generate Pattern** to create a tiled preview of the pattern in the preview area.

11. Click **Generate Again** to create additional patterns. You can generate up to twenty patterns. After generating patterns, you preview them and decide which ones you want to add to the Pattern Library.

PREVIEW AND SAVE PATTERNS

1. Click the **buttons** at the bottom of the preview window in the Tile History section to preview the patterns you've generated. Alternatively, you can type the number of the pattern you want to view, and then press **ENTER**.

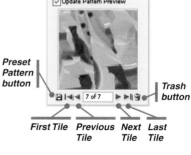

Tile History

Preset
Pattern
button

Trash
button

First Tile   Previous   Next   Last
             Tile   Tile   Tile

2. Click the **Trash button** to delete a tile.

3. Click the **Preset Pattern button** to open the Pattern Name dialog box.

4. Type a name for the pattern, and then click **OK**. After saving the pattern, it appears in the Pattern Library for future use.

Use the Art History Brush

The Art History Brush makes it possible for you to create stylized artwork by painting into an image using a history state. As a rule, you'll open an image, apply a filter to the image, and then use that history state as the basis for the Art History Brush.

1. Open the desired image.

2. Apply the desired filters to the image.

3. Select the **Art History Brush**.

4. In the Options bar, select a brush tip and diameter as outlined previously.

5. Specify the **Mode** and **Opacity**.

6. Open the **Style** drop-down list, and choose an option from the drop-down list. Each option is a description of the type of brush stroke the tool will create.

7. Type a value for **Area**. This value designates the area covered by a brush stroke with the tool. If you specify a large value, the tool covers a large area and creates numerous brush strokes.

8. Type a value for **Tolerance**. Specify a low value to paint anywhere in the image, a high value to paint only in areas where the color of the history state varies greatly from the image's original color.

9. Select **Window | History** to open the History palette.

10. Click the **Open** history state. This returns the image to its original state; however, the filter is still applied until you use the Art History Brush.

11. Click the blank square in the Set Source For The History Brush column to the left of the image state that you want the Art History Brush to sample.

12. Drag inside the image to paint with the tool. Figure 5-1 shows an image before and after a makeover with the Art History Brush.

Figure 5-1: You can create stylized artwork by painting inside an image with the Art History Brush.

Use the Preset Manager

The Preset Manager enables you to manage presets for every preset library in Photoshop. You use the Preset Manager to rename presets, load preset libraries, save presets, and more.

SELECT A PRESET TYPE

1. Select **Edit | Preset Manager** to open the Preset Manager dialog box.
2. Click the button to the right of the **Preset Types** field, and select the desired type from the drop-down list.
3. Click a preset to select it. After selecting a preset, you can do one of the following:

   • Click **Rename** to open the Rename dialog box and rename the preset.

   • Click **Delete** to delete the preset.

4. Click **Done** to exit the Preset Manager and apply your changes.

CREATE A PRESET GROUP

1. Select **Edit | Preset Manager** to open the Preset Manager dialog box.
2. Click the **button** to the right of the **Preset Types** field, and select the desired type from the drop-down list.
3. Select the presets you want to combine as a group. Click the first preset, and then press **CTRL** while clicking additional presets you want to add to the group.
4. Click **Save Set** to open the Save dialog box. The file format will vary depending on the preset group you're editing. For example, the file format for styles is ASL.
5. Type a name for the preset group, and then click **Save**.

LOAD A PRESET GROUP

1. Select **Edit | Preset Manager** to open the Preset Manager dialog box.
2. **Click** the **button** to the right of the **Preset Types** field, and select the desired type from the drop-down list.
3. Click **Load** to open the Load dialog box.
4. Select the desired preset group.
5. Click **Load** to load the desired group.

Work with Filters

Photoshop has many filters that you can use to add artistic touches to images. If you've ever felt the need to unleash the repressed artist within you, the Filter Gallery is your source for artistic materials. You can apply a single filter to create an image that looks like a watercolor painting. If you're into distorting images for fun and profit, you'll love the Liquify Filter. It's like virtual silly putty.

Use the Filter Gallery

You use the Filter Gallery to apply one or more filters to an image to achieve a desired look. Each filter has parameters that you can modify to suit your individual taste. When you apply multiple filters to an image, you can arrange the order in which they are applied to the image.

APPLY FILTERS INDIVIDUALLY

1. Select the desired image.
2. Select **Filter | Filter Gallery** to display the image in the Filter Gallery.
3. Select the desired filter from one of the filter groups. To display the contents of a filter group, click the **right-pointing triangle** to view all filters within a group.
4. Adjust the filter parameters to suit your taste.
5. Click **OK** to apply the filter.

APPLY MULTIPLE FILTERS WITH THE FILTER GALLERY

1. Select the desired image
2. Select **Filter | Filter Gallery**.
3. Apply a filter as outlined previously.
4. Press the **ALT** key while clicking another filter. Figure 5-2 shows an image with multiple filters applied to it.

Figure 5-2: You can achieve a desired effect by applying multiple filters to an image.

5. After applying multiple filters, you can do the following:

 • Click the **Eyeball icon** to the left of a filter's name to temporarily disable it.

 • Drag a filter to a different position in the hierarchy. Drag it up the list to apply it before filters beneath it or down the list to apply it after other filters.

 • Select a filter, and click the **Delete Effect Layer button** to remove the filter.

6. Click **OK** to apply the filters to the image.

Use the Liquify Filter

If you like Salvador Dali's painting with the melting watches, *The Persistence of Memory*, you'll love the Liquify Filter. The Liquify Filter is a great tool which you can use to achieve surreal effects. It's also a great tool for distorting your former significant other's image into something that will make you laugh.

Forward Warp Tool
Reconstruct Tool
Twirl Clockwise Tool
Pucker Tool
Bloat Tool
Push Left Tool
Mirror Tool
Turbulence Tool
Freeze Mask Tool
Show Mask Tool
Hand Tool
Zoom Tool

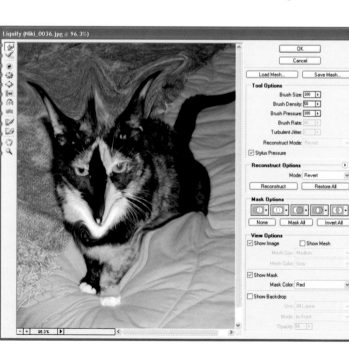

1. Select the image you want to liquify.

2. Select **Filter | Liquify** to open the Liquify dialog box.

3. In the Tool Options section, type values in the applicable boxes to set the following parameters:

 • **Brush Size** sets the size of the brush you'll use to distort the image.

 • **Brush Density** determines the range of the brush from the center point. Specify a low value and the transformations occur at the center of the brush without radiating outward, a high value and the tool distorts pixels at a greater distance from the center.

 • **Brush Pressure** sets the rate at which the transformations occur when you drag the brush across an image. Specify a low value and the transformations occur at a slower rate, a high value and the transformations occur at a faster rate.

 • **Brush Rate** determines how quickly transformations occur when you hold a tool such as the Twirl Clockwise tool stationary in the image. Specify a low value and transformations occur slowly, a high value and transformations occur more rapidly.

- **Turbulent Jitter** determines how tightly the Turbulence tool scrambles pixels.

4. Open the **Reconstruct Mode** drop-down list, and select an option to determine how the Reconstruct Tool reconstructs the area of the preview image you drag the tool across. Your options are:

   - **Revert** returns the area of the image over which you use the Reconstruct tool to its original state without any smoothing of pixels.

   - **Rigid** restores the reconstructed area to its original state while maintaining the right angles between frozen and unfrozen areas.

   - **Stiff** configures the Reconstruct tool to act as a weak magnet between frozen and unfrozen edges, thus reconstructing the edge area without disturbing any distortions in the frozen areas.

   - **Smooth** causes pixels between edges of distortions and edges between frozen and unfrozen areas to be smoothed while reconstructed.

   - **Loose** is similar to the Smooth option, reconstructing the edges between frozen and unfrozen areas with even greater continuity.

   - **Displace** reconstructs unfrozen areas while matching the level of distortion at the start point. If you are not reconstructing near a frozen area, this option causes the tool to create an interesting clone effect of the undistorted areas near the area in which you initially begin using the tool.

   - **Amplitwist** reconstructs areas near the initial use of the Reconstruct tool, using the start point displacement, rotation, and scale.

   - **Affine** causes areas near the point at which you initially use the Reconstruct tool to be reconstructed using all distortions that are present at the start point.

5. Click the **Stylus Pressure check box** if you're using the tool with a digital stylus. When you select this option, the Brush Pressure setting for the tool is amplified by the amount of pressure you use while pressing the digital stylus on the digital tablet.

6. Select and drag a **Liquify** tool across the image in the preview window. Use as many tools as often as needed to achieve the desired distortion level.

7. Select the **Reconstruct Tool** to selectively reconstruct areas of the image using the current Reconstruct Mode.

8. Click **OK** to apply the Liquefy Filter to the image.

How to...

- *Rotate and Flip the Images*
- *Straighten a Photo with Free Transform*
- *Straightening a Photo with the Measure Tool + Rotate Canvas*
- *Resize and Trim Images*
- *Using the Crop Command*
- *Using the Eyedropper Tool*
- *Use a Histogram to View the Tonal Range*
- *Adjust the Tonal Range with Levels*
- *Use the Curves Command*
- *Color Correct Images*
- *Using Color Balance*
- *Edit in 16-bit Mode*
- *Working with Adjustment Layers*
- *Sharpen and Blur Images*
- *Fine-tuning with the Sharpen, Blur, and Smudge Tools*
- *Retouch and Repair Images*
- *Changing Image Colors*
- *Use Dust and Scratches Filter*
- *Creating a Sepia Tone from a Color or Grayscale Photo*

Chapter 6

Color Correcting, Retouching, and Repairing Images

This chapter shows you how to use powerful Photoshop menu commands and tools to resample and resize images. You'll also learn to repair defective images and use the Photoshop toolkit to sharpen photos and add pizzazz to images.

Perform Simple Image Corrections

Simple image corrections make it possible for you to correct faults, such as skewed images resulting from originals being incorrectly placed in a scanner. You can also rotate an image. If you shoot images with a digital camera and rotate the camera to take a portrait, the image may come into your computer in landscape (horizontal) format. You can rotate these images so they display properly. You can use the Crop command to remove unwanted material around your center of interest.

Rotate and Flip the Images

If an image is not properly oriented, you can rectify this by rotating the image. You can rotate an image 90 degrees in a clockwise or counterclockwise direction or rotate an image 180 degrees. You can also flip an image horizontally or vertically.

1. Open the image you need to reorient.

2. Select **Image | Rotate Canvas** and select one of the following options:

   - **180°** rotates the image 180 degrees.

   - **90° CW** rotates the image 90 degrees in a clockwise direction.

   - **90° CCW** rotates the image 90 degrees in a counterclockwise direction.

   - **Arbitrary** opens a dialog box in which you can enter the number of degrees to rotate the canvas. Click the CW button to rotate the image clockwise or the CCW button to rotate the image counterclockwise.

   - **Flip Canvas Horizontal** flips the canvas horizontally (from left to right).

   - **Flip Canvas Vertical** flips the canvas vertically (from top to bottom).

Straighten a Photo with Free Transform

If an image is slightly skewed, you can easily straighten it using the Free Transform command. First enable the grid, which provides a visual reference in the form of straight vertical and horizontal lines. After selecting the Free Transform command, you can rotate the image, aligning a feature such as the edge of a building that should be vertical or horizontal to the grid.

1. Open the image you want to straighten.

2. Select **View | Show | Grid** to display the grid, shown in Figure 6-1.

3. Select **Edit | Free Transform**. Alternatively you can press **CTRL + T**. After invoking the Free Transform command, eight handles appear around the image perimeter. If you cannot see the handles, maximize the image.

4. Move your pointer beyond the border of the image until it becomes a curved line with two arrowheads.

TIP

If you need to rotate an image that resides on a layer, select the image and select **Edit | Transform** and then select one of the rotate or flip commands from the submenu.

Figure 6-1: Use the grid to straighten an image.

NOTE

Before you can apply the Transform command, you must first unlock the Background layer. (See Chapter 4, "Using Layers," for additional information.)

STRAIGHTENING A PHOTO WITH THE MEASURE TOOL + ROTATE CANVAS

If you have an image that is askew and has a straight edge, such as the edge of a roof or side of a building, you can quickly straighten the image using the Measure Tool and a menu command. If you need to straighten a photo quickly, this is the ideal method to use.

1. Open the image you want to straighten.

2. Select the **Measure Tool**.

3. Drag the tool along an edge that should be vertical or horizontal.

Eyedropper Tool   I
Color Sampler Tool   I
Measure Tool   I

4. Select **Image | Rotate Canvas | Arbitrary** to open the Rotate Canvas dialog box. Notice that a value is already entered, and a rotation direction has been selected in the dialog box. Photoshop determined that rotating the image this number of degrees will straighten it.

Rotate Canvas
Angle: 1.94   ○ °CW   ⊙ °CCW   OK   Cancel

5. Click **OK**. Figure 6-2 shows an image after straightening.

6. Use the **Crop** tool to remove the non-image areas at the edge of the canvas. See "Crop a Photo with the Crop Tool".

Figure 6-2: You can straighten an image with the Measure Tool.

5. Drag left or right to rotate the image, releasing the mouse button when the image is straightened as desired.

6. Press **ENTER** to apply the transformation.

7. Use the **Crop tool** to remove non-image areas at the edge of the canvas. See "Crop a Photo with the Crop Tool" later in this chapter.

8. Select **File | Save**.

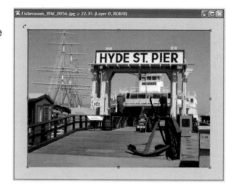

Resize and Trim Images

When you edit images, you often have more information than you need. An image may have undesirable objects that detract from your center of interest, or it may simply be too large for the intended destination. After all, you don't post a 4-MB image on a web site. Other times you may need additional canvas area to add text and other elements. Photoshop has a plethora of tools that you can use to resize and trim images.

CROP A PHOTO WITH THE CROP TOOL

Use the Crop tool to trim an image to the desired size. You can make a freehand selection, or you can specify the resolution and the size of the area the tool will crop to.

1. Open the image you want to crop.

2. Select the **Crop** tool.

Crop Tool

3. Drag diagonally inside the image to define the size of the cropped image. Photoshop displays a cropping rectangle inside the image. Eight handles appear on the perimeter of the rectangle, as shown in Figure 6-3.

4. If the cropping rectangle is not sized as desired, do one of the following:

- **Drag a corner handle** to resize the width and height of the cropping rectangle. Hold down the **SHIFT** key to resize proportionately.

- **Drag the middle handle** on the left or right border to change the width of the cropping rectangle.

Figure 6-3: Adjust the cropping rectangle to the desired size.

- **Drag the center handle** on the top or bottom border to change the height of the cropping rectangle.

- **Drag inside the cropping rectangle** to move it to a different position.

5. Press **ENTER** to crop the image.

RESIZE AN IMAGE: RESOLUTION AND IMAGE SIZE

You can use menu commands to resize an image to specific dimensions. You can also change the image resolution to suit the intended destination. For example, if you're going to print the image, select a resolution between 150 and 300 pixels per inch.

1. Open the image you want to resize.

2. Select **Image | Image Size** to open the Image Size dialog box.

3. Under Pixel Dimensions, type values for Width and Height. Alternatively you can type values under Document Size to size an image for a printer. After you type new values, the document file size is updated near the top of the dialog box. The old file size appears in parentheses.

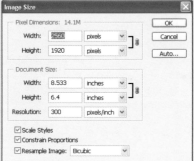

4. Click **Auto** to open a dialog box that enables you to type the desired resolution value in a text field. Other options appear depending on the image file type you're editing. For example, a JPEG file has three quality options: Draft, Good, and Best.

5. If you have layers with styles applied, accept the default **Scale Styles** option; otherwise, click the **Scales Styles** check box to deselect the option.

6. Accept the default **Resample Image** options, and select one of the following interpolation options from the drop-down menu:

   - **Nearest Neighbor** is the quickest, yet least precise, method of interpolation. Use this method when resizing illustrations with no embedded bitmaps (full-color images) as this method of interpolation does not apply anti-aliasing to edges. This interpolation method results in the smallest file size.

   - **Bilinear** is acceptable for bitmaps and produces a medium-quality image.

- **Bi-Cubic** is a more precise method of interpolation, resulting in smooth gradations between tones.

- **Bi-Cubic Smoother** should be used when you're increasing the size of an image. This method smoothes the pixels in an attempt to avoid the blocky pixelated look sometimes seen when an image is upsized.

- **Bi-Cubic Sharper** should be used when you decrease the size of an image. This method of interpolation sharpens the image to maintain detail. If the resized image is too sharp, select the Bi-Cubic method.

7. Click **OK**.

CHANGE THE CANVAS SIZE

When you open an image in Photoshop, the canvas size and the image size are the same. You can, however, increase the size of the canvas, which gives you more working area around the image. You can change canvas size to display a color border around your image. When you change the canvas size, you can specify where the additional canvas is added to the document.

1. Select **Image | Canvas Size** to open the Canvas Size dialog box. The current canvas dimensions are listed in the Canvas Size section.

2. Type new values in the Width and Height text boxes. Alternatively, you can click the **Relative** check box, which enables you to type values that will be added to the current canvas width and height.

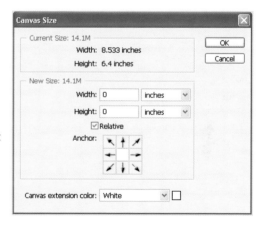

3. In the Anchor section, click the direction from which you want the canvas extended. If you accept the default option, the canvas will be extended equally from the center out; if you click the arrow in the upper-left corner of the Anchor icon, the canvas will be extended from the upper-left corner with the new canvas appearing below and to the right of the original image, as shown in Figure 6-4; and so on.

NOTE

You can select a different unit of measure by which to resize the canvas by clicking the button to the right of the unit of measure field and choosing a different option from the drop-down menu.

Figure 6-4: You can modify the canvas size to add additional area to the image.

QUICKSTEPS

USING THE CROP COMMAND

You use the Crop command to crop an image to an area selected with one of the Marquee selection tools. The Crop command has no parameters; it crops the image to the specified area. Even though you can create an elliptical selection, Photoshop will not crop to the elliptical section leaving blank canvas around the ellipse.

1. Use one of the **Marquee** selection tools to create a selection.

2. Select **Image | Crop** to crop the image to the selected area.

4. Click the **button** to the right of the Canvas Extension field, and select one of the following options:

- **Foreground** uses the current foreground color as the canvas extension color.

- **Background** uses the current background color as the canvas extension color.

- **White** uses white as the canvas extension color.

- **Black** uses black as the canvas extension color.

- **Gray** uses gray as the canvas extension color.

- **Other** gives you the option of specifying a color from the Color Picker.

TRIM A PHOTO WITH TRIM

When you increase the canvas size, you add solid areas of color around the image (or images if you're working on a multi-layer collage). Typically, you use the extra canvas area to add text to identify an image or perhaps shapes created with one of the drawing tools (the Brush, Pencil, or Pen Tool). When the image is ready to save, you may find that you have more canvas than you need. You can easily remove excess canvas with the trim command, while preserving text and other items you have added to the document.

1. Select **Image | Trim**. The Trim dialog box appears.

2. Select the method by which the image is trimmed:

- **Transparent Pixels** trims the image by removing transparent pixels from the specified trim area.

- **Top Left Pixel Color** trims the image by removing all pixels matching the color of the top left pixel from the specified trim area.

- **Bottom Right Pixel Color** trims the image by removing all pixels matching the color of the bottom right pixel from the specified trim area.

3. Select one or more of the Trim Away options: **Top**, **Bottom**, **Left**, or **Right**.

4. Click **OK** to trim the image.

Trim

Based On
- Transparent Pixels
- ○ Top Left Pixel Color
- ◉ Bottom Right Pixel Color

Trim Away
- ☑ Top   ☑ Left
- ☑ Bottom   ☑ Right

[OK]
[Cancel]

USING THE EYEDROPPER TOOL

When you create text or shapes, you often need to match the color of the object you are creating with another color in your document. You can easily do this using the Eyedropper Tool. You can use the Eyedropper Tool to set the Foreground or Background color in the toolbox. After sampling a color with the Eyedropper Tool, use it with each subsequent drawing tool or the text tool until you change the Foreground or Background color. When you use the Eyedropper Tool, you can specify the size of the area sampled with the tool.

1. Select the **Eyedropper** Tool.

2. In the Options bar, click the **button** to the right of the Sample Size field, and select one of the following options:

- **Point Sample** samples the color from the pixel directly under the tool.

- **3 x 3 Average** selects a color based on the average pixel hue in a 3 x 3 pixel area surrounding the pixel the tool is over.

- **5 x 5 Average** selects a color based on the average pixel hue in a 5 x 5 pixel area surrounding the pixel the tool is over.

3. Do one of the following:

- To specify the Foreground color, click inside the image. If you drag while holding down the mouse button, the Foreground color swatch refreshes to the color of the sample area under the tool. Release the pointer to set the Foreground color.

- To specify the Background color, press **ALT** while clicking the desired area. If you drag while holding down the mouse button, the Background color swatch refreshes to the color of the sample area under the tool. Release the pointer to set the Background color.

Color Correct with Curves and Levels

Whether you acquire your images directly from a digital camera, scan them into Photoshop, or acquire them from clip art CDs, you'll probably need to do some color correction. Sometimes you're dealing with a slight color cast, while other times the image is too dark or too light. You can manually perform sophisticated corrections to your images with the Curves and Levels commands, or you can let Photoshop take the reins with Auto Color and Auto Levels commands.

Use a Histogram to View the Tonal Range of an Image

A *histogram* is a graph that shows the distribution of color pixels at each color level. There are 256 color levels ranging from 0 to 255. The distribution is in three ranges: shadows, which are on the left side of the histogram; midtones, which occupy the middle of the histogram; and highlights, which are on the right side of the histogram.

ANALYZE AN IMAGE WITH A HISTOGRAM

The distribution of pixels on a histogram consists of peaks and valleys. Whenever you see a large peak, there are a large number of pixels in that tonal range. If the histogram graph is flat or has very few pixels in the shadows, the image is overexposed. If the histogram graph is flat or has very few pixels in the highlights tonal range, the image is underexposed.

1. Open the image you want to color correct.

2. Select **Window | Histogram**. This illustration shows the histogram of a properly exposed image.

3. Click the button with the **right-pointing triangle** to reveal the Histogram palette menu. Select one of these options:

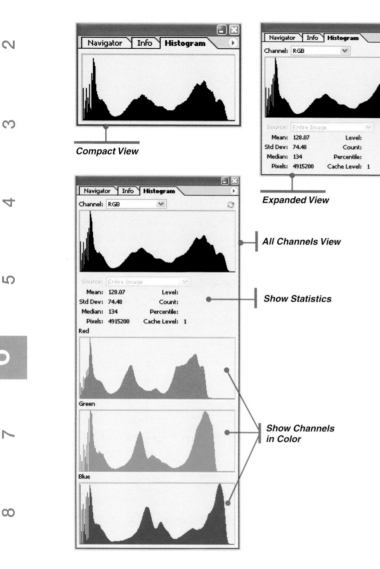

Compact View

Expanded View

All Channels View

Show Statistics

Show Channels in Color

- **Compact View** displays the histogram of the image with no statistical information, as shown here.

- **Expanded View** displays the histogram of the image along with statistical information as shown here.

- **All Channels View** displays the histogram of the entire image, plus one for each channel. Note that the channels will be different depending on the color model used for the image. This histogram shows the color channels for an RGB image.

- **Show Statistics** displays the statistical information for the histogram.

- **Show Channels in Color** displays the color channel histograms in the appropriate color. For example, if you're viewing a histogram for an RGB image, the color channel histograms will be red, green, and blue.

USE THE HISTOGRAM CHANNELS MENU

When you're viewing a histogram in expanded or all channel view, you can view the histogram for a specific channel by clicking the button to the right of the Histogram Channels menu and choosing one of these options:

- Select **RGB**, **CMYK**, or **Composite**, depending on the color model for the image whose histogram you are viewing.

- Select a **specific color channel** to view a histogram for that channel. Again your choices will vary depending on the color model for the image you are analyzing.

- Select **Luminosity** if the image is RGB or CMYK to view a histogram displaying the luminance (intensity) values in the composite channel.

- Select **Colors** if the image is RGB or CMYK to view a composite histogram of all channels. Each channel is displayed in its native color.

VIEW STATISTICAL INFORMATION

If you view a histogram in expanded or all channels view, you can view the statistical information. Certain information, such as level or count, changes depending on where you position your pointer in the histogram. The following statistical information is listed in a window below the histogram:

- **Mean** shows the average intensity value.

- **Std Dev** (Standard Deviation) shows the variance of intensity values.

- **Median** shows the middle value in the intensity range exhibited by the image.

- **Pixels** shows the number of pixels used to calculate the histogram.

- **Level** shows the intensity level of the histogram area underneath the pointer.

- **Count** shows the number of pixels corresponding to the intensity level underneath the pointer.

- **Percentile** shows the cumulative number of pixels below the level currently under the pointer. This value is expressed as a percentage of pixels in the image, ranging from the value 0 at the far left of the histogram to 100 at the far right.

- **Cache Level** shows the current image cache being used to display the histogram. If you enable the Cache For Histograms option in the Memory and Image Cache preferences, Photoshop displays the histogram faster. The original cache is Level 1. Each subsequent cache level uses the average of four adjacent pixels as a single pixel, effectively halving the dimension of each subsequent cache level. Disable the Cache For Histograms option when you need a highly accurate histogram to check for posterization (color reduction in areas of an image that show up as solid blocks of a hue instead of a gradation of hues).

Adjust the Tonal Range with Levels

When you adjust the tonal range with the Levels command, you can select the shadow, midpoint, and highlight colors from within the image using the Eyedropper tools. The shadow color you select is mapped to black (0), the midpoint to gray (128), and the highlight to white (255). You can eyeball the color choice or use a combination of the Info palette, Color Sampler tool, and Threshold adjustment layer to accurately select shadow, midpoint, and highlights from within the image you are correcting.

ADJUST THE TONAL RANGE WITH AUTO LEVELS

You use the Auto Levels command to adjust the black point and white point of an image. This command maps the lightest pixels of each color channel to pure white (255) and the darkest pixels to pure black (0). The intermediate pixels are redistributed proportionately, which effectively increases the contrast of an image. Because this command does alter color information, an unwanted color

---

TIP

You can use the Eyedropper Tool to sample a color from anywhere on the screen.

TIP

Press **ALT** to temporarily select the Eyedropper Tool while using any of the painting tools.

cast may occur after you apply this command. To adjust tonal range with Auto Levels, under Image move your pointer over **Adjustments**, and select **Auto Levels**.

MANUALLY ADJUST LEVELS WITH THE LEVELS COMMAND

You can manually adjust levels using the sliders in the Levels dialog box. It's helpful if you view the histogram for the image while you're adjusting levels.

1. Select **Window | Histogram**.

2. Then select **Image | Adjustments | Levels** to open the Levels dialog box.

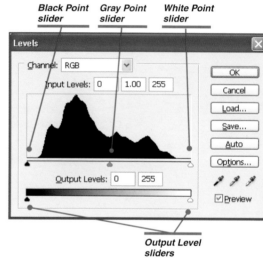

Black Point slider   *Gray Point slider*   *White Point slider*

Output Level sliders

3. Under the Channel menu, select the channel for which you want to adjust levels. Your choices will vary depending on the type of image you're editing. For an RGB image, your choices are Red, Green, and Blue.

4. Drag the **Black Point** slider to the edge of where the pixels start to leave the floor of the histogram.

5. Drag the **White Point** slider to the edge of where the pixels start to leave the floor of the histogram.

6. Drag the **Gray Point** slider to change the gamma (the brightness and contrast of image midtones produced when the image is displayed on a device such as a computer monitor) of the image. Move the slider to the left to lighten the image or the right to darken the image.

7. Drag the **Output Level Black** and **White Point** sliders to set new shadow and highlight values. As you adjust levels, a gray band appears in the Histogram palette showing you how the histogram will look when the new levels are applied, as shown in this illustration.

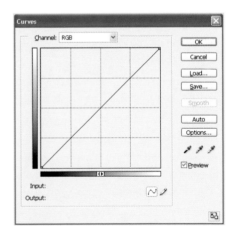

8. Click **OK** to apply the new levels settings. After you apply the settings, an information icon appears in the Histogram palette. This signifies that the histogram has changed.

9. Click the **Information** icon in the Histogram palette to update the histogram.

Use the Curves Command

To use the Curves command to alter the tonality and color of an image, modify the curve for the composite of all image channels or modify an individual channel to change the characteristics of that color in an image. The default curve in the Curves dialog box is a diagonal line from left to right, bottom to top. You alter the curve by adding points. When you add a point and move the point, you modify the pixels at a specific level. When you add points near the top of the curve, you modify the highlights of the image; points in the middle of the curve modify the midtones; points near the bottom of the curve modify shadows. Drag a point up to lighten pixels at the level, down to darken them.

1. Open the image you want to color correct.

2. Select **Image | Adjustments | Curves** to open the Curves dialog box.

3. Open the **Channel** drop-down list, and select the channel or channels you want to modify. The default option modifies the curves for all channels.

4. Click the **curve** to add a point. Alternatively, with an RGB image, you press **CTRL** while you click a pixel in the image to add a point to the curve. You can add as many as fourteen points to a curve. Points are anchored until you move them.

5. To move a point, drag it to a new position in the dialog box. The illustration shows a curve with several points.

6. Click **OK** to apply the changes.

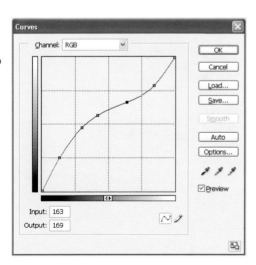

When you select Auto Color, Auto Contrast, Auto Levels, or the Auto option in the Levels or Curves dialog boxes, the black, gray and white points are mapped to default levels of 0, 128, and 255 respectively. The gray point is perfect for removing color casts. However, the black and white default values may be too dark or too light depending on the type of images you're editing and your personal taste. You can, however, change the default to suit your tastes.

1. Select **Image** | **Adjustments**, | **Levels** or **Curves**.

2. Click the **Options** button to open the Auto Color Correction Options dialog box.

3. Select one of these options:

- **Enhance Monochromatic Contrast** lightens highlights and darkens shadow to improve overall contrast.

- **Enhance Per Channel** maximizes contrast in each channel to greatly enhance image contrast. As this algorithm changes color values in each channel, this option may introduce a color cast. The Auto Levels command uses this algorithm.

- **Find Dark & Light Colors** finds the average darkest and lightest pixels in an image and maps these values to the black and white points. The Auto Color command uses this algorithm.

4. Select the **Snap Neutral Midtones** option if you want the gamma values of the image snapped to a neutral midtone. The Auto Color command uses this option.

5. Click the **Shadows** color swatch to open the Color Picker.

6. Enter the desired values. Note that you must enter identical values in the R, G, B, fields to create a neutral shadow color. The values you enter are a matter of personal taste. This determines the value to which the darkest areas of the image will be mapped. Settings of 8, 8, 8 produces pleasing shadows.

7. Click the **Highlights** color swatch to open the Color Picker.

8. Enter the desired values. Enter identical values in the R, G, B fields to specify a neutral highlight color. Again, these values are a matter of personal taste. Settings of 245, 245, 245 produce pleasing highlights.

9. In the Shadows and Highlights Clip text boxes, accept the default values, or enter different values. The values you specify determine to what extent white and black pixels are clipped. A value between 0.0 % and 1.0 % is recommended.

NOTE

The Midtones color is used for removing color casts from images. Therefore, you should leave it at the default setting.

10. Click **Save As Defaults** to save these settings as your default color corrections settings.

MANUALLY ADJUST LEVELS AND CURVES WITH THE EYEDROPPERS

Within the Levels and Curves dialog box are three Eyedroppers: Black Point, Gray Point, and White Point. You select each Eyedropper and then click inside the image to map image colors to black, gray, and white. When used in conjunction with the Info palette and a Threshold adjustment layer, you can accurately select the colors to map to the black, gray, and white points.

1. Open the image you want to color correct with the Levels or the Curves command.

2. Select **Window Info** to open the Info palette.

3. Click the **triangle** to the left of the Eyedropper in the upper-left quadrant, and select **Total Ink** from the drop-down list. When the Info palette is in Total Ink mode, the palette displays the intensity of the color value of the pixel you sample with the Color Sampler tool.

4. Select **Window | Layers** to open the Layers palette.

5. Click the **Create New Fill Or Adjustment Layer button** shown here.

6. Select **Threshold** to open the Threshold dialog box. The image you are color correcting is displayed as a black and white image.

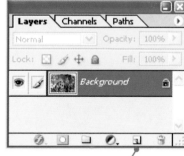

7. Drag the **Threshold Level** slider to the left until there are only a few black areas in the image. These are the image's darkest parts, which you will map to the black point.

Create New Fill Or Adjustment Layer button

8. Click **OK** to exit the Threshold dialog box.

9. Select the **Color Sampler Tool**.

10. Click inside one of the dark areas to position a crosshair with the number 1 at that spot in the image.

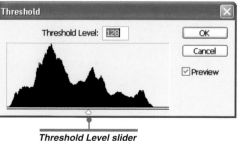

Threshold Level slider

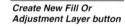

> ### TIP
> Set the Color Sampler Tool sample size to Point Sample in order to sample the color directly under the pointer.

11. In the Layers palette, double-click the **Threshold** layer to display the Threshold dialog box.

12. Drag the **Threshold Level** slider to the right until only a few white areas remain. These are the image's lightest areas, which you will map to the white point.

13. Select the **Color Sampler Tool**.

14. Click inside one of the white areas to position a crosshair with the number 2 at that spot in the image.

15. Click **OK**.

16. Select the **Threshold** layer and drag it to the **trash can** icon in the Layers palette.

17. Select the **Color Sampler Tool**.

18. Drag inside the image while viewing the Info palette. Your goal is to locate an area in the image with the value 128, the same value as the gray point. This removes any color cast from the image.

19. Click the area of the image with a value of 128 or thereabouts.

20. Select **Image** | **Adjustments** | **Levels** or **Curves**.

21. Select the **Set Black Point Eyedropper,** and click inside the first point you created with the Color Sampler Tool. The point will be mapped to the black point value, and all values in the image will be adjusted as well.

22. Select the **Set Gray Point Eyedropper**, and click inside the second point you created with the Color Sampler Tool. The point will be mapped to the gray point value, and all values in the image will be updated to reflect the change.

23. Select the **Set White Point Eyedropper**, and click inside the third point you created with the Color Sampler Tool. The point will be mapped to the white point value, and all values in the image will be updated to reflect the change.

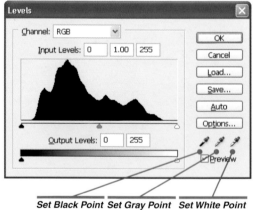

Set Black Point *Eyedropper* Set Gray Point *Eyedropper* Set White Point *Eyedropper*

NOTE

The Levels and Curves dialog boxes have the same Eyedroppers. You'll get the same results using either command.

Figure 6-5: You can correct the colors of an image using Eyedroppers.

24. Click **OK** to exit the Curves or Levels dialog box. Figure 6-5 shows an image before and after color correction.

Color Correct Images

Another task you can accomplish with Photoshop is color correcting images. Using Photoshop tools and menu commands, you can remove red-eye, adjust the hue and saturation of an image, adjust color balance, and much more. If the Levels and Curves commands intimidate you, you can eyeball color corrections using the Variations command. If you're editing a digital photograph where the subject is in heavy shadow but the rest of the image is properly exposed, you can easily fix this using the Shadow/Highlight command.

CURE RED-EYE WITH THE COLOR REPLACEMENT TOOL

When you take a portrait of a person with a standard flash, the flash bounces off the person's retina, producing what is known as red-eye. This can ruin an otherwise interesting portrait. You can easily remove red-eye with the Color Replacement Tool.

1. Open the image you want to repair.

2. Zoom in on the eyes.

3. Select the **Color Replacement Tool**.

4. In the Options bar, adjust the brush size so that it is slightly smaller than the red area of the eye, as shown on the next page.

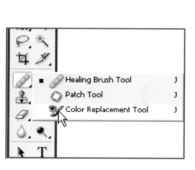

5. In the Options bar, select the following parameters:

- For Mode, select **color**.

- For Sampling, select **Once**. This option removes only the color you target.

- For Limits, select **Discontiguous**. This option removes all instances of the target color under the brush.

- For Tolerance, select a low value. The default value of 30 percent works well in most cases.

6. Set the **Foreground** color to black or a very dark gray.

UICKSTEPS

USING COLOR BALANCE

Yet another tool in your color correction arsenal is the Color Balance command. Use this command when you need to balance the mix of colors in an image.

1. Open the image you want to color correct.

2. Select **Image | Adjustments | Color Balance** to

Color Balance	
Color Balance	OK
Color Levels: 0 0 0	Cancel
Cyan ——○—— Red	☑ Preview
Magenta ——○—— Green	
Yellow ——○—— Blue	
Tone Balance	
○ Shadows ⊙ Midtones ○ Highlights	
☑ Preserve Luminosity	

open the Color Balance dialog box.

3. In the Tone Balance section, select the tonal range for which you want to balance color. Your choices are **Shadows, Midtones,** or **Highlights**.

4. Select **Preserve Luminosity** (the default) to prevent changing the tonal balance in the image.

5. Drag the sliders to balance the color. Drag a slider away from a color you want to decrease, towards a color you want to increase. As you make adjustments, the values above the color sliders update to show the increase or decrease for the red, green and blue values. If you're working with an LAB image, you balance greens and blues, which changes the balance in the A and B channels.

6. Click **OK** to apply the changes.

NOTE

The Color Balance command is only available when the composite channel is selected in the Channels palette.

7. Click inside the red area of the eye, and then drag across the area to repair the image.

8. Repeat for the other eye.

REMOVE UNWANTED COLOR CAST

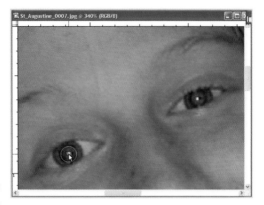

You can use the Set Gray Point Eyedropper in either the Levels or Curves dialog box to remove a color cast from an image. You do so by identifying the area of the image that should be a neutral tone and then mapping it to the gray point.

1. Open the image from which you want to remove the color cast.

2. Select **Image Adjustments Levels** or **Curves.**

3. Click the **Set Gray Point** Eyedropper, and then click an area inside the image that should be a neutral gray. This should correct the color cast for the entire image. If the color cast is predominantly in the shadow areas of the image, click the **Set Black Point** Eyedropper, and then click an area inside the image that should be black. If the color cast is in the highlights, click the **Set White Point** Eyedropper, and then click an area inside the image that should be white.

EYEBALL IT WITH THE VARIATIONS COMMAND

If you're visually oriented and don't like dealing with curves, histograms, or levels, Photoshop has a wonderful command that lets you eyeball a color correction. This gem is an image adjustment command known as Variations. With Variations, you can remove a color cast or highlight by clicking a variation of the original image and then comparing the original to the modified version.

1. Open the image you want to edit.

2. Select **Image | Adjustments | Variations** to open the Variations dialog box, shown in Figure 6-6. The Show Clipping option is selected by default. This option identifies areas of the image that will be out of gamut with a neon-like overlay if a variation is applied.

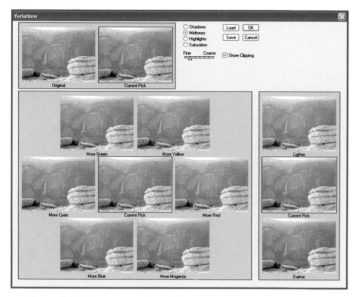

Figure 6-6: You can use the Variations command to correct the color of an image.

3. Select the type of adjustments you'd like to make.

- **Shadows**, **Midtones**, and **Highlights** adjust the dark, middle, and light tones in your image.

- **Saturation** increases or decreases the hue of the image.

4. Drag the **Fine/Coarse** slider to determine the degree of correction you want to apply. As you drag the slider, the variation thumbnails change. Fine settings produce subtle changes while coarse setting produce pronounced changes.

5. To adjust the image, do one of the following:

- To adjust the brightness of the image, click a thumbnail in the right window.

- To add a color to an image, click the appropriate variation thumbnail.

- To remove a color cast from an image, click the opposite variation thumbnail. For example, if the image has a green cast, click the **More Yellow** variation thumbnail.

6. Click **OK** to apply the changes.

CHANGE HUE AND SATURATION

Use the Hue/Saturation command to adjust the hue and saturation for an entire image or a specific color component. This command is an excellent tool to correct color deficiencies. You can also use this command to change the hue of specific colors and achieve special effects.

CHANGE HUE/SATURATION FOR THE ENTIRE IMAGE

1. Open the image for which you want to adjust hue and saturation.

2. Select **Image |Adjustments | Hue/ Saturation** to open the Hue/Saturation dialog box.

3. Accept default Edit option of **Master**.

4. Drag the **Hue** slider until the colors appear as desired. Alternatively, you can enter a value in the Hue text field.

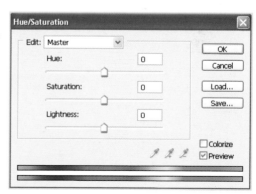

TIP

Start with the default Fine/Coarse setting to make your initial adjustments; and then drag the slider all the way to Fine to make your final adjustments.

TIP

To restore the Current Pick to the original image, click the **Original Image** thumbnail.

1   2   3   4   5   6   7   8   9   10

5. Drag the **Saturation** slider to achieve the desired result. Drag to the right to increase saturation, left to decrease saturation. Alternatively, you can enter a value in the Saturation text field.

6. Drag the **Lightness** slider to darken or lighten the image. Alternatively, you can enter a value in the Lightness text field.

7. Press **OK** to apply the settings.

CHANGE HUE/SATURATION FOR A SPECIFIC COLOR

1. Open the image for which you want to adjust the hue and saturation.

2. Select **Image | Adjustments | Hue/Saturation** to open the Hue/Saturation dialog box.

3. Open the Edit drop-down list, and select the color for which you want to adjust hue and saturation. The Hue/Saturation dialog box changes to the configuration shown here. Notice that a range of color has been selected in the dialog box.

Eyedropper tool

Eyedropper Add To Sample tool

Eyedropper Subtract From Sample tool

4. Modify the range of colors by doing one of the following:

   ● Drag the **inner vertical** sliders to change the range of colors.

   ● Drag the **outer triangular** sliders to increase or decrease the range fall-off. This setting determines how many similar colors will be affected by your edits.

   ● Select the **Eyedropper** tool, and click inside the image to define the color.

   ● Select the **Eyedropper Add To Sample** tool, and click inside the image to add colors to the range.

   ● Select the **Eyedropper Subtract From Sample** tool, and click inside the image to remove colors from the range.

5. Drag the **Hue** slider to change the color of the range. If needed, drag the **Saturation** and/or **Lightness** sliders to change the lightness and saturation of the color range.

6. Click **OK** to apply your changes. Alternatively you can modify additional colors.

USE PHOTO FILTERS

If you're an avid 35-mm photographer, you may have used photo filters to warm or cool an image. Another popular photo filter you may have used is a color filter to tint an image. In Photoshop you can apply the same filters digitally to cool, warm, or tint an image.

1. Open the image to which you want to apply a photo filter.

2. Select **Image | Adjustments | Photo Filter** to open the Photo Filter dialog box.

3. Select **Filter** and select one of the following options:

TIP

If you can't find a color filter to suit your needs, click the **Color** check box, click the color swatch, and select the desired color from the Color Picker.

- **Warming Filter (85)** warms up the color tones in a cool image that has a bluish color cast.

- **Cooling Filter (80)** cools an image that has a yellowish cast by making the colors bluer.

- **Warming Filter (81)** warms the color tones of a bluish image by making them more yellow.

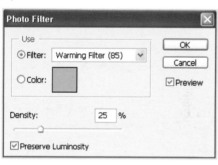

- **Cooling Filter (85)** cools an image with a yellow cast by making the colors bluer.

- **Color Filters** tint an image. You can remove a color cast from an image by selecting a filter with a complimentary color. You can also use a color filter for special effects.

4. Drag the **Density** slider to determine how much color is applied to the image. Alternatively, you can enter a value in the Percentage text box. Select a higher density for a more pronounced effect.

5. Click **OK** to apply the filter.

NOTE

Accept the default Preserve Luminosity option unless you want the image to be darkened by the filter.

If you have two images that were photographed in different lighting conditions but of the same subject, you can use the Match Color command to make it appear that the images were shot with the same lighting conditions. This command is especially useful if consistency is important when preparing a portfolio of several images.

1. Open the images you want to match.

2. Select the image whose colors you want to match to other open images.

3. Select **Images | Adjustments | Match Color** to open the Match Color dialog box.

4. Click the **button** to the right of the Source field, and choose the image to which the selected image will be matched.

5. Click the **Neutralize** check box to remove any color cast in the target image.

6. Drag the **Luminance** slider to increase or decrease brightness in the target image. Alternatively, you can enter a value between 1 and 200 in the **Luminance** text box.

7. Drag the **Color Intensity** slider to modify color saturation in the target image. Alternatively, you can enter a value between 1 (grayscale) and 200. The default setting is 100.

8. Drag the **Fade** slider to determine how much the target image is changed. Drag the slider to the right to reduce the effect the command has on the target image.

9. Click **OK** to apply the changes.

NOTE

If the source image has multiple layers, you can select the layer you want used for matching purposes by clicking the button to the right of the Layer field and then choosing the desired layer from the drop-down list.

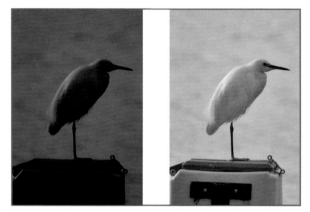

Figure 6-7: You can use the Shadow/Highlight command to brighten subjects that are in shadow.

ADJUST SHADOWS AND HIGHLIGHTS

If you've ever tried to correct an image where the subject was in deep shade or backlit, you know what a difficult process it can be. Fortunately, Photoshop has a command to adjust shadows and highlights. Figure 6-7 shows an image before and after the Shadow/Highlight command was used.

1. Open the image you want to adjust.
2. Select **Image | Adjustments | Shadow/Highlight** to open the Shadows/Highlights dialog box.
3. Drag the **Amount** sliders to determine how much correction is applied to shadow and highlight areas. As you drag the sliders, your image updates to reflect the new settings.
4. Click **OK** to apply the changes.

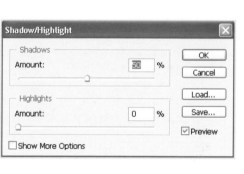

Edit in 16-Bit Mode

When you perform extensive editing on an image, you may notice that the histogram starts looking a little ragged, with gaps in the tonal curve. This is because of the limited number of values available with the default 8-bit mode. Each pixel in an 8-bit image has 256 possible values. A pixel in a 16-bit image has roughly 24 million possible values. This means that a 16-bit image has more color information, which ensures a smooth blending of adjacent pixels. You achieve better results when you edit an image in 16-bit mode, especially when working with curves and levels. The additional color information safeguards against clipping colors.

1. Open the image you want to edit.
2. Select **Image | Mode | 16 Bits/Channel**.
3. Edit the image as needed using the techniques discussed previously in this chapter.
4. If desired, print the Image. When you print a 16-bit image, the results are stunning.
5. Save the image in a format that supports 16-bit mode.

WORKING WITH ADJUSTMENT LAYERS

When you edit an image, pixels are modified. When you continue to make changes, more pixels are modified. Later you may decide you made an error. You can use the History palette to restore the image to a previous state. When you do this, you lose all edits from that point forward. You can alleviate this problem by using adjustment layers. When you apply an adjustment layer, you can use many other commands. If you decide to tweak a command, do so by activating the layer and modifying the parameters.

1. Open the image you want to modify.

2. Select **View | Layers** to open the Layers palette.

3. Click the **Adjustment Layers** button, and select the desired option from the pop-up menu.

4. Make the desired changes, and click **OK**. After applying an adjustment layer, it appears in the layers list. The following image shows several adjustment layers that were applied in the Layers palette.

5. Add other adjustment layers as needed.

6. Double-click any **adjustment layer** to open the dialog box. You can edit an adjustment layer at any time.

7. After you finish editing the image, select **Flatten** from the Layer menu.

Sharpen and Blur Images

Sharpening and blurring—the yang and the yin. If you have a blurry image, you can sharpen it in Photoshop. On the other hand, you can blur a perfectly sharp image for artistic purposes. You control the amount of sharpening or blurring applied. You can take the Zen approach, that less is more, or apply these effects lavishly.

SHARPEN WITH THE UNSHARP MASK FILTER

Photoshop has many filters that you can use to sharpen an image. The Unsharp filter is undoubtedly the best of the lot. This filter controls the amount of sharpening applied to "unsharp" edges.

1. Open the image you want to sharpen.

2. Select **Filter | Sharpen | Unsharp Mask** to open the Unsharp Mask dialog box.

3. Drag the **Amount** slider to determine the amount of sharpening to be applied to the image. A value between 150 and 200 is an excellent choice for an image that will be printed; otherwise, select a value between 85 and 150.

4. Drag the **Radius** slider to determine the number of pixels surrounding an edge that will be sharpened. Experiment with values from two to four.

5. Drag the **Threshold** slider to determine how different edge-pixels must be from surrounding pixels before they are actually considered edge-pixels. Alternatively, you can enter a value in the Threshold text field. As you experiment with different values, pay close attention to the image. If the edges become posterized, lower the value. Experiment with values from 1 to 12.

6. Click **OK** to sharpen the image.

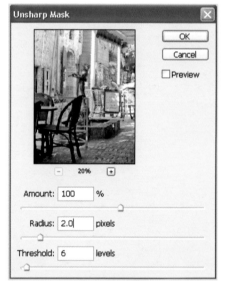

FINE-TUNING WITH THE SHARPEN, BLUR, AND SMUDGE TOOLS

When you edit an image, you often want to touch up small areas. For example, you can draw attention to a subject's eyes with the Sharpen Tool. You can also smudge or blur an area in that you want to de-emphasize. With these tools you brush on the effect; hence, you can control the opacity of the brush, size, and so on.

1. Select the **Sharpen, Blur** or **Smudge Tool** from the toolbar.

2. In the Options bar, specify the brush size, brush tip, mode, and strength.

3. Drag the tool over the area you want to touch up.

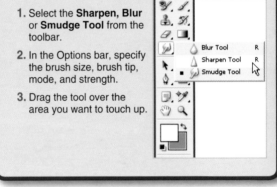

USE THE GAUSSIAN BLUR FILTER

You can apply an artistic blur to an image to achieve a dreamlike effect with the Gaussian Blur command. When you apply this blur to an image, you determine the extent of the blur by specifying the radius beyond each pixel that is blurred.

1. Open the image you want to blur.

2. Select **Filters** | **Blur** |**Gaussian Blur** to open the Gaussian Blur dialog box.

3. Drag the **Radius** slider to determine the extent of the blur.

4. Click **OK** to blur the image.

USE THE MOTION BLUR FILTER

With the Motion Blur filter, you can make a photograph of a stationary object appear as if it were moving at high speed when the picture was taken. You can use the filter to add a sense of realism to an object such as a car or truck that was photographed at a high shutter speed and appears to be parked instead of moving.

1. Open the image you want to blur.

2. Select **Image** | **Blur** | **Motion Blur** to open the Motion Blur dialog box.

3. Drag the **Angle** slider to determine the direction the subject in the image will appear to be traveling. Alternatively, you can enter a value from 0 to 360.

4. Drag the **Distance** slider to determine the intensity of the blur.

5. Click **OK** to apply the motion blur to the image.

Figure 6-8: Use the Clone Stamp Tool to copy pixels from one area to another.

Retouch and Repair Images

If you need to retouch a small area of an image, you can do so with a myriad of Photoshop tools. With the Clone Stamp Tool, you can copy pixels from one area to another. The tool works wonders on scanned images with small tears. It's also a great tool for a digital face lift. You can repair large areas of an image with the Patch tool.

USE THE CLONE STAMP TOOL

The Clone Stamp Tool makes it possible to copy pixels from one part of an image to another or from one image to another as long as the images are both the same color model. You can control the size of the brush for the tool and, therefore, the size of the area you clone.

1. Open the image from which you want to clone.

2. Select the **Clone Stamp Tool**.

3. In the Options bar, select the brush size, mode, opacity, and flow.

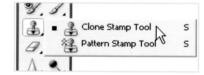

4. Select **Aligned** (the default) to sample pixels from the current sampling point. If you deselect this option, you sample pixels from the original sampling point each time you resume painting.

5. Select **All Layers** to sample pixels from all layers in the image. If you deselect this option, pixels are only sampled from the currently selected layer.

6. Press **ALT** while you click the desired area inside the image to set the anchor point for sampling.

7. Drag inside the selected image or another image to clone pixels from the anchor point, as shown in Figure 6-8.

USE THE HEALING BRUSH TOOL TO FIX SMALL AREAS

The Healing Brush Tool makes it possible for you to touch up small areas. If you need to remove minor imperfections in an image or features such as crow's-feet from a subject's face, this is the ideal tool.

1. Open the image you want to repair.

2. Select the **Healing Brush Tool**.

3. In the Options bar, set the brush diameter, hardness, spacing, angle, and roundness options. If you're using a digital tablet, select an option from the **Size** drop-down menu. Select **Pen Pressure** to vary the size of the stroke based on pen pressure; use **Stylus Wheel** to vary the brush size according to the position of the pen thumbwheel; or don't set either of these to create strokes that don't vary in size.

4. In the Options bar, select a **Mode** option to determine how the pixels are blended.

5. In the Options bar, select **Aligned** to align sampled pixels to the current pointer position. Deselect this option to paint from the initial anchor point.

6. In the Options bar, select **All Layers** to sample pixels from all layers. Deselect this option to sample pixels from the currently selected layer.

7. In the Options bar, select a source option. Select **Sampled** to sample pixels from the image, or select **Pattern** to sample pixels from a pattern. If you select **Pattern**, select a pattern from the Pattern drop-down menu.

8. Press **ALT** while you click to set the anchor point.

9. Drag the **Healing Brush Tool** across the area you want to repair.

USE THE PATCH TOOL TO FIX LARGE AREAS

The Patch Tool works like the Healing Brush in that it copies pixels and texture from one source to another. The Patch Tool, however, lets you define the size of the area that you want to repair. You can use the tool to clone pixels or a pattern.

1. Open the image you want to repair.

2. Select the **Patch Tool**.

3. In the Options bar, select one of the following:

- **Source** copies pixels from the destination to the source.

- **Destination** copies pixels from the source to the destination.

4. Drag inside the image to define the source area, as shown at the left.

5. Drag to the destination.

CHANGING IMAGE COLORS

If you want to change an image from color to grayscale or colorize a grayscale photo, you can easily do so in Photoshop. You can also apply a sepia tone to an image to make it look like an antique photograph.

CREATE A GRAYSCALE PHOTO FROM A COLOR PHOTO

The easiest way to create a grayscale photo from a color image is to change the mode to grayscale. You can also convert an image from color to grayscale using a layer adjustment.

1. Open the image you want to convert to grayscale.

2. Select View | **Layers**.

3. Click the **Layer Adjustment** button, and select **Channel Mixer** to open the Channel Mixer dialog box.

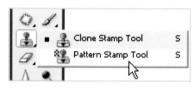

4. Click the **Monotone** check box. The image is converted to grayscale, and the Red Channel value is 100 percent. If this is acceptable, you can click **OK**.

5. Adjust the channel mix as desired. You can mix the channels to achieve a slightly different looking grayscale image. For example, use a value of 60 for the red channel, 20 for the green channel and 20 for the blue channel. As long as the total value of all three channels equals 100, you're good to go.

6. Click **OK** to exit the Channel Mixer dialog box.

7. Flatten the image.

Continued...

USE THE PATTERN STAMP TOOL

With the Pattern Stamp Tool, you can paint patterns on an image. You can select a preset pattern from the Pattern Library.

1. Select the **Pattern Stamp Tool**.

2. In the Options bar select a brush tip, and specify brush size, mode, opacity and flow.

3. Click the **Pattern** icon and select a pattern.

4. In the Options bar, select **Aligned** to align pixels sampled from the pattern to the current sampling point, even if you release the mouse button. Deselect **Aligned** and pixels will be sampled from the pattern at the initial sampling point.

5. In the Options bar, select **Impressionist** to paint impressionistic patterns.

6. Drag inside the image to paint the pattern.

Use Dust & Scratches Filter

If you're working with old photos that have damage in the form of dust speckles or scratches, you can easily remove them with the Dust & Scratches filter. The filter performs its magic by blurring dissimilar pixels.

1. Open the image you want to repair.

2. Select **Filters** | **Noise** | **Dust & Scratches** to open the Dust & Scratches dialog box.

3. Drag the **Radius** slider to the right until the "noise" begins to disappear. Alternatively, you can enter a value between 1 and 16. Don't select a value higher than needed, as you'll excessively blur the image.

CHANGING IMAGE COLORS: *(Continued)*

COLORIZE A GRAYSCALE PHOTO

You can use the Hue/Saturation command to colorize a grayscale photo. This technique can be used when you want to create a stylized collage similar to movie posters.

1. Open the image you want to colorize.

2. Select **Image | Mode | RGB Color**.

3. Select **Image | Adjustments | Hue/ Saturation** to display the Hue/Saturation dialog box.

4. Click the **Colorize** check box.

5. Drag the **Hue** and **Saturation** sliders to achieve the desired level of colorization. Figure 6-10 shows an image that has been colorized.

Figure 6-10: You can add color to a grayscale image.

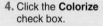

After using the History Brush Tool or, for that matter, any Brush tool, if you find the result is a bit overdone, select **Edit | Fade History Brush Tool** (or the name of the brush you just used). This opens the Fade dialog box. Drag the slider to change the Opacity, which in essence fades the amount of paint applied by the brush.

4. Drag the **Threshold** slider to the right to specify the highest possible value that eliminates the dust marks and scratches. This setting determines how dissimilar pixels must be before the filter eliminates them.

5. Click **OK** to apply the repair.

USE THE HISTORY BRUSH TO MAKE SELECTIVE TOUCH-UPS

If you use Photoshop to edit images of people, you end up using a variety of filters to bring out the best in your subject. For example, to smooth the skin of a subject, you can apply a slight Gaussian blur. However, you don't want to blur the fine details of your subject's hair, mouth, or eyes. You can restore detail to these areas using the History Brush.

1. Open the image you want to retouch.

2. Apply the desired filters.

3. Select **View | History** to open the History palette. At the right you see a History palette after a Gaussian blur has been applied to an image.

4. Click the blank square in the **Set Source For The History Brush** column to the left of the image state that you want to selectively restore. For example, if you want to selectively restore a Gaussian blur to parts of the image, click the blank square to the left of Gaussian Blur in the History palette. After selecting an image state, the History Brush icon appears in the Set Source For The History Brush column.

Set Source For the History Brush column

5. Select the **History Brush Tool**.

6. In the Options bar, set the brush size, select the brush tip, and then specify mode, opacity, and flow.

7. Paint over the areas of the image you want to restore to a previous state.

QUICKSTEPS

CREATING A SEPIA TONE FROM A COLOR OR GRAYSCALE PHOTO

When you convert a color or grayscale photo to a sepia tone photo, it has a warm brown tone reminiscent of old photos. People pay good money to have sepia tone photos taken in mall kiosks. You can quickly create a sepia tone photo in Photoshop without cracking a sweat.

1. Open the image you want to convert to sepia tone.

2. Select **Window | Actions** to open the Actions palette.

3. Click the **right-pointing triangle** to the left of the Default Actions folder.

4. Scroll to the **Sepia Toning** title, and select it.

5. Click the **Play** button in the Actions palette. The image is converted to sepia tone.

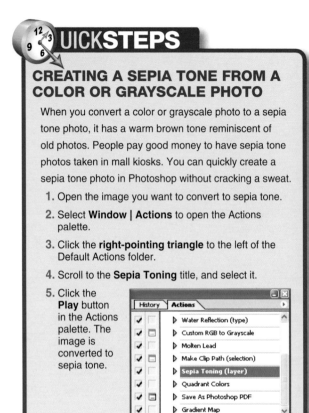

Play button

REDUCE COLOR NOISE IN DIGITAL PHOTOGRAPHS

If you're a digital photographer and you frequently shoot in low-light conditions without flash, you end up selecting a high ISO setting to increase the sensitivity of the camera. When you increase the sensitivity of a digital camera, you can introduce noise in the form of color artifacts. You can easily remove this noise in Photoshop by performing a few simple steps.

1. Open the image that contains the digital noise.

2. Select **Image | Mode | Lab Color**.

3. Select **Window | Channels** to open the Channels palette.

4. Click the **A** in the Channels palette to display the A channel in the working space.

5. Select **Filter | Blur | Gaussian Blur**.

6. Drag the **Radius** slider until the noise in the image begins to disappear.

7. Click **OK** to apply the blur.

8. Click the **B Channel** to display the B channel in the working space.

9. Press **CTRL+F** to copy the Gaussian blur filter into the B channel.

10. Select **Image | Mode | RGB Color**. You should notice a substantial reduction in digital noise. Figure 6-9 shows an image before and after this technique was applied.

Figure 6-9: You can easily reduce digital noise in images.

How to...

- *Create Text*
- *Edit Type*
- *Committing Type*
- *Hyphenating and Justifying Type*
- *Use Check Spelling*
- *Transforming Type*
- *Find and Replace Text*
- *Warp Text*
- *Create Text on a Path*
- *Edit Text on a Path*
- *Create Text within a Closed Path*
- *Finding and Using Layer Styles*
- *Add Special Type Effects with Layer Styles*
- *Create Text Masks*

Chapter 7
Using Type and Type Effects

An important aspect of working in Photoshop is making your type as effective and dramatic as the myriad effects you can create with images. In this chapter you will discover how to create and edit type on images, with typical formatting, hyphenation, and justification. You will see how to perform the commonly needed tasks of spell check and find and replace. Then, with the mundane but critical tasks out of the way, you will see how to play with your type, warping it, transforming it by rotating, skewing, and resizing. You will find out how to use layer styles that let you create special effects like drop shadows, beveling and embossing, inside and outside glows, and gradient fills. Finally, you will learn how to mask your type, enabling you to copy images as fill for type, and how to make a *selection* of type, which can then be manipulated just like any other selection.

Create and Edit Text

When you enter text, it creates its own text layer, which is available to be edited until you *rasterize* it. Initially, text is vector-based; however, when you rasterize it, it becomes a bitmap object. At this point, it can no longer be accessed as editable text. However, some of the special tools and effects, such as the paint tools and filter effects, can be used once the text is rasterized.

When you select the Type Tool, the Options toolbar becomes a formatting toolbar. Figure 7-1 shows the tools available to you for creating and editing text.

Figure 7-1: The Options toolbar contains formatting tools when you select the Type Tool.

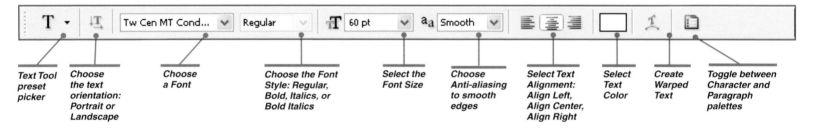

Text Tool preset picker | Choose the text orientation: Portrait or Landscape | Choose a Font | Choose the Font Style: Regular, Bold, Italics, or Bold Italics | Select the Font Size | Choose Anti-aliasing to smooth edges | Select Text Alignment: Align Left, Align Center, Align Right | Select Text Color | Create Warped Text | Toggle between Character and Paragraph palettes

Create Text

You can enter text in two ways—as point type or as paragraph type. Use point type when you have only a word or so to enter. Use paragraph type when you are working with more than a few words.

ENTER POINT TYPE

Point type becomes a new type layer. As you are entering text, it doesn't wrap to the next line; it continues on the same line.

1. Set attributes for the text. See "Format Type with the Character Palette."

2. Select either the **Horizontal Type Tool** or the **Vertical Type Tool**.

Figure 7-2: Point type entered using the Vertical Type Tool creates a useful label for photos.

3. Click in the image area and the pointer will morph into an I-beam pointer. Place it where you want the text to begin. For horizontal type, the small intersecting line marks where the bottom of the type will appear.  For vertical type, the intersecting line identifies the center of the type.  Figure 7-2 shows vertical text entered onto a photo.

4. Select any formatting you want from the Type Options in the Options bar, or the Character palette, or the paragraph palette (see "Edit Type" later in this chapter).

5. Type your characters. Press **ENTER** to begin a new line.

6. Click **Commit** on the Options bar. (See "Committing Type.")

ENTER PARAGRAPH TYPE

You type a paragraph of text into a *bounding box* that contains the text and creates a separate text object on its own layer. Set attributes for the paragraph. See "Format Paragraphs with the Paragraph Palette."

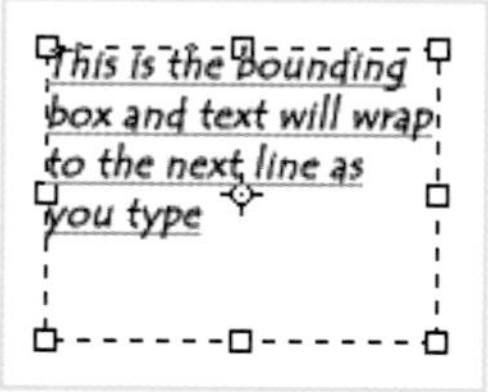

NOTE

You can resize the bounding box using the handles on the perimeter of the bounding box. Or, if you press **ALT** as you drag to form a bounding box for paragraph text, the Paragraph Text Size dialog box will be displayed. Type in the **Height** and **Width** for the bounding box, and click **OK**.

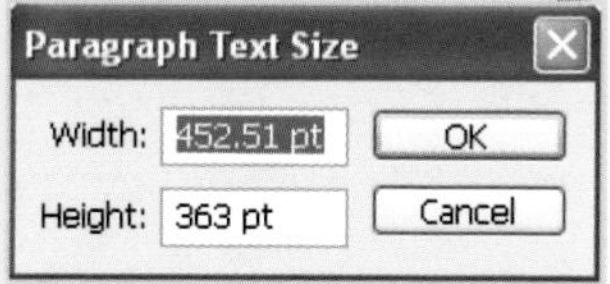

Paragraph Text Size

Width: 452.51 pt   OK
Height: 363 pt   Cancel

1. Select either the **Horizontal Type Tool** or the **Vertical Type Tool**.

2. Drag the pointer diagonally so that a bounding box is created.

3. Select any formatting you want from the type options in the Options bar, or the Character palette, or the Paragraph palette (see "Format Type with the Character Palette" later in this chapter).

4. Type your characters. Press **ENTER** to begin a new line.

5. Click **Commit** on the Options bar. (See "Committing Type.")

This is the Bounding box and text will wrap to the next line as you type

You can change from point type to paragraph type or vice versa. Select the type layer (not the text itself), click **Layer | Type | Convert To Point Text** or **Convert To Paragraph Text**.

QUICKSTEPS

COMMITTING TYPE

After your text has been entered and you are satisfied with the results, you *commit* the text to accept the changes. Do one of these to accept or commit the changes:

- Click **Commit** in the Options toolbar.
- On the numeric keyboard, press **ENTER.**
- On the main keyboard, press **CTRL+ENTER.**
- Select another tool, or select a menu option.
- Choose an interface palette.

Edit Type

To edit your text, you can change the font, text color, font size and style, leading, and kerning. Much of this can be done with the toolbar shown in Figure 7-1. All can be done with the Character or Paragraph palettes.

FORMAT TYPE WITH THE CHARACTER PALETTE

The Character palette allows you to edit the most common text attributes.

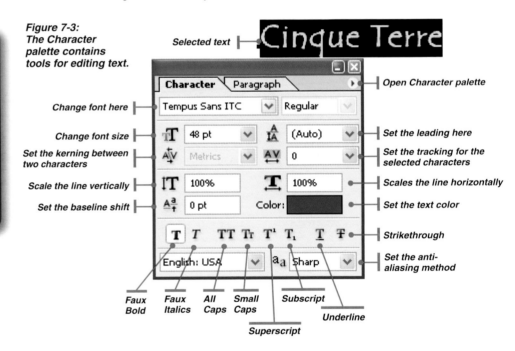

Figure 7-3:
The Character palette contains tools for editing text.

Selected text

Open Character palette

Change font here

Change font size — Set the leading here

Set the kerning between two characters — Set the tracking for the selected characters

Scale the line vertically — Scales the line horizontally

Set the baseline shift — Set the text color

Strikethrough

Set the anti-aliasing method

Faux Bold · Faux Italics · All Caps · Small Caps · Subscript · Superscript · Underline

1. If it is not already showing, display the Character palette by selecting **Window | Character**. The Character palette will open, as shown in Figure 7-3.

2. Click the text layer, and then select the text by highlighting it

3. Select from among these options:

- **Font** to change the name of the font used.

- **Font Style** to change to Bold, Italics, Bold Italics or None.

HYPHENATING AND JUSTIFYING TYPE

HYPHENATE WORDS

On the Paragraph palette, place a check mark in the **Hyphenate** check box to have Photoshop automatically hyphenate words.

SET HYPHENATION RULES

1. Open the **Paragraph** palette, and click **Hyphenation.** The Hyphenation dialog box will open.

2. Select from among these options.

- **Words Longer Than __ Letters** will hyphenate only words longer than the given number of letters; default is 5 letters.

- **After First __ Letters** requires a given number of letters before hyphenating.

- **Before Last __ Letters** requires hyphenation to occur at least that many letters from the end.

- **Hyphenate Limit __ Hyphens** limits the number of hyphens in adjoining lines; 0 provides no limit.

- **Hyphenation Zone** defines the distance from the end of the line that hyphenation will occur.

- **Hyphenate Capitalized Words** allows/restricts the hyphenation of capitalized words.

3. Click **OK.**

Continued...

- **Font Size** to change the point size of the characters.

- **Leading** to change the space between lines of text. Auto is the default. Usually you want to select a leading larger than the size of the text. So if the point size is 20 points, you might use leading of 24 or larger. You can use this to overlap lines of text for special effects.

- **Kerning** changes the space between two characters. Place the pointer between the two characters you want to manipulate. You can squish characters close together or set them farther apart.

- **Tracking** changes spacing for selected characters. Using a higher number increases space; a negative number decreases spacing.

- **Scale Vertically** adjusts the height of selected text.

- **Scale Horizontally** adjusts the width of selected text.

- **Baseline Shift** moves the selected characters above or below the baseline, such as in subscripts and superscripts

- **Text Color** sets the color of text.

- A line of character attributes can be chosen for selected characters: **Faux Bold** (when your font has no bold typeface), **Faux Italics** (when your font has no italics), **All Caps**, **Small Caps**, **Superscript**, **Subscript**, **Underlining**, and **Strikethrough**.

- **Language** establishes the language being typed.

- **Anti-aliasing** adjusts the smoothness of the letters, from the least adjustment of None, to the most of Smooth.

FORMAT PARAGRAPHS WITH THE PARAGRAPH PALETTE

When you type a paragraph into a bounding box, you have a Paragraph palette available for formatting line and paragraph spacing. Figure 7-4 shows the tools available with the Paragraph palette.

1. Click **Window | Paragraph** to display the Paragraph palette if it is not already showing.

HYPHENATING AND JUSTIFYING TYPE *(Continued)*

SPECIFY NO BREAK

To prevent a group of letters from being broken during word wrap:

1. Select the letters that are not to be broken.
2. Open the **Character** palette, and click **No Break**.

SET JUSTIFY RULES

You can set the spacing between words, letters, and glyphs (any characters or symbols in a font including nontext characters, such as Wingdings font characters).

1. Open the **Paragraph** palette, and click **Justification.** The Justification dialog box will open.

2. Set the values to define the spacing between words, letters, and glyphs as described in Table 7-1.
3. Click **OK**.

2. Set your paragraph parameters before typing text by clicking the attribute or by filling in a text box.

3. Create paragraph text by selecting the Horizontal Type Tool or Vertical Type Tool and dragging a bounding box.

4. Begin to type the paragraph.

5. To change paragraph settings, select the paragraph and move your pointer over the option, such as Indent Left Margin. When your pointer becomes a pointing hand with a two-headed arrow, click and drag to change the value. (Dragging horizontally seems to work better.)

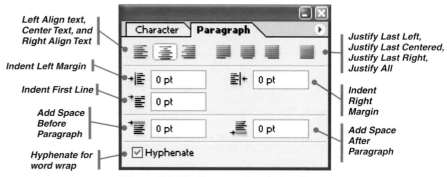

Figure 7-4: The Paragraph palette allows you to define paragraph attributes such as alignment, spacing and indentation.

Use Check Spelling

To check whether the words in your paragraph are correct, use Check Spelling.

1. Select the text to be tested.
2. Open **Edit | Check Spelling**.
3. If a word cannot be found in the Photoshop dictionary, the Check Spelling dialog box will be displayed, as shown in Figure 7-5. If the word is not in the dictionary, Photoshop thinks the word has been misspelled. Choose among these options:

- **Ignore** to skip the word identified as a mistake.
- **Ignore All** to skip all occurrences of a word.
- **Change** to replace the word under Not In Dictionary with the one in Change To.

TRANSFORMING TYPE

You can transform type by manipulating the bounding boxes:

SELECT A BOUNDING BOX

To display the bounding box with handles for rotating and resizing:

- In Edit mode, select the **Type Tool** and click the text.
- Select the **Type Tool**, select the layer with the type, and click in the text.

RESIZE A BOUNDING BOX

1. Place your pointer over the bounding-box handles until you see a double-headed arrow.

2. Drag the handles until the bounding box is the size you want.

3. To change the size proportionally, press **SHIFT** while you drag.

ROTATE A BOUNDING BOX

1. Place the pointer outside the bounding box until the pointer morphs into a curved double-headed arrow.

2. Drag the pointer in the direction the box is to be rotated.

3. Press **SHIFT** while you drag to change the rotation in 15 degree increments.

4. Press **CTRL** while you drag the center point to another place, even outside the bounding box. Then you can rotate the bounding box around a wider circle.

Continued...

Continued...

TIP

You can tell when you are in Edit Mode by looking for the Commit and Cancel Transform tools in the Option toolbar. If these tools are there, you are in Edit Mode.

- **Change All** to replace all occurrences of the identified word with the one in Change To.

- **Add** to add the word in Not In Dictionary to the dictionary.

4. Click **Done** to close the dialog box. Or if the spelling checker finds no more misspelled words, it will display a message that the Spell Check Is Complete.

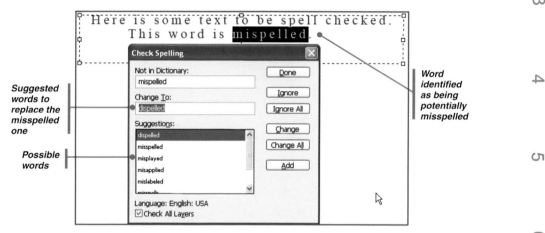

Figure 7-5: The Check Spelling feature identifies all words that are not in the Photoshop dictionary as potential misspellings.

Find and Replace Text

To find text and replace it with other text:

1. Click **File | Find And Replace**. The Find And Replace Text dialog box will open.

2. Under Find What, type in the text to be searched for and replaced.

3. Under Change To, type the new text.

4. Click options if they apply:

- **Search All Layers** to search for the text in all layers of an image

- **Forward** to search forward from one text object to another

- **Case Sensitive** to restrict the search to the case in the Find What text box

- **Whole Word Only** to search only for whole words that match the Find What text

TRANSFORMING TYPE (Continued)

SKEW A BOUNDING BOX

Press **CTRL** while you drag a corner handle. The pointer morphs into an arrow that can be used to skew the shape of the bounding box.

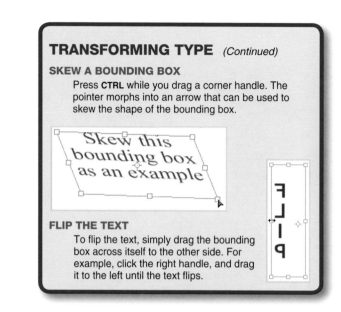

FLIP THE TEXT

To flip the text, simply drag the bounding box across itself to the other side. For example, click the right handle, and drag it to the left until the text flips.

- **Find Next** to search for the next occurrence
- **Change** to change the found text to the Change To text
- **Change All** to change all occurrences of the Find What text

5. Click **Done**.

Warp Text

You can create interesting effects with text by warping it.

1. In the Layers palette, click the layer containing the text to be warped.

2. Select **Layer | Type | Warp Text**. The Warp Text dialog box, shown in Figure 7-6, will open.

- Open the **Style** drop-down list, and select a warp style.
- Click **Horizontal** or **Vertical** to orient the text horizontally or vertically.
- Drag the **Bend slider** to exaggerate or lessen the warp of the text. Alternatively, you can type a percentage of **Bend** to set the degree of warp.
- Drag the **Horizontal Distortion slider** to increase or decrease the horizontal warp, or type in a percentage in the text box.
- Drag the **Vertical Distortion slider** to increase or decrease the vertical warp, or type in a percentage in the text box.

3. Click **OK** when the warp effect is as you want.

Create Text on a Path

You can type text along a path, such as seen in Figure 7-7. First you create a path and then type text, pulling it along the path.

1. Create a layer for your path and text.

2. Select a tool, such as the Pen Tool or Freeform Pen Tool, to create a path. (See Chapter 5 for additional information on creating paths.)

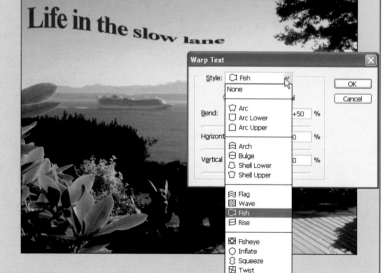

Figure 7-6: The Warp Text dialog box presents options for the style of warp you want.

Figure 7-7: Type text on a path for special effects.

![CAUTION]

If your text does not conform to the path or if the path disappears, make sure you are on the right layer.

![TIP]

The text will appear in the direction that the path is drawn; so if you draw a line left to right, that is how the letters will be inserted. Also, if the path is too short or the text comes to the end of the path before all letters are on the path, the letters will follow the path and curve around the end of it.

![NOTE]

If your letters seem to disappear as you type, you may need to *pull* the text string along the path. Select the Path Selection Tool, and where the text disappears, drag an anchor point along the path in the direction the text is to flow. As you release the Path Selection Tool, the missing letters will appear.

3. Click **Paths** on the Options toolbar.

4. Select the **Horizontal Type Tool**, for text parallel to the path, or **Vertical Type Tool**, for text perpendicular to the path.

5. Place the pointer above the path until it morphs into an I-beam. Click the path and an insertion point will appear.

6. Type your text.

Edit Text on a Path

To edit the text on a path, inserting and deleting letters and making formatting changes:

1. Select the text layer that the text to be edited is on.

2. Click either the **Horizontal Type Tool** or the **Vertical Type Tool**.

3. Click the text string to place the insertion point, or highlight the text.

4. Make your changes.

Create Text within a Closed Path

To type text with a closed path, such as a circle or ellipse, you create a path around a shape and type text, dragging the text where you want it.

1. Select a shape tool, and draw a shape, such as the oval in Figure 7-8.

2. Click **Path** to make it into a path.

3. Click the **Horizontal Type Tool** or the **Vertical Type Tool**, and place the insertion point on the shape.

4. Type the text.

5. Adjust the positioning by using the **Path Selection Tool** or the **Direct Selection Tool** to pull the text string one way or the other. You will also want to rotate the text, format it, or apply layer styles to it before you finish.

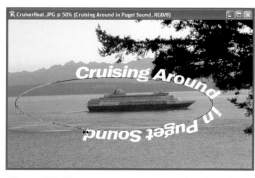

Figure 7-8: You can type text around a closed path to create unusual effects.

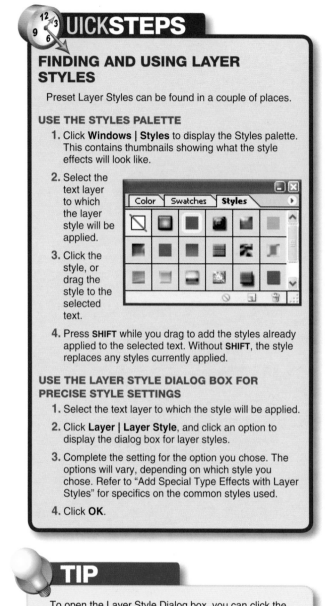

QUICKSTEPS

FINDING AND USING LAYER STYLES

Preset Layer Styles can be found in a couple of places.

USE THE STYLES PALETTE

1. Click **Windows | Styles** to display the Styles palette. This contains thumbnails showing what the style effects will look like.

2. Select the text layer to which the layer style will be applied.

3. Click the style, or drag the style to the selected text.

4. Press **SHIFT** while you drag to add the styles already applied to the selected text. Without **SHIFT**, the style replaces any styles currently applied.

USE THE LAYER STYLE DIALOG BOX FOR PRECISE STYLE SETTINGS

1. Select the text layer to which the style will be applied.

2. Click **Layer | Layer Style**, and click an option to display the dialog box for layer styles.

3. Complete the setting for the option you chose. The options will vary, depending on which style you chose. Refer to "Add Special Type Effects with Layer Styles" for specifics on the common styles used.

4. Click **OK**.

TIP

To open the Layer Style Dialog box, you can click the Layer Style button at the bottom of the Layers palette.

Add Special Type Effects with Layer Styles

You can apply special effects to your text with options from Layer Styles. Photoshop has several predefined, or preset, styles that can be used to create drop shadows, embossing or beveling, inside and outside glows, gradient coloring, patterns and more. Figure 7-9 shows examples of some effects described in this section. Three commonly used styles are described next.

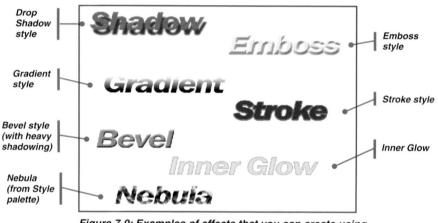

Figure 7-9: Examples of effects that you can create using layer styles.

DROP SHADOWS

To create a slight shadow on the type:

1. Select the text to be given the drop shadow.

2. Select **Layer | Layer Style | Drop Shadow**. The Layer Style dialog box will appear with the Drop Shadow options, as shown in Figure 7-10. (You can also click the **Layer Style** button on the Layer palette, and then click **Drop Shadow** to display its options on the Layer Style dialog box.)

3. Experiment with the options and view the results in the Preview box. If you have a question about what the options are, refer to Chapters 4 and 6 for additional information.

- **Blend Mode** is by default Multiply. The default color is black.

- **Opacity**, because of the Blend Mode, makes the shadow lighter or darker.

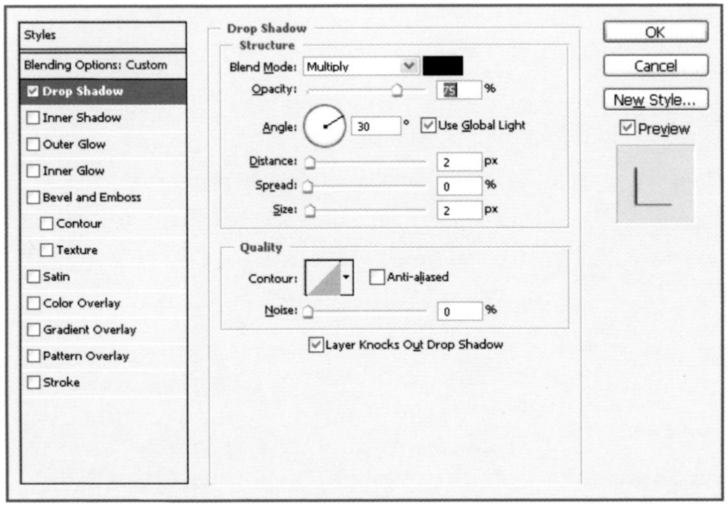

Figure 7-10: The Drop Shadow options allow you to control the shadowing very precisely.

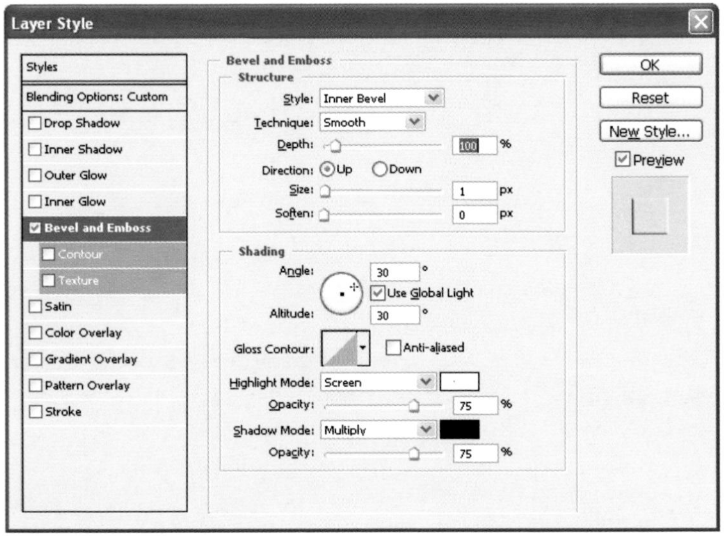

Figure 7-11: Bevel And Emboss can give your text depth and a more professional look.

- **Angle** is the direction of the light source. **Global Light** places a light source on all the type.

- **Distance** is how far the shadow is offset from the type.

- **Spread** relates to the percentage of thickness a shadow has, and it is related to Size.

- **Size** is how sharp or fuzzy the shadow is.

- **Contour** opens a submenu of shadow curves or shapes.

- **Anti-aliased** specifies whether the jaggedness of letters is to be smoothed.

- **Noise** makes the shadow smoother, clumpier, or noisier.

- **Layer Knocks Out Drop Shadow** pertains to whether the shadow will be visible on a semitransparent layer. When the option is checked, the type layer knocks out the shadow, so if you turn the layer fill down, you can still see where the type cuts the shadow. If unchecked and you turn the layer fill down, as the type disappears, the shadow still shows fully—a shadow with no type. It is similar to a stencil.

4. When you are satisfied, click **OK**.

BEVEL AND EMBOSS

To create either beveling or embossing on the type:

1. Select the layer containing the text to be given the special effect.

2. Select **Layer | Layer Style | Bevel And Emboss**. The Layer Style dialog box will appear. (You can also click the **Layer Style** button on the Layer palette, and then click **Bevel and Emboss** to display the Layer Style dialog box.)

3. The options for controlling the beveling and embossing are displayed on the dialog box, as shown in Figure 7-11. As you select options, you can view the results in the Preview box. If you have a question about the options, refer to Chapters 4 and 6 for additional information.

- **Style** displays a menu of styles you can use: Outer Bevel bevels the edge of the type; Inner Bevel gives a more rounded look to the bevel; Emboss makes the type look as if it were stamped, or standing apart from the background; Pillow Emboss is a more rounded look; Stroke Emboss adds an edge to the outline.

TIP

To copy an effect from one layer to another, arrange both layers so that you can see them. Select the layer containing the effect. From the Layers palette, drag the layer containing the effect to the layer to be copied to. When you release the pointer, the effect will be applied to the text on the layer.

TABLE 7-1: *Defines Justification Rules*

Element	Minimum	Maximum	No Effect
Word Spacing	0%	1000%	100%
Letter Spacing	−100%	500%	0%
Glyph Spacing	50%	200%	100%

- **Technique** displays three options: Smooth blurs the edges; Chisel Hard makes it look very crisp and defined; Chisel Soft is less sharp than Chisel Hard but more defined than Smooth.

- **Depth** sets the depth of the bevel or embossing.

- **Direction** determines whether the surface of the type is Up and rounded, or Down and indented.

- **Size** determines the size of the shading, how deep into the text it is.

- **Soften** blurs the shaded part of the bevel or embossing.

- **Angle** establishes the degree of the light source and whether all the type has the same light source.

- **Altitude** determines how high the light source is.

- **Gloss Contour** displays a menu of options for the shape or contour of the bevel.

- **Anti-aliased** smoothes the edges of the contour.

- **Highlight Mode** is applied to the highlights of the bevel or embossing. By default it is Screen blend mode and white in color.

- **Opacity** is connected to Highlight Mode and varies it. Drag the sliders to set the values.

- **Shadow Mode** is applied to the shadows of the bevel or embossing. By default it is set to Multiply blend mode and is black in color.

- **Opacity** can be varied for the Shadow Mode. Drag the sliders to set the values.

4. When you are satisfied, click **OK**.

MAKE TYPE GLOW INSIDE AND OUT

Inside Glow and Outside Glow make your type look as if there were a light source inside or behind the type:

1. Select the layer containing the text to be given the special effect.

2. Select **Layer | Layer Style | Inner Glow**. The Layer Style dialog box will appear. (You can also click the **Layer Style** button on the Layer palette, and then select Inner Glow to display its options on the Layer Style dialog box.)

3. The options for controlling the inside and outside glow are displayed on the dialog box, as shown in Figure 7-12. As you select options, you can view the results in the Preview box. You can see that many of the options are the same as either Drop Shadow or Bevel And Emboss. Here are the options unique to Inner Glow:

- **Noise** makes the glow harsher, more clunky.
- The fill for the glow can be solid, or you can select a graduated color scheme from the drop-down list.
- **Technique** can be Softer or Precise for keeping or blurring the detail.
- **Source** locates whether the source of light will be coming from the center of the type or from the inside edges.
- **Choke** increases or decreases the perimeter of the matte of the glow.
- **Size** defines the size of the glow.
- **Contour** pertains to the pattern of the fading of the glow.
- **Range** describes where the contour will be applied to the glow.
- **Jitter** increases and decreases the variations around the layer.

4. When you are satisfied, click **OK**.

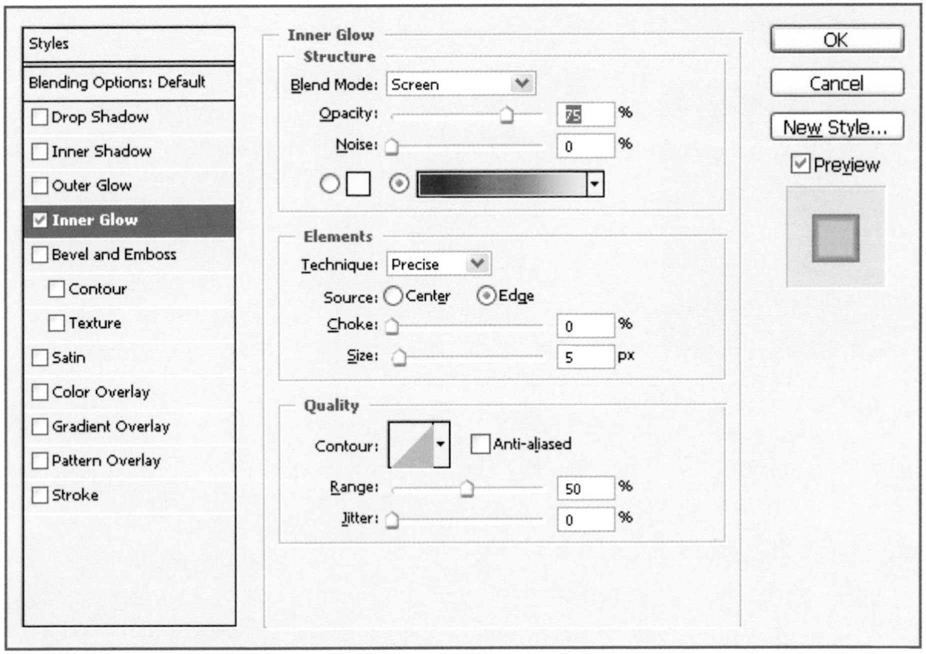

Figure 7-12: Inner Glow makes your type look as if there were an inside source of light.

Create Text Masks

You can use a text mask either to create a selection of type or to fill type with the background from one image or layer that you want to use on another image or layer. It is like making a cutout of one image to use in another.

Figure 7-13: The words "Puget Sound" were first cut out of the sunset part of the picture, using a type mask, and then enlarged and are now available to be moved to another image.

1. In the Layers palette, select the layer that contains the image you want to use.

2. Select the **Horizontal Mask Type Tool** or the **Vertical Mask Type Tool**.

3. Set your formatting the way you want, as described previously in this chapter. Click the image to set the insertion point. The canvas will be filled with a protective red masking layer.

4. Type the words you want to mask, and then click **Commit**.

5. You can do several tasks:

   ● Copy and paste the masked type to place it on its own layer without removing or cutting the type from the background image. While the type mask is selected, it can be moved, copied, filled, or treated like another selection as shown in figure 7-13.

   ● Move the masked type using the Move Tool, and it will remove or cut the type pattern from the image so you have a cutout of the text. You can stretch the selection box and otherwise distort the type, but it cannot be edited as type.

How to...

- 🗨 *Preparing the Image for Printing*
- *Print Images with a Desktop Printer*
- 🗨 *Printing a Single Copy of a Page*
- *Print Vector Graphics*
- 🗨 *Printing Part of an Image*
- *Use Color Management When Printing*
- *Create a Contact Sheet*
- *Create a Picture Package*
- 🗨 *Saving a Document*
- *Use the Save As Command*
- *Save a Layered File*
- *Add File Information and MetaData*
- *Create a Digital Copyright*
- 🗨 *Importing Document Metadata*
- *Save Document Metadata as a Template*
- *Create a PDF Presentation*

Chapter 8
Printing and Exporting Images

After you use the powerful Photoshop toolset to hone your image to perfection, you're ready to print your image or save it for future use. In this chapter, you'll learn valuable information about printing and saving images. You'll see how to save your images as noncompressed files and as Photoshop PSD files. You'll also learn to save a document while preserving layers. You'll find out how to print your images on a desktop inkjet printer and use the powerful Print With Preview command to resize the document and set other parameters within a single dialog box.

Print Your Work

Editing your image and applying special effects puts your creative muse to work. However, Photoshop also lets you be creative on the print end. You can print your image to your local printer or create a picture package that includes several different sizes of the same image on a single sheet.

PREPARING THE IMAGE FOR PRINTING

1. Select **Image | Image Size** to open the Image Size dialog box.

2. In the Document Size section, type the desired values for **Width** or **Height**. As a rule, you'll type a value to match the document size to the paper size in your printer paper tray.

3.

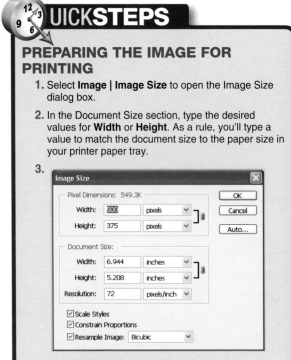

Accept the default document resolution, or enter a different value in the Resolution field. You should not exceed the current document resolution; otherwise, pixelation may occur when Photoshop resamples the image. You can, however, select a lower resolution to match your desktop printer.

4. Click **OK** to size the image.

NOTE

Many printers have a built-in margin which you'll have to subtract from the Width or Height value. You can find the margins for your default printer by accessing the Page Setup dialog box. If you haven't maximized the image to the workspace, click the **bottom border** of the document window, and from the shortcut menu select **Page Setup**.

When you print an image from within Photoshop, you can print a single image, print multiple images, preview an image prior to printing, and much more. When you print an image from within Photoshop, you can use the powerful Page Setup command. From within the Page Setup dialog box, you can specify the size and orientation of the printed image. If you prefer to set all parameters for printing within a single dialog box, you can do so using the Print With Preview command.

Print Images with a Desktop Printer

One of the easiest ways to see the fruits of your creative labor in Photoshop is to print a copy of the image on your local printer. If you own a printer that is capable of using photo paper, you can create an image suitable for framing on glossy or matte paper. The results can be stunning, especially if you own one of the new six-color inkjet printers. These gems are capable of mixing about any color you can throw at them. If your monitor is properly calibrated, what you see on the screen is what you'll take out of the printer tray.

USE THE PAGE SETUP COMMAND

1. Select **File | Page Setup** to open the Page Setup dialog box.

2. Open the **Size** drop-down list, and select the desired paper size.

3. Open the **Source** drop-down list, and select the paper source.

4. In the Orientation section, click **Portrait** or **Landscape**. This determines how your image will be mapped to the printed page. Select Portrait if your image is taller than it is wide, Landscape if your image is wider than it is tall.

NOTE

When you enter a different resolution, deselect the Resample Image check box. If you don't, Photoshop will change the pixel dimensions of the image, which involves interpolation when redrawing the image. When Photoshop redraws pixels, image degradation may occur and the file size will increase. When you deselect the Resample Image option and change image resolution, the image print-size is changed accordingly. For example, if you have an 800 × 600 pixel image at 72 PPI, the document will print at 11.111 × 8.333 inches. When you change the resolution with the Resample Image check box deselected and change the image resolution to 300 PPI, the pixel dimensions are still 800 × 600, but the document will print at 2.66 × 2 inches.

TIP

If you're printing an image on a photo-size paper with perforations, you can set the Crop Tool width, height, and resolution to match the paper size. Resize the image to the approximate size of the paper, and then use the Crop Tool to crop the image to the paper size. See Chapter 6 for more information on the Crop Tool.

5. Click **Printer** to open the second Page Setup dialog box.

6. Open the **Name** drop-down list, and select the desired printer.

7. Click **Network** to select a printer on your network.

8. Click **Properties** to set properties for the selected printer. This opens a dialog box that you use to specify settings for the selected printer. The illustration shows the Epson Stylus Photo 925 Properties dialog box.

9. Specify the settings for your printer.

10. Click **OK** to exit the second Page Setup dialog box, and then click **OK** to exit the first Page Setup dialog box.

PRINT AN IMAGE

After setting up the page, you're ready to print the image.

1. Select **File | Print** to open the Print dialog box.

2. Open the printer **Name** drop-down list, and select the desired printer. This step is not necessary if you've already invoked the Page Setup command.

3. Click **Properties** to reveal the dialog box for the selected printer's properties. This step is not necessary if you've already invoked the Page Setup command.

4. In Copies, type the number of copies you want to print. Alternatively, you can click the spinner buttons to set the value.

5. Click **OK** to print the document.

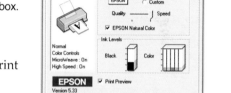

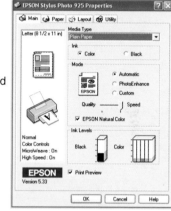

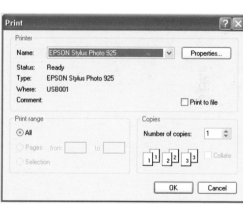

NOTE

The Print dialog box shows a Page Range and Collate section. Photoshop does not support multipage documents. These sections are carryovers from the generic Windows Print dialog box.

NOTE

If the image is bigger than the currently selected printer media, the handles will not be visible. Move your pointer over the top or bottom border of the bounding box. When the pointer becomes a vertical line with a dual-headed arrow, drag to resize the image.

TIP

To change the unit of measure, open the unit of measure drop-down list, and select an option.

USE THE PRINT WITH PREVIEW COMMAND

1. Select **File | Print With Preview** to open the Print with preview dialog box.

2. Drag one of the corner handles of the image preview to rescale the image. The white area around the image thumbnail represents the printer media size.

3. Accept the default Position options, or click the **Center Image** check box to deselect the option. If you deselect this option, the Top and Left text fields become available, enabling you to enter the value you want for the image offset from the top and the left border of the page. Alternatively, you can drag the thumbnail preview to determine where the image will appear on the printed page.

4. Under Scaled Print Size, accept the default value, which will be 100 percent, or a different value if you manually scaled the image preview. Alternatively, you can select from the following options:

   • **Scale** enables you to enter a value to which you want the image scaled. This is a percentage of the image's original size.

   • **Scale to Media** scales the document to fit the printer media.

   • **Width** enables you to enter a value to which you want the width of the document sized. After entering a value, the height of the document is scaled proportionately.

   • **Height** enables you to enter a value to which you want the height of the document sized. After entering a value, the width of the document is scaled proportionately.

   • **Show Bounding Box** (enabled by default) displays a bounding box around the image thumbnail with four handles that you use to resize the document.

   • **Print Selected Area** becomes available if you select a region of the document with one of the marquee select tools. This technique will be covered in a forthcoming section.

5. After setting print options, do one of the following:

- Click **Print** to print the image. Click **Cancel** to cancel printing.
- Click **Done** to exit the dialog box and preserve the current options.
- Press **ALT** and click **Print One Copy** to print one copy of the image with the current settings
- Press **ALT** and click **Reset** to reset the dialog box to the default settings for the image.
- Press **ALT** and click **Remember** to save the current print options without exiting the dialog box.

Print Vector Graphics

To create a document with vector graphics, such as shapes or text, you can print
the image to a PostScript printer such as an Adobe Acrobat PDF file. In this
case, Photoshop sends the vector information as separate images for each type
layer and vector shape, so that the vector graphics can print at full resolution,
regardless of the resolution of the background image.

1. Click **File | Page Setup** to open the Page Setup dialog box.

2. Click **Printer** to select a postscript printer and specify other print options.

3. Click **OK** to exit the Page Setup dialog box.

4. Select **File | Print With Preview** to open the Print dialog box.

5. Click the **Show More Options** check box.

6. Open the drop-down list beneath the check box, and select **Output**.

7. Click the **Include Vector Data** check box.

8. If necessary, select a postscript encoding option from the **Encoding** drop-down list.

9. Click **Print**.

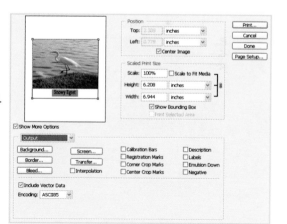

QUICKSTEPS

PRINTING PART OF AN IMAGE

There may be times when you want to print part of an image without altering the original with the Crop Tool. You can easily print the desired portion of an image by selecting the area and then invoking the Print With Preview command.

PRINT A SELECTION

1. Select the **Rectangular Marquee Tool**, and drag inside the image to define the area you want to print, as shown in the following image.

2. Click **File | Print With Preview** to display the Print dialog box.
3. Click the **Print Selected Area** check box.
4. Click **Print**.

NOTE

You can also include vector data when you save an image with vector objects in the EPS format.

Use Color Management When Printing

When you print an image, you can let the printer take the reins and perform color management, or you can override the printer's color management by specifying a color management profile. A color profile describes the color space of a device, such as a monitor or printer, and the color space of the actual document itself. A color management profile is embedded with the document. You decide whether to accept the embedded color profile or use the specified Photoshop color profile. A device color profile does not change the document color values; it is merely a method used by the device to interpret color values in the document.

1. Click **File | Print With Preview** to open the Print with preview dialog box.
2. If the drop-down list below the thumbnail image doesn't read Color Management, open it and click **Color Management**.
3. Under Source Space, accept the default **Document** option to print the document with the color profile currently assigned to the document.
4. If necessary, click **Page Setup** to access the Page Setup dialog box, and select a printer, media size, and so on.
5. Under Print Space, open the **Profile** drop-down list, and select an option. Your list will vary depending on the devices you have attached to your system. If you select an option other than Same As Source or Printer Color Management, the Intent option becomes available.
6. If necessary, open the **Intent** drop-down list, and select one of the following options:

   - **Perceptual** attempts to preserve color values to produce a print with colors that appear natural to the human eye. This rendering option may change color values and is useful for photographic images that may contain out of gamut colors.

Printer Color Management
Working RGB - Adobe RGB (1998)
Working CMYK - U.S. Web Coated (SWOP) v2
Working Gray - Dot Gain 20%
Lab Color
Adobe RGB (1998)
Apple RGB
ColorMatch RGB
sRGB IEC61966-2.1
Euroscale Coated v2
Euroscale Uncoated v2
Japan Color 2001 Coated
Japan Color 2001 Uncoated
Japan Standard v2
Japan Web Coated (Ad)
U.S. Sheetfed Coated v2
U.S. Sheetfed Uncoated v2
U.S. Web Coated (SWOP) v2
U.S. Web Uncoated v2
Dot Gain 10%
Dot Gain 15%
Dot Gain 20%
Dot Gain 25%
Dot Gain 30%
Gray Gamma 1.8

- **Saturation** renders a print with vivid saturated colors. This rendering intent will change color values and is especially useful for documents that contain graphics, such as graphs or bar charts, where visual impact is more important than preserving the relationship between colors.

- **Relative Colormetric** renders an image by comparing the extreme highlight of the image color space to the color space of the selected color profile. This option shifts out of gamut colors to the closest reproducible color in the destination color space. This option preserves more of the image's original colors than does the Perceptual rendering intent.

- **Absolute Colormetric** does not alter image colors that fall within the destination gamut. This rendering intent clips out of gamut colors and does not scale colors to the destination white point. Use this color intent to maintain color accuracy while creating a proof to simulate the output of a particular device. Note that this rendering intent may not preserve the color relationship between colors.

7. Click **Print** to print the document.

Create a Contact Sheet

If you're a digital photographer, you download your pictures from a media card to your hard drive before editing them in Photoshop. Many digital photographers archive their original images to CD disks for future use. Before archiving the images to disk, you can create a contact sheet, which can be used to identify the images stored on the disk. Figure 8-1 shows a contact sheet.

1. Select **Window | File Browser** and navigate to the folder of images you're going to archive to disk.

2. Select **File |Automate | Contact Sheet II** to display the Contact Sheet II dialog box. Alternatively, if you're working with the File Browser, open choose **Automate | Contact Sheet II** from the File Browser menu.

8

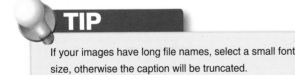

Figure 8-1: Create a contact sheet of images stored in a folder.

TIP

If your images have long file names, select a small font size, otherwise the caption will be truncated.

3. Open the **Use** drop-down list, and select one of the following options:

   • **Current Open Documents** to create a contact sheet using the documents you currently have open in Photoshop.

   • **Folder** to create a contact sheet using images stored in a folder. If you select this option, the Browse button becomes available, which you use to navigate to the desired folder.

   • **Selected Images From Browser** to create a contact sheet using the images currently selected in the File Browser. If no images are selected, the contact sheet is created using images from the folder currently displayed in the File Browser.

4. Under Document, specify the size of the media to which you'll be printing the contact sheet as well as the resolution at which the contact sheet thumbnails will be printed. If your printer uses default margins, the default 8 × 10 inch size works well with 8 ½ × 11 inch paper.

5. Type a value in the **Resolution** field. This is the resolution at which the thumbnails will be created and therefore printed. The default value of 72 pixels won't give you much detail. Type a value of about 150 to create thumbnails with better detail.

6. Open the **Mode** drop-down list, and select one of the following color mode options: Grayscale, RGB Color, CMYK Color, or Lab Color.

7. Accept the **Flatten All Layers** option to create a composite thumbnail of all layers.

8. Under Thumbnails, click the **Place** drop-down option, and select one of the following: Across First or Down First.

9. Accept the default **Use Auto-Spacing** option, and Photoshop evenly spaces the thumbnails across rows and columns. If you disable this option, the Vertical and Horizontal text boxes become available, enabling you to enter the value by which you want the thumbnails spaced.

10. Type values in the **Rows** and **Columns** text boxes to determine how many thumbnails will be placed in each row and how many columns will comprise the contact sheet.

11. Click the **Rotate For Best Fit** check box to have thumbnails rotated for best fit. This option will rotate any portrait thumbnails to landscape mode, which might make them difficult to view if you pack several rows and columns of thumbnails on a contact sheet.

12. Accept the default **Use Filename As Caption** option, and Photoshop will list the applicable file name beneath the thumbnail. If you deselect this option, the contact sheet will display only images.

NOTE

Alternatively, you can click a thumbnail in the File Browser, and select **Automate | Picture Package** from the File Browser menu.

NOTE

You can also create a picture package by selecting a folder of images or an individual image file, options you'll find on the Use drop-down list, in the Picture Package dialog box.

13. Open the **Font** drop-down list, and select the font that will be used to display the caption text.

14. Open the **Size** drop-down list, and select a size. Alternatively, you can enter a value in this field.

15. Click **OK** to process the contact sheets. Note that this may take some time depending on the number of images you are committing to the contact sheet.

16. Select each contact sheet in turn, and then select **File | Print**.

Create a Picture Package

If you use Photoshop to edit photos for clients or create images for friends and relatives, you can create a picture package. A picture package prints more than one copy of an image on a sheet. You can mix different sizes, for example, one 5 × 7 inch and two 3 × 5 inch photos on one 8 × 10 sheet. Figure 8-2 illustrates a picture package.

1. Open the desired image.

2. Click **File | Automate | Picture Package** to display the Picture Package dialog box.

3. Accept the default **Foremost Image** option to create a picture package from the currently active document.

4. Open the **Page Size** drop-down list, and select the desired size.

Figure 8-2: You can create a Picture Package with multiple images on a single sheet.

UICKSTEPS

SAVING A DOCUMENT

When you open an image in Photoshop, after editing the file, you'll want to save it. You can save the file using its native format. If the image's native format does not support layers, you'll need to flatten layers before you can save the file in its native format.

1. Open the desired image file.

2. Edit the file using the techniques shown in Chapter 6, "Correcting Color, Retouching, and Repairing Images."

3. If necessary, flatten the image.

4. Select **File | Save**.

5. Open the **Layout** drop-down list, and select the desired layout.

6. Type the desired print resolution in **Resolution**. Specify a resolution no greater than the resolution of the image for which you're creating the picture package.

7. Under Label, click the **Content** drop-down box, and select an option. Note that the last four items are derived from the file's metadata. If you select Custom Text, the Custom Text field becomes available, enabling you to enter the text you want displayed as an image caption.

8. If you select one of the caption options, select the remaining options for Font, Font Size, Color, Opacity, Position, and Rotate.

9. Click **OK** to create the Picture Package.

10. Click **File | Print** to print the picture package.

Save Images

After editing an image in Photoshop, your next step is to save the file. You can save an image to most of the currently available image file formats. If you're going to edit the image at a future date, you can save the image in Photoshop's native PSD format to preserve the layers. You can also save the image in another format that supports layers for editing in another "layer friendly" image editing application.

Use the Save As Command

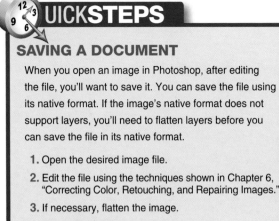

After editing a file in Photoshop, you may want to save the file using a different image format. If you're a digital photographer and you edit RAW images in Photoshop, this will almost always be the case. You can save an edited image using any of the popular image file formats (found in the Format drop-down list) for print or monitor display.

1. Select **File | Save As** to open the Save As dialog box.

2. Enter the desired file name.

3. Open the **Format** drop-down list, and select a format.

4. Click **Save**. Depending on the image format, an additional dialog box appears enabling you to specify file format options for the document you are saving.

5. If necessary, click **OK** to exit the selected format's options dialog box, and save the file.

Resource Scheduling

Processing meeting requests

Use these options if you are responsible for coordinating resources, such as conference rooms.

☑ Automatically accept meeting requests and process cancellations

☐ Automatically decline conflicting meeting requests

☐ Automatically decline recurring meeting requests

You must give users permission to view and edit this calendar if you want these options to work offline.

Set Permissions...

OK   Cancel

NOTE

A detailed discussion of each file format is beyond the scope of this book. For in-depth information on each file format, press F1 to summon Photoshop's online help.

Save a Layered File

If you add layers when editing an image, you can preserve the layers when you save the file. You can save a layered file in any format that supports layers. However, if you're going to edit the document exclusively in Photoshop, save the layered file using Photoshop's native PSD file format.

1. Select **File | Save As** to open the Save As dialog box.

2. Enter a file name for the document.

3. Click the **Format** drop-down box, and select one of the options shown here. To preserve layers, save the file in one of the following formats: Photoshop (*PSD, PDD), Photoshop PDF **(**PDF, PDP), and TIFF (*TIFF, *TIF). Note that the second format is Adobe's PDF (Portable Document Format).

4. Under Save Options, select **Save As A Copy** to save a copy of the original document.

5. **Click Save** to save the document with layers intact.

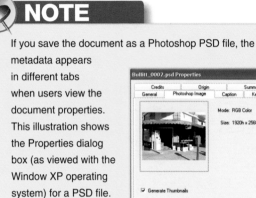

Add File Information and Metadata

When you save an image you've edited in Photoshop, you can add information to the file that can be read by other Photoshop users. In addition, some of the information you enter as metadata can be viewed by users who access the image's properties dialog box after selecting the file outside of Photoshop.

1. Open the desired image.

2. Select **File | File Info** to open the file information dialog box shown here.

3. Under **Description**, type a title for the document, the author's name, a description of the image, and keywords.

4. Click **OK** to add the metadata to the document.

Create a Digital Copyright

When you create a digital copyright, it appears in the Summary dialog box when the images properties are accessed. Other Photoshop users can also view your digital copyright by selecting File | File Info.

1. Open the image you want to copyright.

2. Click **File | File Info** to open the file information dialog box.

3. Under **Description**, enter the desired metadata as outlined in the previous section.

4. Open the **Copyright Status** drop-down list, and select **Copyrighted**.

5. In the **Copyright Notice** text box, type the desired information—for example: Copyright 2004, Doug Sahlin, All rights reserved.

6. In the **Copyright Info URL** text box, type the URL to the copyright owner's Web site. After entering this information, the Go To URL button becomes active. Other Photoshop users can click this button to view the URL while they are online.

7. Click **OK** to apply the digital copyright.

Save Document Metadata as a Template

If you frequently use the same metadata, you can save it as a template. After saving metadata as a template, it appears on a list in the file information dialog box.

1. Open a document.

2. Click **File | File Info**.

3. Type the information you want to save as a Metadata template.

4. Click the **triangle icon** in the upper-right corner of the dialog box, and click **Save Metadata Template** to open the Save Metadata dialog box.

5. Type a name for the metadata template, and then click **OK**.

Create a PDF Presentation

You can quickly create a PDF presentation using one of the Automate commands. The PDF Presentation command enables you to add transitions between slides and to specify which images are used to create the PDF document. A PDF presentation is viewed in Full-screen mode without the Acrobat interface.

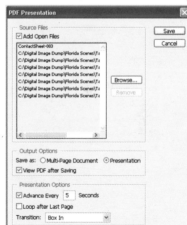

1. Open the desired files.

2. Click **File | Automate | PDF Presentation** to display the PDF Presentation dialog box.

3. Click **Add Open Files** to include all open files in the PDF.

4. Click **Presentation** in the Output Options section.

5. Click the **View PDF After Saving** check box to display the PDF document in Adobe Acrobat or Acrobat Reader after it is saved.

6. Accept the default advance options, which will automatically advance the presentation to the next page after five seconds. If you deselect the Advance option, viewers of the PDF document need to press **PAGE DOWN** or the **DOWN ARROW** key to advance to the next page of the presentation.

PDF Options dialog box showing:

- Encoding
  - ZIP
  - JPEG (selected)
  - Quality: 10 Maximum
  - small file — large file
- Save Transparency
- Image Interpolation
- Downgrade Color Profile
- PDF Security — Security Settings...
- Include Vector Data
  - Embed Fonts
  - Use Outlines for Text
- OK
- Cancel

Transition drop-down list:
Blinds Horizontal
Blinds Vertical
Box In
Box Out
Dissolve
Glitter Down
Glitter Right
Glitter Right-Down
None
Random Transition
Split Horizontal In
Split Horizontal Out
Split Vertical In
Split Vertical Out
Wipe Down
Wipe Left
Wipe Right
Wipe Up

TIP

If desired, click **Browse** to display the Open dialog box. Navigate to any additional image files you want to include in the PDF presentation.

NOTE

You can also create a multipage PDF document by clicking the Multi-Page Document button in the Output Options section.

7. Click the **Loop After Last Page** check box to loop the PDF presentation back to the first page after the last page is displayed.

8. Open the **Transition** drop-down list, and select a transition option.

9. Click **Save** to open the Save dialog box.

10. Click **Save** to open the PDF Options dialog box.

11. Under **Encoding,** click **Zip** or **JPEG**. Zip is lossless compression, which means no color data is lost when images are compressed. If you select JPEG, specify the image quality by dragging the Quality slider or by entering a value from 1 to 12 in the Quality text box. Higher values apply less compression to the image, ensuring higher quality at the expense of a larger file size.

12. Click the **Save Transparency** check box to preserve transparency when the file is opened in Adobe Acrobat. This check box is disabled if no transparency exists in the images used to create the PDF presentation.

13. Click the **Image Interpolation** check box to anti-alias low resolution images.

14. Click **Downgrade Color Profile** to downgrade the ICC color profile from PDF version 4 to PDF version 2.

15. Click the **PDF Security** check box to enable the Security Settings button. Click the button to open the PDF Security dialog box, which enables you to password protect the document, select the version of Acrobat security you are applying to the PDF file, and set viewer permissions for printing, copying, or changing the document.

16. After setting security options, click **OK** to exit the PDF Security dialog box and add security to the document.

17. Click the **Include Vector data** check box to optimize any vector graphics in the document. If you select this option, you can embed fonts with the document, which will enable viewers who do not have installed on their system the fonts you've used in the document to view the document by using the fonts embedded with the document. Alternatively, you can select Use Outlines For Text to convert the text into noneditable vector graphics.

18. Click **OK** to save the presentation as a PDF file.

How to...

- Optimize Using the Save For Web Dialog Box
- Making Part of an Image Transparent
- Creating Your Own Optimization Settings
- Work with Image Maps
- Work with Hexadecimal Values for Color
- Using Layers to Create Image Maps
- Set Output Options
- Slice an Image
- Use Rollovers and States
- Saving Sliced Images
- Preview Images in a Browser
- Export Layers as Files
- Create an Animation

Chapter 9
Preparing Your Art for the Web

This chapter works with Photoshop's and ImageReady's tools for creating and editing images for the World Wide Web. You will learn how to optimize images and to create image maps and apply rollover effects using Photoshop and ImageReady.

Optimize Images for the Web

Images for use on the Web need to be efficient—the file size needs to be as small as possible without a noticeable loss in image quality. Smaller size means the images are transmitted and displayed faster, reducing the time it takes a web page to load. Three factors determine the file size of an image (for a set width and height): the file format (usually GIF, JPEG, or PNG), the number of colors (determined, in part, by the file format chosen), and the resolution of the image (in pixels per inch). Of the file types, GIF and JPEG formats are the most common. PNG is not as widely supported, though newer browsers do support it. Here are some characteristics of these common file types:

- **GIF (Graphic Interchange Format)** images use an indexed palette of a maximum of 256 colors. Images with large areas of solid colors and sharp detail work best as GIFs. GIF also supports transparency, allowing the area under the transparent portions of the GIF to be visible.

- **JPEG (Joint Photographic Experts Group)** format compresses an image to reduce the file size. This is a lossy system, one where colors are removed from the image in compression. JPEG supports 24-bit color, which yields approximately 16 million colors.

- **PNG (Portable Network Graphic Specifications)** comes in two flavors: PNG-8, which is similar to GIF, and PNG-24, which is similar to JPEG but uses lossless compression (no colors are removed).

You set the file type, number of colors, and resolution when you save images.

Optimize Using the Save For Web Dialog Box

Photoshop gives you two methods for saving images for the Web. The first is to use the Save As option in the File menu, selecting either the CompuServe GIF or JPEG formats. (This method is not available in ImageReady.) A more complete set of options is available using the Save For Web dialog box.

1. With an image open in Photoshop, click **File | Save For Web**. The Save For Web dialog box will open, as shown in Figure 9-1.

2. Depending on your image type, read one of the following sections to learn how to optimize your image. The optimization options vary by file type.

OPTIMIZE A GIF OR PNG-8 IMAGE

GIF and PNG-8 images are very similar and use an indexed color palette. The optimization options are shown in Figure 9-2.

To optimize a GIF or PNG-8 image in Photoshop:

1. With your image open in Photoshop, click **File | Save For Web**.

2. Click the **2-Up** tab so that you can see both the original and modified images side-by-side.

3. Open the **Optimized File Format** drop-down list, and select **GIF** or **PNG-8**.

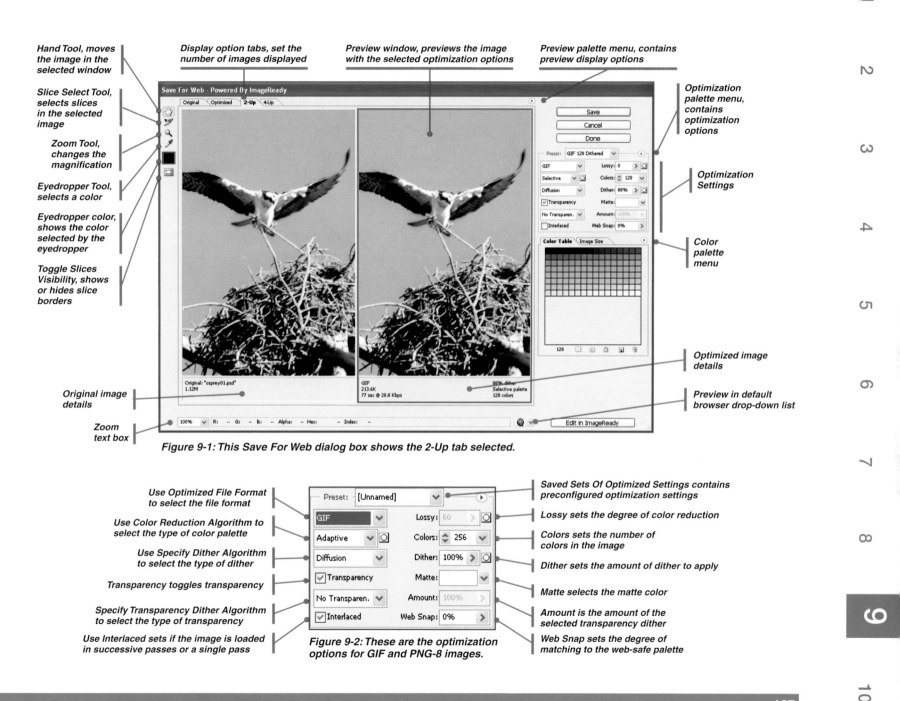

Hand Tool, moves the image in the selected window

Display option tabs, set the number of images displayed

Preview window, previews the image with the selected optimization options

Preview palette menu, contains preview display options

Slice Select Tool, selects slices in the selected image

Optimization palette menu, contains optimization options

Zoom Tool, changes the magnification

Eyedropper Tool, selects a color

Optimization Settings

Eyedropper color, shows the color selected by the eyedropper

Toggle Slices Visibility, shows or hides slice borders

Color palette menu

Original image details

Optimized image details

Preview in default browser drop-down list

Zoom text box

Figure 9-1: This Save For Web dialog box shows the 2-Up tab selected.

Use Optimized File Format to select the file format

Saved Sets Of Optimized Settings contains preconfigured optimization settings

Use Color Reduction Algorithm to select the type of color palette

Lossy sets the degree of color reduction

Use Specify Dither Algorithm to select the type of dither

Colors sets the number of colors in the image

Transparency toggles transparency

Dither sets the amount of dither to apply

Specify Transparency Dither Algorithm to select the type of transparency

Matte selects the matte color

Use Interlaced sets if the image is loaded in successive passes or a single pass

Amount is the amount of the selected transparency dither

Figure 9-2: These are the optimization options for GIF and PNG-8 images.

Web Snap sets the degree of matching to the web-safe palette

TIP

Not all of Photoshop's editing options are available in indexed color mode, so it can be advantageous to work in RGB mode and convert the image to indexed color when it is saved. Photoshop will convert the image to indexed color when the image is saved as a GIF or PNG 8.

QUICKSTEPS

MAKING PART OF AN IMAGE TRANSPARENT

With GIF, PNG-8, and PNG-24 images, you can select a color to be transparent in the final image. This allows you to have images that appear to have irregular borders, among other effects.

SELECT A COLOR TO BE TRANSPARENT

1. If your image is not in Indexed Color mode, click **Image** | **Mode** | **Indexed Color**. The Indexed Color dialog box opens.

2. Click **Palette** and select **Custom** from the drop-down list. This opens the Color Table dialog box.

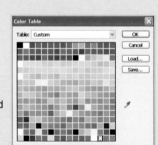

3. If your image is already in Indexed Color mode, click **Image** | **Mode** | **Color Table** to display the Color Table dialog box.

4. Select the **Eyedropper Tool** and click the color you want to be transparent.

5. Click **OK** to close the **Color Table** dialog box. If necessary, click **OK** to close the **Indexed Color** dialog box.

4. Select the options you need.

- Select the color reduction algorithm in the Color Reduction Algorithm drop-down list. See Table 9-1.

- Select the dither algorithm in the Dither Algorithm drop-down list. See Table 9-2.

- If you want an area of your GIF or PNG-8 to be transparent, select the **Transparency** check box.

- If you are using transparency, select the transparency dither algorithm in the Transparency Dither Algorithm drop-down list.

- If you want your GIF or PNG-8 image to be interlaced, select the **Interlaced** check box. Interlace loads the image in several passes rather than a single pass.

- For GIF images, use the **Lossy** slider to select the amount of color removal you want. The more colors you remove, the higher the Lossy value and the smaller the file will be.

- Use the **Colors** spinner to select the number of colors you want in your GIF or PNG-8 image. Fewer colors mean a smaller file size.

- Click **Matte** and select your matte color from the drop-down list. See Table 9-3. The matte color sets the color that transparent pixels will be dithered against. This blends the edges of the transparent pixels with the background.

- If you've selected a matte option, set the amount with the **Amount** slider.

- Set the amount of web snap using the **Web Snap** slider. Web Snap shifts the colors in the image to the closest web-safe color. The higher the value, the more colors will be shifted.

5. When you're satisfied with your selections, click **Save**. The Save Optimized As dialog box opens.

6. In the Save In drop-down list, select the location for your image, type the file name in the File Name text box, and verify the File Type. Then click **Save**.

OPTIMIZE A JPEG IMAGE

JPEG files are recommended for photographs and continuous tone images because they support more colors than the GIF format.

1. With your image open in Photoshop, click **File** | **Save For Web**.

2. Open the Optimized File Format drop-down list, and click **JPEG** from the drop-down list.

3. Choose the options you want:

- Select the degree of compression you want from the **Compression** drop-down list. Higher compression settings produce fewer colors and smaller images.

- If you want the image to download in successive passes rather than in one pass, select the **Progressive** check box.

- If you want to preserve the ICC profile (the color space) for the image, select the **ICC Profile** check box.

- If you want the image optimized, select the **Optimized** check box. This feature, which is not supported by older browsers, creates a slightly smaller file.

- If you want to use a compression setting not specified in the Compression Quality drop-down list, use the **Quality** slider to set the compression amount.

- Use the **Blur** slider to set the amount of blur. This applies a Gaussian-type blur (an adjustable hazy effect caused by adding detail to the pixels) to the image and decreases the file size. Recommended values are 0.1 to 0.5.

- Use the **Matte** drop-down list to select the matte color. The matte color is the fill color for pixels that were transparent in the original image.

4. When you're satisfied with your selections, click **Save**. The Save Optimized As dialog box opens.

5. Use the **Save In** drop-down list to select the location for your image, enter the file name in the File Name text box, and click **Save**.

OPTIMIZE A PNG-24 IMAGE

PNG-24 images are similar to JPEG images, but PNG-24, unlike JPEG, uses a lossless compression algorithm. This means that PNG-24 images tend to be larger, but PNG-24 can preserve 256 levels of transparency.

1. With your image open in Photoshop, click **File | Save For Web**.

2. Open the Optimized File Format drop-down list, and click **PNG-24**.

3. To preserve any areas of transparency in the image, select the **Transparency** check box.

- If you want the image to load in successive passes, select the **Interlaced** check box.

- If you haven't selected the transparency option, open the **Matte** drop-down list to select a matte color. This color replaces the transparent pixels.

TABLE 9-1: *Color Reduction Algorithms*

NAME	WHAT IT DOES
Perceptual	Creates a palette that gives precedence to colors for which the eye has greater sensitivity.
Selective	Favors broad areas of color and the preservation of web-safe colors.
Adaptive	Samples and uses the colors in the image rather than creating a full-spectrum palette.
Restrictive (Web)	Limits the palette to the 216 web-safe colors.
Custom	Allows you to create a custom palette by selecting the colors for the palette from the Color Table dialog box.
Black & White	Uses only black and white, which produces an effect similar to the halftones used in newspapers.
Grayscale	Uses only shades of gray, including black and white.
Mac OS	Uses the default Macintosh 8-bit system palette.
Windows	Uses the default Windows 8-bit system palette.

TABLE 9-2: *Dithering Algorithms*

NAME	WHAT IT DOES
Diffusion	Applies a random pattern across adjacent pixels. You control the amount of dither using the Dither slider. More dither increases the number of colors
Pattern	Applies a square pattern similar to a halftone.
Noise	Applies a random pattern similar to Diffusion without diffusing the pattern across adjacent pixels.

NOTE

Dithering is a technique that Photoshop uses to combine pixels of different colors to create new colors that are unavailable in the image or a color table. Dithering is used to prevent banding or to smooth distortions in color blending in images.

4. When you're satisfied with your selections, click **Save**. The Save Optimized As dialog box opens.

5. Open the **Save In** drop-down list, select a location for your image, type the file name in the File Name text box, and click **Save**.

SAVE OPTIMIZED IMAGES

Saving optimized images is similar to saving any other images.

1. Click **Save** in the **Save For Web** dialog box. The Save Optimized As dialog box will be displayed.

2. Open the **Save In** drop-down list to select a location for the file, and type the file name in the File Name text box.

3. Open the **Save As Type** drop-down list, and select the format you want.

4. Open the **Settings** drop-down list, and select your output settings. Click **Other** to view and select additional options.

5. If there are slices in your image, open the **Slices** drop-down list, and select an option:

   - **All Slices** to save all the slices in the image
   - **Selected Slices** to save only the selected slices
   - **All User Slices** to save only the user slices in the image

6. Click **Save**.

To save an optimized image in ImageReady:

1. Click **File | Save Optimized** or **Save Optimized As** if you wish to preserve the original image.

2. If you select **Save Optimized As**, the Save Optimized As dialog box is displayed. Otherwise, the image is simply saved.

3. Open the **Save In** drop-down list, select a location for the file, and type the name of the file in the File Name text box.

4. Open the **Settings** drop-down list, and select your output settings. Choose **Other** to specify additional options.

5. If there are slices in your image, open the **Slices** drop-down list, and select an option.

6. Click **Save**.

TABLE 9-3: *Matte Descriptions*

NAME	WHAT IT DOES
None	Makes pixels with more than 50 percent transparency fully transparent and pixels that are 50 percent or less fully opaque.
Eyedropper color	Uses the color selected with the Eyedropper Tool.
Black and White	Uses black or white, respectively, for the matte color.
Other	Allows you to select a color using the Color Picker dialog box.

NOTE

Matte, working the opposite of Transparency, fills transparent pixels with a chosen color to display a solid background, rather than a transparent one.

TIP

Use these three tools to define hotspots (the area in the image that has a hyperlink) in an image:

- The Rectangle Image Map Tool for defining rectangles and squares.
- The Circle Image Map Tool for defining ovals and circles.
- The Polygon Image Map Tool for defining irregular areas.

Work with Image Maps

Image maps allow you to define one or more areas of an image as web-page hyperlinks. You can make image maps by selecting areas using the Image Map tools (ImageReady only) or by using layers where each layer is a single hyperlink. Image maps can be either client-side or server-side. Client-side image maps are interpreted by the browser (the client), and server-side image maps are interpreted by the server. Client-side image maps are the default in ImageReady and are faster than server-side image maps, since it's not necessary to contact the server to execute. Server-side image maps do not work with multiple-slice images.

To create an image map using the Image Map tools:

1. Open your image in ImageReady, or if it's open in Photoshop, click the **Edit In ImageReady** button.

2. Select the appropriate image map tool in the toolbox.

3. With the **Square** or **Circle Image Map** tools, click to set one corner of the image map area, and drag to the opposite corner. With the **Polygon Image Map** tool, click to set the start of the image map area, move the pointer to the end of the segment, and click again. Repeat until the desired area is selected.

4. Click **Window | Image Map** to open the Image Map palette, and enter a name for the image map in the Name text box.

5. Open the **URL** drop-down list, and type the URL for the image map. If you've previously entered a URL, it will appear in the drop-down list. The URL can be an absolute reference (including the protocol, such as http, and the domain name) or a relative reference (the page and directory name, if applicable).

6. Open the **Target** drop-down list, and if desired, select a target frame. If the page is part of a frameset, this can be the name of one of the frames in the frameset. Select among these options:

   - **_blank** opens a new browser to display the page.
   - **_self** displays the page in the same frame as the calling file.

9

1 2 3 4 5 6 7 8 9 10

TIP

Using _blank always opens a new browser to display the page. This is useful when you want to keep the browser with your web site open while displaying a page from another web site.

TIP

Web accessibility standards require text descriptions for all graphic elements, so providing alternate text for all your graphics is a good habit. Speech software reads these descriptions for users with low vision.

- **_parent** displays the page in the current top-level (parent) frame.
- **_top** replaces all the current frames with the new page.

7. Type the alternate text for the image in the Alt text box. The alternate text may be displayed in place of the image or as a tool tip (depending on the user's browser settings).
8. Click **File** | **Save Optimized As**. The Save Optimized As dialog box is displayed. Open the **Save In** drop-down list, and select the location for your files.
9. Open the **Save As Type** drop-down list, click **HTML And Images (*.html)**. This will save your image and the generated image map HTML code. You can save just the image or just the HTML code by selecting the appropriate option in the Save As Type drop-down list.
10. If you already have a web page for your image map, select it from the list. If you are creating the web page, enter the name in the File Name text box. Click **Save**.
11. To add areas to your image map, use the Image Map tools, and resave your work. Click **File** | **Update HTML** to update your HTML code as you work.

Work with Hexadecimal Values for Color

In web pages and Cascading Style Sheets (CSS), it's common practice to specify RGB color values in hexadecimal notation. Hexadecimal is a base-16 numbering system, while the decimal system is base 10. The hexadecimal system uses the numbers zero through nine and the letters *A* through *F* (#00 to #0F to count from zero to fifteen). Hexadecimal color values are specified in the format #RRGGBB where RR is the value of the red component, GG is the value of the green component, and BB is the value of the blue component. For example, green is #00FF00 in hexadecimal and 0 255 0 in decimal; yellow, #FFFF00 and 255 255 0.

In the Color Picker, shown in Figure 9-3, the selected color values are displayed in both decimal (in the RGB text boxes) and hexadecimal (in the # text box). The hexadecimal value can be copied and pasted into web pages or other documents, such as style sheets.

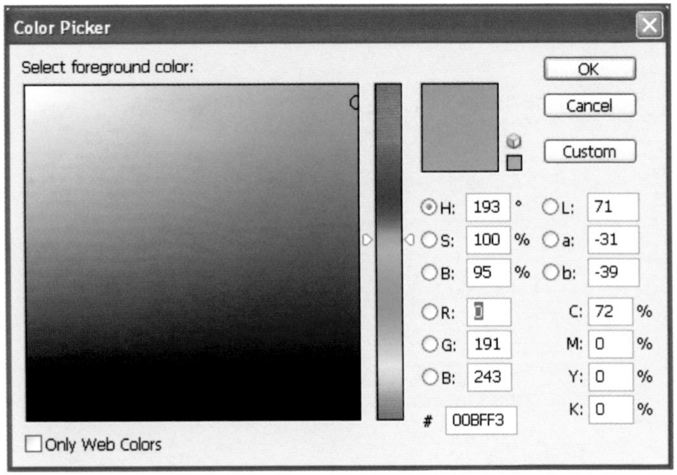

Figure 9-3: Color Picker shows the selected color in RGB and hexadecimal notation.

USING LAYERS TO CREATE IMAGE MAPS

When you use layers to create an image map, each hotspot is the shape of the content of the layer. If the content changes in size, so does the hotspot. This allows you to create very precise irregular-shaped hotspots that don't require modification if the image is edited. The Layers palette is used extensively; so if it is not open on the screen, click **Window | Layers**.

1. Select the layer to use for the hotspot in the Layers palette.

2. To create a hotspot from a layer, you:

- Click **Layer | New Layer Based Image Map**.

  –Or–

- Click the **Image Map** palette menu, and select **Promote Layer Based Image Map Area**.

3. Type the **URL** and other information in the Image Map palette.

TIP

To open the Output Settings dialog box from the Save Optimized or Save Optimized As dialog boxes, open the **Settings** drop-down list, and click **Other**.

Set Output Options

Use the Output Settings dialog box to set the output options for Photoshop and ImageReady. In ImageReady, you can also apply your saved output settings to other files. In Photoshop, open the Output Settings dialog box from the Save Optimized, Save Optimized As, or the Save For Web dialog boxes. Only the Save For Web dialog box allows you to save and load your settings.

1. With an image open in Photoshop, click **File | Save For Web**.

2. Click **Optimize | Edit Output Settings**. The Output Settings dialog box is opened.

You can select the different groups of output options from the drop-down list in the upper-left corner. The HTML options are listed in Table 9-4.

3. Select **Saving HTML Files** from the drop-down list. The options you may choose to select are:

- **Use Long File Name Extension (.html)** uses the HTML extension rather than the shorter HTM extension. In actual use, it makes no difference which is used.

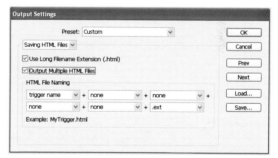

- **Output Multiple HTML Files** creates an HTML file for each selected state in rollover images. Whether to use single or multiple output files depends on the action triggered by each state.

- **HTML File Naming** offers a number of options through drop-down lists for automatically generating file names when Output Multiple HTML Files is selected.

4. Select **Slices** from the drop-down

TABLE 9-4: *HTML Settings*

NAME	DESCRIPTION
Output XHTML	Ensures the generated code conforms to the XHTML standard. If selected, some other options (such as Tag Case) are unavailable due to XHMTL requirements. XHTML has more stringent syntax than HTML
Tag Case	Sets the case of the HTML tags. The options are Lowercase, Uppercase, and Mixed Case (leading caps).
Attribute Case	Sets the case of the HTML tag attributes. The options are Lowercase, Mixed Case, Mixed With Initial Lower, and Uppercase.
Indent	Sets the type and amount of indent for indented lines. The options are Tabs, None, 1 Space, 2 Spaces, 4 Spaces, and 8 Spaces.
Line Endings	Sets the line endings for different operating systems. The options are Automatic, Mac (Macintosh), Win (Windows), and Unix.
Encoding	Sets the character encoding for the generated code. The options are Automatic (iso-8859-1), Western (iso-8859-1), Mac OS Roman (x-mac-roman), and Unicode™(utf-8). The iso-8859-1 character set is the standard set of characters used in Western European languages. Unicode™(utf-8) is a better choice if you need to support other languages.
Include Comments	Includes HTML comments within the HTML <!-- --> delimiters. Comments help understand what is happening on the page.
Always Add Alt Attributes	Includes the ALT attribute for those HTML tags where it is applicable, such as the image (IMG) tag. Web accessibility standards require the ALT attribute for all non-text elements. The ALT value will be empty, so you will need to enter the tag information separately.
Always Quote Attributes	Places quotes around the values of HTML tag attributes. HTML does not require quotes, but XHMTL and XML (Extensible Markup Language) do.
Close All Tags	Inserts the closing HTML tags for all tags that require them. HTML is generally forgiving of unclosed tags, but XHTML and XML are not.
Include Zero Margins on Body Tag	Adds the Margin attribute set to 0 (zero) to the BODY tag. This starts the page content in the upper-left corner of the browser with no margin. This is not supported by all browsers.

list. Select an option:

- **Generate Table** creates an HTML table for displaying the slices.

- **Empty Cells** sets the rules for how empty table cells are generated: GIF, IMG W&H (GIF spacer image, using the Image tag, IMG, with width and height specified); GIF, TD W&H (GIF spacer image, using the Table Data tag with width and height specified); and NoWrap, TD W&H (text is not wrapped, using the Table Data tag with width and height specified).

- **TD W&H** sets when width and height values will be generated. The options are Auto, Always, and Never.

- **Spacer Cells** controls whether or not a row of spacers cells will be generated. Some browsers allow space between cells, which destroys the effect of slices. A row of spacer cells at the top or bottom of the table can help ensure that the table will have the overall width specified. The options are: Auto, Auto (Bottom), Always, Always (Bottom), and Never.

- **Generate CSS** generates a Cascading Style Sheet to display the slices rather than a table. Not all browsers fully support style sheets, which limits this method. You should test this with your target browser.

- **Referenced** sets how the CSS elements will be referenced in the code—By ID (a unique ID value set in the code), Inline (style elements set in the DIV tag), or By Name (classes referenced by a unique ID).

- **Default Slice Naming** provides options, through a series of drop-down lists, for automatically generating file names for each slice.

5. Select **Image Maps** from the drop-down list to select the type of image map and the placement in the web page of the image map code. Client-side image maps are recommended because they don't require a trip to the server to work. Server-side image maps can be either NCSA (Na-

tional Center for Supercomputing Applications) or CERN (European Organization for Nuclear Research—the birthplace of the World Wide Web) standard. If you plan to use server-side image maps, you should check with your Internet service provider (ISP) to find which standards are supported. The image map code can be placed at the Top, in the Body, or at the Bottom of the web page. This is a matter of personal preference and makes no practical difference.

6. Select **Background** from the drop-down list to place a background image on the web page. The background can be an image or a solid color. If you want to use an image, then the path to the image is entered in the

Path text box. The Choose button allows you to browse to an image file. If you prefer a solid color, set the color with the BG Color drop-down list. You can choose None, Matte (the current matte color), Foreground, Background, one of the current palette colors, or a color chosen with the Color Picker.

7. Select **Saving Files** from the drop-down list. There are options for saving optimized files, automatic file naming, and file name compatibility.

- **Put Images In Folder** allows you to select a folder to put your optimized images in.

- **Use Long Filename Extensions** uses the longer extensions (such as JPEG instead of JPG). This is a matter of personal preference and has no practical effect.

- **Copy Background Image When Saving** saves the page background image (if used) with the optimized image.

- **File Naming** offers a number of options through drop-down lists for automatically generating file names.

- **Filename Compatibility** ensures any file names will be compatible with the selected operating systems.

- **Metadata** provides information about the image. Information about an image can be saved with the image as metadata.

- **Add Custom ImageReady Metadata (Backward Compatibility)** includes copyright and image description from the Image Info dialog box.

Output Settings

Preset: Custom

Metadata

☑ Add Custom ImageReady Metadata (Backward Compatible)
☐ Add EXIF Metadata (JPEG Only)
☑ Add XMP Metadata

XMP Options
☐ Write Minimal Set of XMP
☐ Include Reference to Source File
☐ Write XMP to Separate Files

[OK]
[Cancel]
[Prev]
[Next]
[Load...]
[Save...]

- **Add EXIF Metadata (JPEG Only)** includes the information from digital cameras such as camera type, date and time of photo, and file size.

- **Add XMP Metadata** is Adobe-specific information that can be shared between Adobe applications.

- **Write Minimal Set Of XMP** is a subset of the metadata that includes file modification and output times, file dimensions, and format.

- **Include Reference To Source File** stores the path to the original document.

- **Write XMP To Separate Files** writes the metadata to a separate file rather than embedding it in the image file.

Working with ImageReady

ImageReady is the workhorse for producing web graphics. Some of its capabilities have been covered in the previous sections; the following sections will cover its advanced features, including slices and rollovers.

Slice an Image

With Photoshop and ImageReady, you can *slice* an image. This means that you can "cut" an image into sections. You can apply different effects to each slice or each could be a hyperlink. To the user, the slices appear as a single image. You have four types of slices to choose from:

- **Auto** slices are created automatically. These are the areas in an image that are not defined by one of the other slice types.

- Use the Slice tool to create **User** slices.

- Select layers in the Layers palette to create **Layer-based** slices.

- Use the Web Content palette to create **Table** slices.

VIEW SLICES

Slices can be viewed in Photoshop, ImageReady, and the Save For Web dialog box. You can distinguish between different types of slices by looking at the lines that define them and the color of their symbols.

NOTE

Slices are always rectangular. You cannot have an oval or irregularly shaped slice.

- User and layer-based slices have solid lines and blue symbols by default.
- Auto slices have dotted lines and gray symbols by default.

Slices are numbered from the upper-left to lower-right of the image—a numeric symbol is in the upper-left corner of each slice. As you add or remove slices, the numbering for individual slices will change to reflect the changes.

Each slice also has a *badge,* or icon, that displays the properties of the slice:

To display or hide the badges in ImageReady:

1. Click the **Web Content** palette menu, and select **Palette Options**. The Web Content Palette Options dialog box is displayed.

2. Select or deselect the **Show Slice Badges** check box.

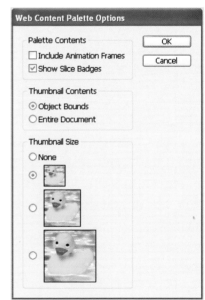

A User slice that has image content   *A slice that is layer-based*   *A slice that has a rollover state*   *A slice that is in a nested table*   *A slice that is a remote target*

A User slice that doesn't have image content   *A slice that is linked*   *A slice that is the active rollover state*   *A slice that is a remote trigger*

CREATE USER SLICES

To create a user slice:

1. Click the **Slice** tool in the toolbox.

2. Open the **Style** drop-down list in the options bar, and select a style.

   - **Normal** uses dragging to set the slice area.

   - **Fixed Aspect Ratio** uses a fixed width-to-height ratio set in the Width and Height text boxes. You set the size of the slice by dragging.

   - **Fixed Size** slices an area defined in pixels by the Width and Height settings.

3. With Normal and Fixed Aspect Ratio slices, drag to select the area of the slice.

4. With a Fixed Size slice, drag the selection outline to the area you want selected.

You can also create user slices using guides:

1. Place the guides on your image.

2. In Photoshop, click the **Slices From Guides** button in the options bar.

3. In ImageReady, click **Slices | Create Slices From Guides**.

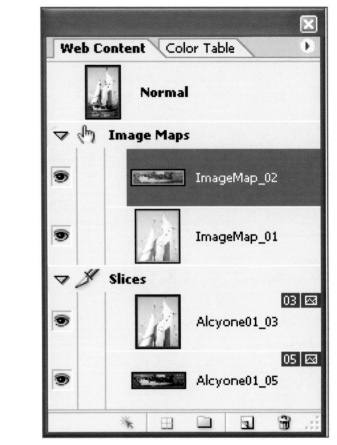

Figure 9-4: The Web Content palette displays slice and image map information.

In ImageReady, you can create a slice from a selection:

1. Use the **Marquee** tool to select an area of the image. The selection area can be any shape.

2. Click **Select | Create Slice From Selection**.

The slice will be a rectangle large enough to contain the entire selected area.

CREATE LAYER-BASED SLICES

A layer-based slice consists of the entire selected layer. These are very useful for rollovers. If you apply an effect, such as a drop shadow, to the layer to create a rollover state, the slice automatically adjusts to include the pixels created by the effect.

To create a layer-based slice in Photoshop or ImageReady, click the layer in the Layers palette. Then click **Layer | New Layer Based Slice**.

USE THE WEB CONTENT PALETTE

The ImageReady Web Content palette has several uses: it displays information about slices, image maps, and animation frames; and it lets you create, edit, and set options for rollovers. Figure 9-4 shows the Web Content palette with slice and image map information displayed. To display the Web Content palette, click **Window | Web Content**.

The Web Content palette menu contains a number of options for working with rollovers, slices, and image maps. You will learn more about the Web Content palette in the following sections.

OPTIMIZE SLICES IN IMAGEREADY

Slices are optimized using the same tools as other graphic files. You can use the Save For Web dialog box in Photoshop or the Optimize palette, shown in Figure 9-5, in ImageReady.

| Dock to Palette Well |
| New Rollover State |
| Duplicate Slice... |
| Delete Slice |
| Delete Rollover |
| Delete All Rollovers |
| Create Layer-Based Rollover |
| Copy Rollover State |
| Paste Rollover State |
| Find All Remote Slices... |
| Find Remote Slices For State... |
| Rollover State Options... |
| ✓ New Layers Visible in All States/Frames |
| Palette Options... |

Figure 9-5: The ImageReady Optimize palette displays the options for optimizing slices.

To optimize a slice in ImageReady:

1. Select one or more slices.

2. Open the Optimize palette and set options as needed.

3. Click the Optimize palette menu, and select **Optimize To File Size.** The Optimize To File Size dialog box will appear.

4. Set the file size in kilobytes in the Desired File Size text box.

5. Select the appropriate option button to use. Under Start With, select either **Current Settings** or **Auto Select GIF/JPEG** to allow ImageReady to automatically select GIF or JPEG settings.

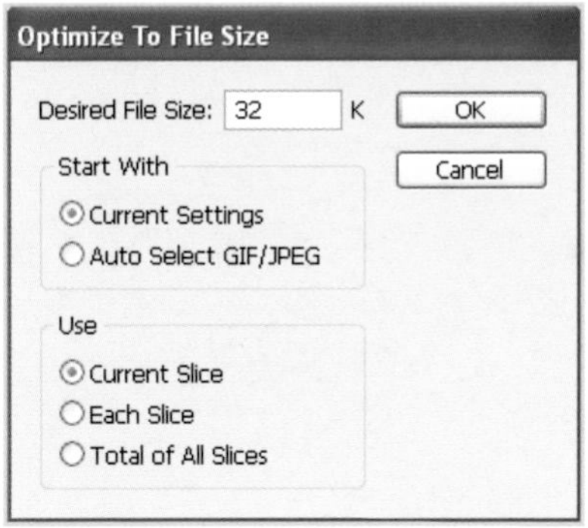

6. Under Use, select the appropriate option to apply the optimization to the **Current Slice**, **Each Slice**, or the **Total Of All Slices**.

7. Click **OK** to apply your settings.

You can also copy optimization settings from one slice to another:

1. Select the slice with the optimization settings to be copied.

2. To apply these setting to a second slice, drag the Droplet icon found on the Optimize palette to the second slice.

Use Rollovers and States

Rollovers are an effect where an event is triggered by some user action. A typical use is to change an image when the pointer is rolled over it. Every image has a normal state—the image that is displayed when the web page is first loaded. Additional states (images) can be displayed based on a mouse action such as rolling or clicking.

Rollovers are a combination of images and HTML and JavaScript code—all of which you can create in ImageReady. Rollovers are commonly used as menu buttons on web pages.

SAVING SLICED IMAGES

Saving slices in ImageReady or Photoshop is virtually the same as saving any other image.

SAVE SLICED IMAGES IN IMAGEREADY

1. Click **File | Save Optimized** or **Save Optimized As**. The related dialog box opens.

2. Open **Slices** and click an option from the drop-down list: All Slices, All User Slices, or Selected Slices.

SAVE SLICED IMAGES IN PHOTOSHOP

1. Click **File | Save For Web**.

2. Click **Save**. The Save Optimized As dialog box opens. Open **Slices** and select an option from the drop-down list: All Slices, All User Slices, or Selected Slices.

3. Click **Save**.

CREATE AND EDIT ROLLOVERS

You can create rollovers from layers, slices, and image maps. The steps are very much the same for each. Layer-based slices work well for rollovers because the dimensions of a layer's content may change as you create a rollover, and layer-based slices automatically include the new pixels.

To create a rollover from a layer-based slice:

1. In Photoshop or ImageReady, create an image with at least two layers. Each layer will be a state in the finished rollover. Applying layer effects is an easy way to create images for rollovers. For example, you could use text with a drop shadow or a glow effect with different settings for each layer. With a drop shadow, you could change the Angle of the light or, for an outer glow, the Spread.

2. Open the image in ImageReady if you created it in Photoshop.

3. Select the normal layer (the layer that will be displayed when the page is first loaded) in the Layers palette, and hide the other layers.

4. Open **Layer** and select **New Layer Based Slice**.

5. In the Web Content palette (click **Windows | Web Content** if it's not open), select the rollover layer that will be displayed when the event is triggered, and click the **Create Rollover State** button. The Over state is chosen by default.

6. In the Layers palette, hide the normal layer and make the rollover layer visible.

7. Click the **Preview In Browser** button in the toolbar. Figure 9-6 shows the rollover in Internet Explorer with part of the JavaScript code that handles the switching of the images. When the pointer is moved over the button, the image changes, as shown here.

8. Right-click the rollover state in the Web Content palette (the pointer must be on the state text). The context menu displays a list of states that can be applied to the rollover, as shown in Figure 9-7.

   - **Over** triggers when the pointer moves over the rollover area.

   - **Down** triggers when the mouse button is pressed. The change of state lasts until the mouse button is released.

   - **Selected** triggers when clicked and remains in the selected state until another rollover state is triggered.

Figure 9-6: This shows the rollover in the normal state in Internet Explorer with JavaScript code displayed.

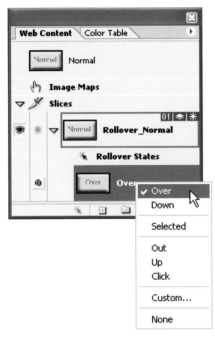

Figure 9-7: The Web Content palette shows the rollover state context menu.

- **Out** triggers when the pointer leaves the rollover area.

- **Up** triggers when the mouse button is released.

- **Click** triggers when clicked and remains in the rollover state until the pointer leaves the rollover area.

- **Custom** triggers the image specified in the Custom State dialog box. You must write your own JavaScript code to handle the event.

- **None** preserves the current state for future use in ImageReady, but no JavaScript code is generated for a web browser.

Preview Images in a Browser

You can easily preview your Photoshop and ImageReady images in any browser installed on your system. To preview an image in Photoshop:

1. Click **File | Save For Web**.
2. In the Save For Web dialog box, click the **Preview In Default Browser** button.

To preview an image in ImageReady, click the **Preview In Browser** button on the toolbar. The image will open in the default browser.

You can add browsers that are installed on your system to the lists of available browsers in both Photoshop and ImageReady. In Photoshop:

1. Click **File | Save For Web**.
2. In the Save For Web dialog box, click the **down-arrow** next to the Preview In Default Browser button to open the Select Browser Menu.
3. Select **Edit List** to open the Browsers dialog box. The browser list will probably be empty.
4. Click **Find All**. All the browsers on your system will appear in the list. Internet Explorer and Netscape are shown here.

5. Select the browser you want as the default, and click **Set As Default**.

6. If you want to have a browser not be available, select it and click **Remove**. This will only remove it from Photoshop's list, not your system.

7. Click **OK**.

8. Click the **down-arrow** next to the Preview In Default Browser button. The Select Browser Menu lists the browsers you have installed. Click the browser you want to use to preview the image.

To preview in ImageReady:

1. Click **File | Preview In | Edit Browser List** to open the Edit Browser List dialog box, which is virtually identical to Photoshop's Browsers dialog box.

2. Click **Find All** to locate the browsers installed on your system, set the default, and remove any browsers you don't want.

3. Click **OK**.

4. Click and hold the **small arrow** in the lower-right corner of the Preview In Browser button to display the list of available browsers.

5. Click the browser you want to use to preview the image.

Export Layers as Files

In ImageReady, you can export individual layers as files.

1. Click **File | Export | Layers As Files** to open the Export Layers As Files dialog box, shown in Figure 9-8. This dialog box is very similar to the Export Animation Frames As Files dialog box, covered in detail in the section "Export Animation Frames as Files". Only the differences are covered here.

2. Open **Export** and select the layers to export from the drop-down list: **All Layers**, **Top Level Layers and Layer Sets**, or **Selected Layers**. Selected Layers is only available if you selected layers before opening the Export Layers As Files dialog box.

3. Open the **Layer** drop-down list, and select a layer, if you are using a separate format for each layer. You can use the navigation buttons to cycle through the layers.

4. Click **Apply** and select **One Format For All Layers** or **Separate Format For Each Layer** from the drop-down list.

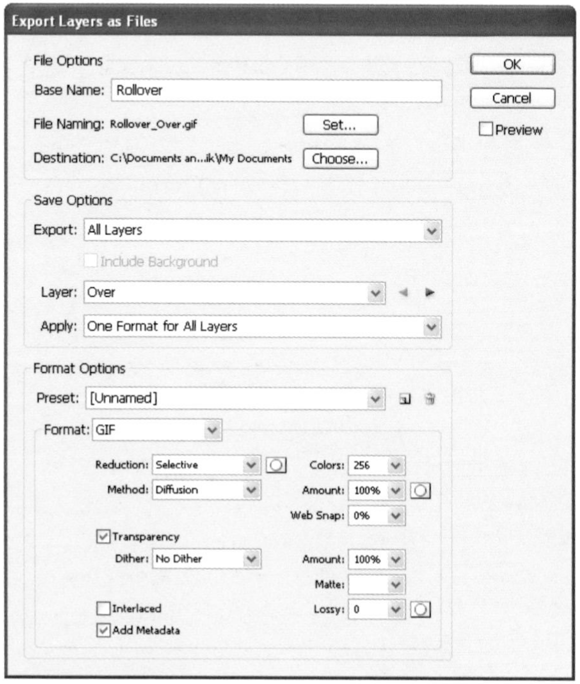

Figure 9-8: The Export Layers As Files dialog box contains the options for exporting layers.

TIP

You can download the free Flash player from Macromedia at **http://macromedia.com**. The Flash player is required to view Flash animations in web browsers and is included with most browser downloads. The free QuickTime player is available from Apple at **http://www.apple.com/quicktime/**. It is required to view QuickTime movies in web browsers.

Animate Your Images

You can create animations as layered images (PSD files) in Photoshop or ImageReady. You can save the finished animation as a GIF, which doesn't require a browser add-in to display properly, a QuickTime movie, or as a Macromedia® Flash™ animation (a SWF file). The latter two require browser add-ins.

Create an Animation

The Animation palette, shown in Figure 9-9, is used in conjunction with the Layers and Web Content palettes to create animations. To create an animation:

1. Create a new layered image in Photoshop or ImageReady.
2. Create a layer for the static elements—the elements that do not move in the animation.
3. Create layers for each frame of the moving elements. In each frame the position and/or shape of the moving object will change slightly.
4. Save the image as a PSD file; then open the image in ImageReady if it's in Photoshop.
5. In the Layers palette, hide all the layers except the static elements and the first frame of the moving elements.
6. Click **Window | Animation** to open the Animation palette, if it's not open; then click the **Duplicate Animation Frame** button. 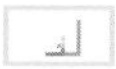
7. In the Layers palette, hide the first frame of the moving objects, and make visible the next frame layer.
8. Repeat steps 6 and 7 for each frame in the animation, successively hiding and making visible each moving object layer.

Figure 9-9: You use the Animation Palette to set options for your animation.

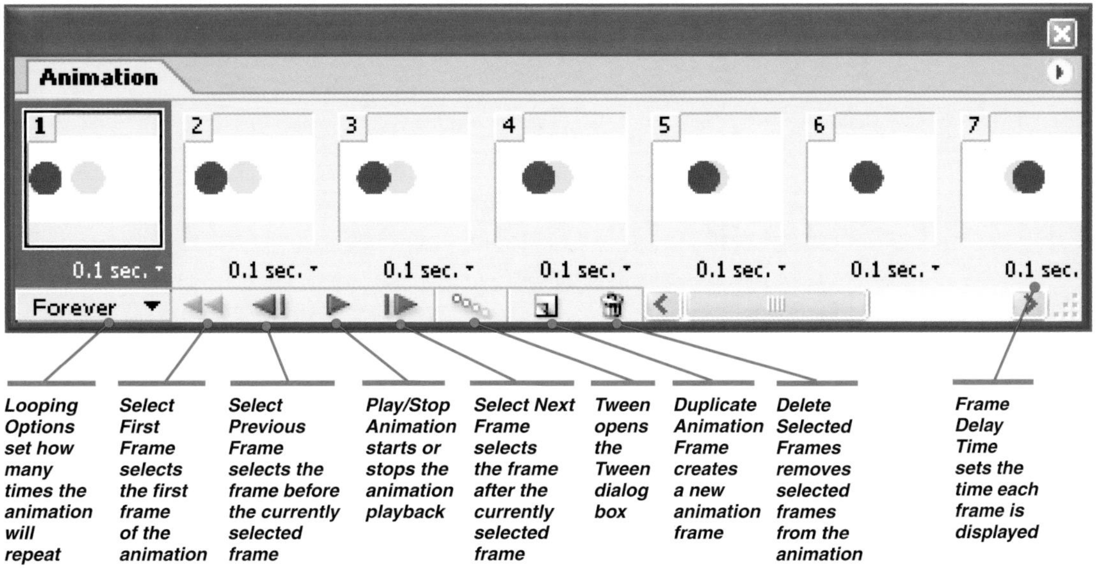
Animation
1
2
3
4
5
6
7
0.1 sec.
0.1 sec.
0.1 sec.
0.1 sec.
0.1 sec.
0.1 sec.
0.1 sec.
Forever
Looping Options set how many times the animation will repeat
Select First Frame selects the first frame of the animation
Select Previous Frame selects the frame before the currently selected frame
Play/Stop Animation starts or stops the animation playback
Select Next Frame selects the frame after the currently selected frame
Tween opens the Tween dialog box
Duplicate Animation Frame creates a new animation frame
Delete Selected Frames removes selected frames from the animation
Frame Delay Time sets the time each frame is displayed

1 2 3 4 5 6 7 8 9 10

9. Set the duration of time each frame will be displayed by clicking the **Frame Delay Time** button and selecting the delay from the menu. Selecting **Other** opens the Set Frame Delay dialog box, where you can set display times not available in the menu.

```
0.1 sec. ▾
```

```
No delay
0.1 seconds
0.2
0.5
1.0
2.0
5.0
10.0
Other...
✔ 0.1 seconds
```

Set Frame Delay

Set Delay: 0.1 seconds   OK

Cancel

10. To set how many times the anima-tion will run, click **Looping Options**. The Looping Options menu opens, and you can select **Once**, **Forever**, or **Other**. If you select Other, the Set Loop Count dialog box opens, and you can set the number of repeats you want.

```
Forever   ▾
```

```
Once
✔ Forever
Other...
```

Set Loop Count

Play: 1 times   OK

Cancel

The creation of animations can be simplified by the use of *tweening*. Tweening creates intermediate frames in an animation. You create the start and end frames, and tweening creates the specified number of frames in be*tween* those frames; hence, the term tweening.

Tweening can be applied to single or contiguous frames:

- If applied to a single frame, you select whether to tween between it and the previous or following frame.
- If you select two contiguous frames, the tweened frames are placed between the selected frames.
- If you select more then two contiguous frames, the intermediate frames are modified.
- If you select the first and last frames, they are treated as contiguous. This is useful for smoothing animations that loop more than once.

1. In the Animation palette, select the frames to tween.

2. Click the **Tween** button to open the Tween dialog box.

TIP

You can set the delay times for single frames or uniformly for a selected group of frames. To set the delay time for a selected group, click the first frame and then press **SHIFT** while you click the last frame. Click the **Frame Delay Time** button in any selected frame to set the time for all the selected frames.

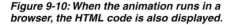

Tween

Tween With: Selection

Frames to Add: 5

Layers
- ⊙ All Layers
- ○ Selected Layers

Parameters
- ☑ Position
- ☑ Opacity
- ☑ Effects

OK

Cancel

Eclipse - Microsoft Internet Explorer

File   Edit   View   Favorites   Tools   Help

Address C:\Documents and Settings\Erik\Local Settings\Temp\ImageReady\TargetPreview2\Eclipse.htm   Go   Links

```
Format: GIF
Dimensions: 300w x 200h
Size: 10.4K
Settings: Selective, 256 Colors, 100% Diffusion Dither, 12 frames, Transparency on, No Transparency Dither,
Non-Interlaced, 0% Web Snap


<html>
<head>
<title>Eclipse</title>
<meta http-equiv="Content-Type" content="text/html; charset=iso-8859-1">
</head>
<body bgcolor="#FFFFFF" leftmargin="0" topmargin="0" marginwidth="0" marginheight="0">
<!-- ImageReady Slices (Eclipse.psd) -->
<img src="images/Eclipse.gif" width="300" height="200" alt="">
<!-- End ImageReady Slices -->
</body>
</html>
```

Done   My Computer

Figure 9-10: When the animation runs in a browser, the HTML code is also displayed.

---

3. Open the Tween dialog box, select the **Tween With** drop-down list, and click the frames to tween. If you selected a single frame, the options Next Frame and Previous Frame are available. If you selected more than one frame, only the Selected option is available.

4. Set the number of frames to create between the selected frames in the Frames To Add text box. This option is not available if you selected more than two frames. In that case only the selected frames are tweened.

5. Select a **Layers** option: **All Layers** to modify all the layers in the selected frames or **Selected Layer** to modify only the layers selected in the Layers dialog box. Static layers do not need to be modified by tweening, but you may have objects on multiple layers that do.

6. Click **Parameters** and select the layers tweening parameters:

   - **Position** varies the position of the objects evenly between the starting and ending frames.

   - **Opacity** varies the opacity of the objects evenly between the starting and ending frames. This is useful for making smooth fades.

   - **Effects** varies the layer effect parameters evenly between the starting and ending frames. For example, a drop shadow effect could be used to give the impression of a light source moving across the animation, changing the angle of the shadow.

7. Click **OK** to apply your settings.

VIEW ANIMATIONS

You can view animations in ImageReady or a web browser. In ImageReady:

1. Open the animation and the **Animation** palette.

2. Click the **Play** button. The animation runs in the document window.

3. While the animation is playing, the Play button changes to the Stop button. Click the **Stop** button to stop the animation.

To view the animation in a web browser, click the **Preview In Browser** button in the toolbox. The animation and generated HTML is shown in the browser, as shown in Figure 9-10.

OPTIMIZE ANIMATIONS

You should only optimize animations as GIF images—this is the only image format that supports animations. If you optimize an animation as a JPEG or PNG, only the current frame of the animation will be displayed. In addition to the optimization options available for all GIF images, with animations you can limit optimization to only the areas that change between frames, which greatly reduces the size of the final file. ImageReady also applies a special dithering algorithm to prevent flickering.

To display the Optimize Animation dialog box, open the **Animation** palette menu, and select **Optimize Animation**.

- **Bounding Box** crops each frame to the area that has changed from the preceding frame. This option is recommended because it makes for a smaller file, but it isn't supported by all GIF editors. If your animations will be edited in other programs, you should determine if this feature is supported or turn it off.

- **Redundant Pixel Removal** makes all pixels that are unchanged from the previous frame transparent. This option is also recommended to reduce the final file size. This feature requires that the Transparency option in the Optimize palette be selected.

SAVE ANIMATIONS

You can save an animation as an animated GIF, a QuickTime movie, or a Macromedia Flash (SWF) file. You can also save each frame of the animation as a separate file.

Saving an animation as a GIF is basically the same as saving any other GIF image. You first optimize the image and then save it.

To save an animation as a QuickTime movie:

1. Click **File | Export | Original Document**. The Export Original dialog box opens.

2. Open **Save As Type**, and click **QuickTime Movie** in the drop-down list.

3. Open **Save In**, select the location to save the file in the drop-down list, and type the name for the file in the File Name text box.

4. Click **Save**. The Compression Settings dialog box is displayed.

5. Select the graphic format from the drop-down list at the top of the dialog box. A number of standard video and graphic formats are available. The default, Photo-JPEG, will work in most situations. The remaining options vary based on the format selected here.

6. If the **Depth** drop-down list is displayed, use it to select the bit depth for the file.

7. If the **Quality** slider is displayed, use it to set the amount of compression for the file. **Best** creates the largest file and **Least**, the smallest.

8. If the **Option** button appears, click it to open a dialog box with options for the selected format. For Photo-JPEG, the only option is **Optimize For Streaming**. If you select this, you can also make the file RFC 2035 Compatible (a format for JPEG compressed video). Streaming video starts playing in a browser before the file has been completely downloaded and continues playing while the full file downloads in the background. The video will start playing in the minimum amount of time, enhancing the user experience.

9. Click **OK** to save the file.

NOTE

RFC stands for Request For Comments. When an Internet standard is proposed, the initial draft is released as a request for comments. Interested parties, such as manufacturers and industry groups, comment on the standard. Eventually the standard is finalized with the RFC number.

Macromedia® Flash™ (SWF) Export

Export Options

☑ Preserve Appearance

SWF bgcolor: ⬜ ▾

☐ Generate HTML

☐ Enable Dynamic Text

Embed Fonts: None ▾

AB ab # ""

Extra: ⬜

Bitmap Options

Format: Auto Select ▾

JPEG Quality: 80 ▾

OK

Cancel

CREATE AN SWF ANIMATION

Macromedia Flash is one of the most popular formats for animations on the Web. ImageReady makes it very easy to create Flash animations (SWF files) that can be imported into Macromedia Flash or added to web pages.

1. Click **File | Export | Macromedia® Flash™ SWF.**

   –Or–

   Click **File | Export | Original Document**. The Export Original dialog box opens. Open **Save As Type**, and select **Macromedia® Flash™ SWF** from the drop-down list. Click **Save.** The Macromedia® Flash™ (SWF) Export dialog box will open.

2. Select the **Preserve Appearance** check box to retain the appearance of text and shape layers that cannot be exported natively to the SWF file. ImageReady will rasterize (convert the text to a graphic) these objects to retain the appearance of the PSD file. These will be lost if this option isn't selected.

3. Open the **SWF Bgcolor** drop-down list, and select a background color.. You can use the current Foreground and Background colors, any color from the current palette, or a color selected with the Color Picker.

4. Select the **Generate HTML** check box to generate the HTML needed to display the animation in a web page.

5. Select the **Enable Dynamic Text** check box to map PSD text to SWF dynamic text. SWF dynamic text is lost when the file in opened in Flash, so this option is only useful if the animation will only be on the Web.

6. If Enable Dynamic Text is selected, use the **Embed Fonts** drop-down list to set the text options. No characters will be embedded if you select **None**. **Full Set** embeds the entire character set. If you select **Partial Set**, you must choose which characters to embed:

   - All uppercase characters
   - All lowercase characters
   - All numbers
   - All punctuation

7. Type other characters you want to embed in the Extra text box.

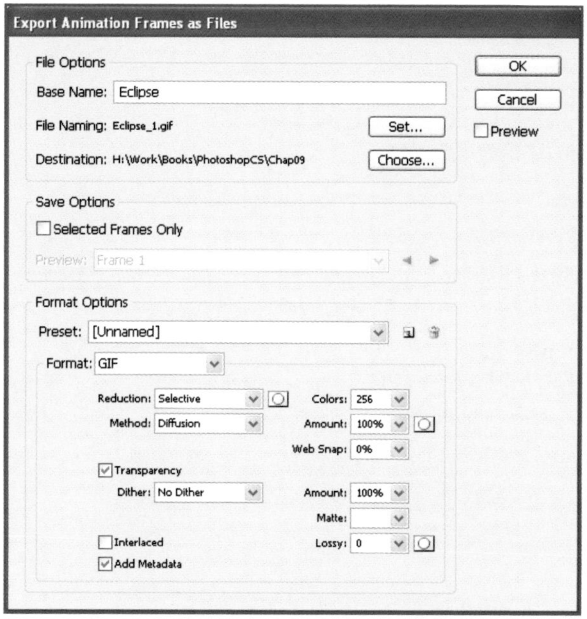

8. Open **Format** and select the format for bitmap images from the drop-down list. **Auto Select** will choose the best format based on the number of colors. **Lossless-8** will generate 8-bit images with no color loss. **Lossless-32** will generate 32-bit images with no color loss. **JPEG** generates JPEG images.

9. If you selected Auto Select or JPEG, open **JPEG Quality** and use the slider to set the amount of compression.

10. Click **OK**. The Export As Macromedia™ SWF dialog box is displayed.

11. Open **Save In**, and select the location for the file from the drop-down list, and type or select the file name in the File Name text box.

12. Click **Save**.

EXPORT ANIMATION FRAMES AS FILES

You can export any or all of the frames of an animation as individual files.

1. Click **File | Export | Animation Frames As Files**. The Export Animation Frames As Files dialog box, shown in Figure 9-11, is opened.

2. Enter the base of the file name for each file in the Base Name text box. File names for each frame will use the base name as the first part of the full file name.

3. Click **Set** to open the Frame File Naming dialog box, which gives you a number of options for constructing a file name for each frame. An Example of the generated file name appears in the lower-left corner of the dialog box.

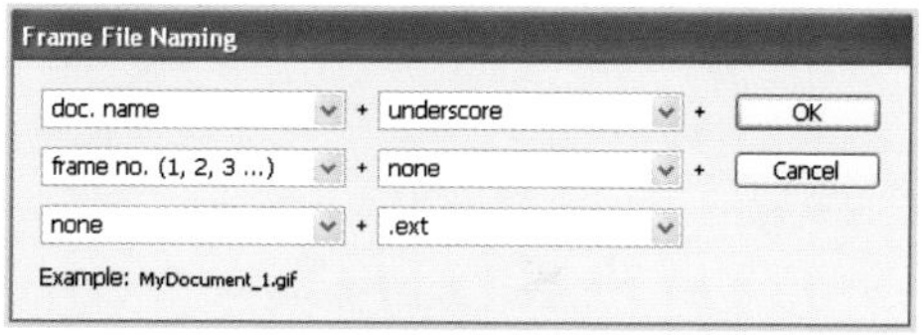

Figure 9-11: The Export Animation Frames As Files dialog box is used to set the options for saving animation frames as files.

4. Click **OK**. The generated file name for the first image appears after the File Naming label.

5. Click **Choose** to open the Browse For Folder dialog box. Select the folder to save the files in, and click **OK**. The path to the folder is displayed after the Destination label.

6. Select the **Selected Files Only** check box if you want to save only the frames that are selected in the Animation palette.

7. Select the **Preview** check box if you want to preview the selected frames in the document window. When you select it, the Preview drop-down list beneath Save Options will be made available. Use the right and left arrows to scroll backwards and forward through the frames.

8. Select any of the remaining **Format Options** as needed. These are the same as in the Save For Web dialog box. If you have questions, refer to "Optimize Using the Save For Web Dialog Box."

9. Click **OK** to save your animation frames as files.

IMPORT FILES AND FOLDERS AS ANIMATIONS

ImageReady can import and edit many animation formats created in other programs. Along with PSD (Photoshop) and GIFs, you can import and edit MOV (QuickTime), AVI (Windows Media), and FLIC (several programs) files. You can also import folders containing bitmap images to use in animations.

To import Photoshop files as frames in ImageReady:

1. Open **File** and select **Open**. The Open dialog box is displayed.

2. Select the Photoshop file to open, and click **OK**.

3. Open the **Animation** palette menu, and select **Make Frames From Layers**.

To import a folder of files as frames in ImageReady:

1. Put only the files you want to be frames in the animation in the folder.

2. Click **File | Import | Folder As Frames**. The Browse For Folder dialog box opens.

3. Select the folder to import, and click **OK**. The files will be placed in the Animation palette as frames and in the Layers palette as layers.

To import MOV, AVI, and FLIC files for editing in ImageReady:

1. Open **File**, select **Open**, and then choose the file to open.

2. Click **OK**. The Open Movie dialog box is displayed.

3. Select the range of frames to import:

- **From Beginning To End** to select all the frames.

- **Selected Range Only** to import some of the frames. Select the frames to import by holding down **SHIFT** and moving the slider or by clicking the previous and next arrows in the animation window.

4. Select the **Limit To Every** check box, click **Frame**, and choose a value in the drop-down list to skip frames in the selected range.

5. Click **OK** to import the selected frames.

NOTE

The number of frames in the resulting animation will be the same as the number of layers in the Photoshop file. The bottom layer of the file will be the first frame of the animation. Select **Reverse Frames** in the Animation palette menu if you want to reverse the order.

NOTE

The files will be imported alphabetically. To ensure the files are placed as frames in the correct order, modify the file names if necessary. You can also reorganize the frames in the Animation palette after they are imported.

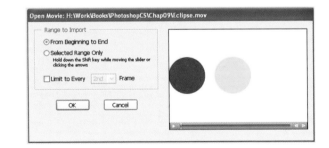

How to...

- *Work with the Actions Palette*
- *Record an Action to Automate a Multistep Task*
- *Play and Undo Actions*
- *Setting Playback Options*
- *Edit Actions*
- *Changing Action Options*
- *Use the Batch Command*
- *Create a Droplet from an Action*
- *Fitting an Image*
- *Crop and Straighten Photos*
- *Use Picture Package*
- *Adding Copyright Information to an Image*
- *Adding Digital Watermarks to an Image*
- *Use Web Photo Gallery*
- *Create a Panorama with Photomerge*

Chapter 10

Saving Time with Actions and Automation

This chapter covers the Photoshop and ImageReady tools for automating repetitive tasks. The Actions palette allows you to create sequences of commands that can be saved and applied to images. Working with Photoshop's Automate menu, which simplifies other complicated tasks, is also covered in this chapter.

Automate Your Images

When working with graphics, you may frequently need to apply the same sequence of commands to a series of images. Resizing to a standard size and applying layer styles or a filter are examples of such tasks. Your images may be processed in a batch (as a group) or individually. The Actions palette, available in both Photoshop and ImageReady, is the most flexible tool to use because you can create and save your own sequences of events.

Work with the Actions Palette

Your primary tool for automating tasks is the Actions palette. The Photoshop Actions palette is shown in Figure 10-1 and the ImageReady Actions palette is shown in Figure 10-2. The palettes are similar and both include a number of default actions, but the Photoshop Actions palette has more user-recordable functionality than ImageReady's. Photoshop also allows you to group actions in sets for better organization, while ImageReady's does not.

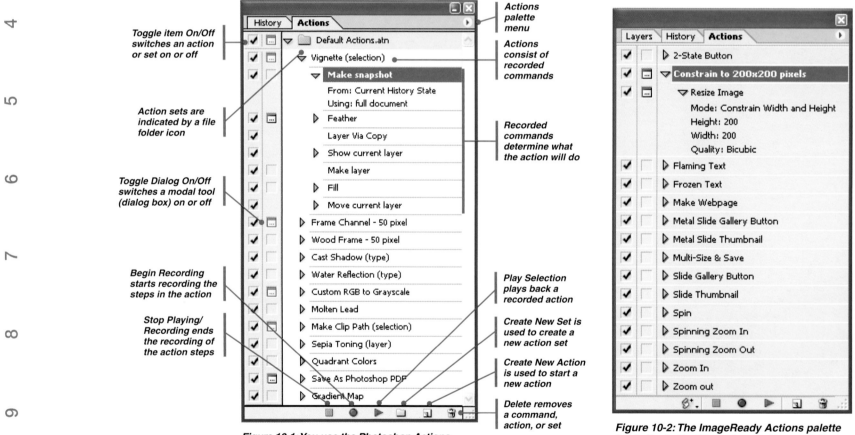

Figure 10-1: You use the Photoshop Actions palette to select and apply actions to your images.

Figure 10-2: The ImageReady Actions palette is similar to the Photoshop Actions palette.

Record an Action to Automate a Multistep Task

You create an action by recording the steps—using the menus and other tools. To record an action:

1. Open an image file.

2. Open the **New Action** dialog box:

   ● In the Actions palette, click the **New Action** button.

   –Or–

   ● Click **New Action** in the Actions palette menu.

The Photoshop New Action dialog box, shown here, has options for the set name and button color. The ImageReady New Action dialog box doesn't have these options because they're not supported.

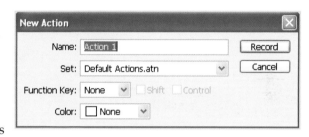

3. In the **New Action** dialog box, type a descriptive name for the action in the Name text box.

4. In Photoshop, you place the new action in a set this way:

   ● Open the **Set** drop-down list box, and choose the set.

   –Or–

   ● Type the name of a new set in the Set drop-down list box.

5. If you want, open the **Function Key** drop-down list, and select a function key combination to run the action or set. This is optional.

6. When you select a function key, you can also choose to use the **SHIFT** and/or **CTRL** keys with it by selecting the Shift and/or Control check boxes. This gives you more keyboard combinations to start the action.

7. In Photoshop, open the **Color** drop-down list, and choose a color for the action in Button mode.

8. Click **Record**.

Your Actions palette is now in Record mode. All the operations you perform from this point until you click the Stop button will be part of your action. When you stop recording, your action will be listed in the Actions palette.

USE MODAL CONTROLS AND TOOLS IN YOUR ACTIONS

A *modal control* is a dialog box when you use it in an action. A *modal tool* is a command that requires you to perform some user action, such as pressing **ENTER** or double-clicking, before continuing. An example of a modal tool is the Crop Tool. After you select an area to crop, you have to press **ENTER** or double-click the selected area to complete the crop.

You can have commands that use modal controls and tools to pause the action and wait for you to enter values in a dialog box or perform the user action, or commands that use the dialog box settings defined in the action and perform the user action automatically (the action doesn't pause).

You set modal controls and tools by clicking the Toggle Dialog On/Off box next to the action name in the Actions palette. The dialog box icon is displayed when a dialog box will be displayed or user actions are required. The Toggle Dialog On/Off box is only available if any of the commands in the action have dialog boxes or user actions associated with them. If all the commands have dialog boxes or user actions, the dialog box icon is gray when selected. If some of the commands don't have dialog boxes or user actions, the icon is red.

Play and Undo Actions

You apply an action to an image by *playing* the action. You can play a single command, an entire action, or a set of actions. You can exclude commands by clearing the Toggle Item On/Off check box for the commands. If a modal control is displayed, you can set values in it as part of the action.

To play an action:

1. Open the image file.

2. To play a complete action, select the action name in the Actions palette.

SETTING PLAYBACK OPTIONS

You can play Actions at three speeds: normal, step by step, and with a set delay between each step. Slowing down an action will help you find any problems with the commands. To set the playback options:

Playback Options

Performance
- ⦿ Accelerated
- ◯ Step by Step
- ◯ Pause For: [   ] seconds

☑ Pause For Audio Annotation

[OK] [Cancel]

1. Click **Playback Options** in the Actions palette.

2. Select a **Performance** option in the Playback Options dialog box:
   - Accelerated, which is the normal (default) speed
   - Step By Step, which stops after each step
   - Pause For, which pauses after each step for the number of seconds you set in the Seconds text box

If you have audio annotations for your action, you can select **Pause For Audio Annotation** to ensure that each annotation will complete before the next command executes.

3. To play part of an action, select the command to start from in the Actions palette.

4. Click the **Play button** or click **Play** in the Actions palette menu.

You can also play single commands in an action:

1. Select the command you want to play.

2. Press **CTRL** while you click the **Play button** in the Actions palette.

   –Or–

   Press **CTRL** while you double-click the command in the Actions palette.

You undo an action using the History palette. Drag the individual commands to the Delete Current State icon. You can also:

- In Photoshop, take a snapshot in the History palette before you start the action, and then restore from the snapshot.

- In ImageReady, click **Edit | Undo** action name.

Edit Actions

You can edit actions in a number of ways. You can:

- **Rearrange** actions and commands
- **Record** additional commands
- **Insert** nonrecordable commands
- **Rerecord and duplicate** actions and commands
- **Delete** actions and commands
- **Change** action options

REARRANGE ACTIONS AND COMMANDS

You can rearrange commands within an action and actions within the Actions palette by dragging them from their current location to a new location in the Actions palette.

RECORD ADDITIONAL COMMANDS

To add additional commands to an action:

1. Select an action in the Actions palette. The new commands will be appended at the end.

   –Or–

   Select a command in the Actions palette. The new commands will be inserted after the selected command.

2. Click the **Record** button, or select **Start Recording** in the Actions palette.

3. Execute the additional commands you want recorded.

4. Click the **Stop** button when the commands have been recorded.

INSERT NONRECORDABLE COMMANDS

You cannot record commands using the painting and toning tools, tool options, and view and window commands. You can, however, insert these commands into your actions, either during recording or after. No values are included when you do this; so, if the command has a dialog box, it will be displayed. You cannot disable the display of any dialog boxes for inserted commands.

To insert a menu item in an action:

1. Select the point in the action where you want to insert the menu item by:

   - Selecting an action name. The menu item will be inserted at the end of the action.

     –Or–

   - Selecting a command. The menu item will be inserted at the end of the command.

2. Click **Insert Menu Item** in the Actions palette menu. The Insert Menu Item dialog box opens.

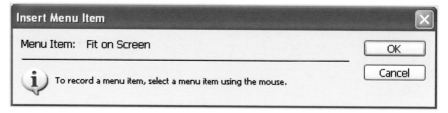

3. Click an item in a menu.

4. Click **OK**.

RERECORD AND DUPLICATE ACTIONS AND COMMANDS

You can change the values used in modal controls or modal tools in an action by Rerecording the action. You can make a copy—and keep the original—by Duplicating the action. To rerecord an action, you first select the action and click **Record Again** in the Actions palette menu. Then, to change a modal control (dialog box):

1. Change the values in the dialog box when it is opened.
2. Click **OK** to set the new values. If you click **Cancel**, the old values are retained.

To change a modal tool, you use the tool differently; then press ENTER to change the effect. You can press ESC to cancel the change.

To rerecord a single command:

1. Double-click the command in the Actions palette.
2. Change the values for the command.
3. Click **OK**.

To duplicate an action or command, you can:

- Press **ALT** while you drag the action or command to a new location in the Actions palette.
- Select the action or command, then click **Duplicate** in the Actions palette.
- Drag the action or command to the New Action button.

DELETE ACTIONS AND COMMANDS

To delete an action or command, you select the action or command in the Actions palette, and then you do one of the following:

- Click the **Delete** button; then click **OK** in the confirmation dialog box.
- Press **ALT** while you click the **Delete** button to skip the confirmation dialog box.
- Drag the action or command to the Delete button.
- Click **Delete** in the Actions palette.

Work with the Automate Menu

The Automate menu in Photoshop contains a number of options for performing complex tasks, with dialog boxes being displayed for entering values during the execution of the operation.

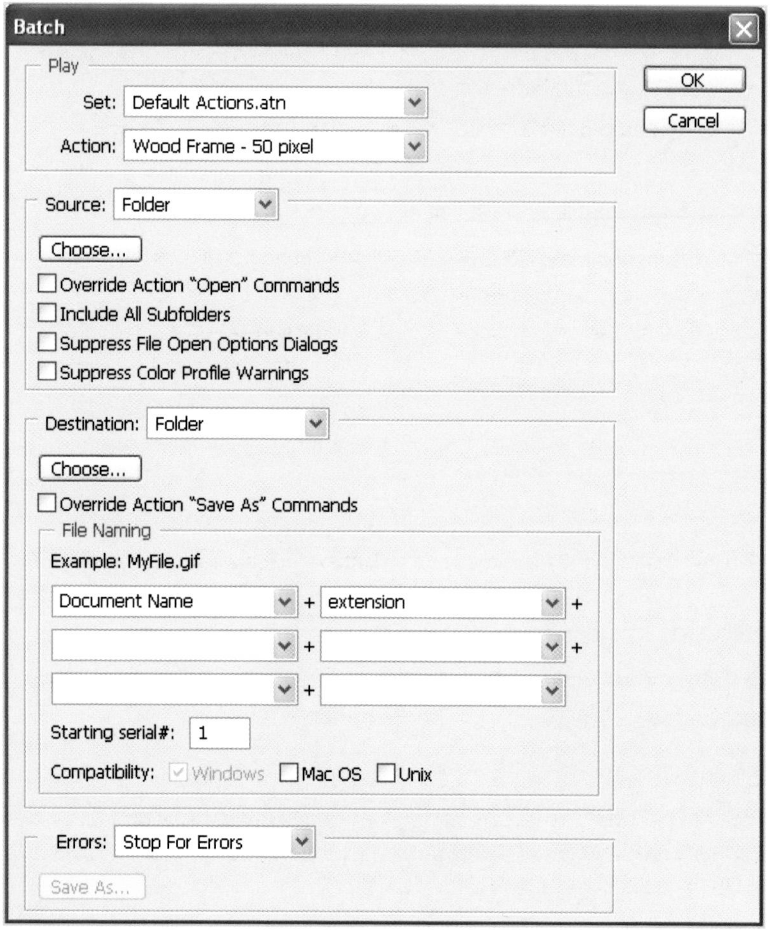

Batch

Play

Set: Default Actions.atn

Action: Wood Frame - 50 pixel

Source: Folder

Choose...

☐ Override Action "Open" Commands
☐ Include All Subfolders
☐ Suppress File Open Options Dialogs
☐ Suppress Color Profile Warnings

Destination: Folder

Choose...

☐ Override Action "Save As" Commands

File Naming

Example: MyFile.gif

Document Name + extension +

+

+

Starting serial#: 1

Compatibility: ☑ Windows ☐ Mac OS ☐ Unix

Errors: Stop For Errors

Save As...

OK
Cancel

Figure 10-3: You use the Batch dialog box to set the options for batch processing.

Use the Batch Command

You apply an action to a folder, including subfolders, with the Batch command. With batch processing, you can leave all the files open, save the changes to the original files, and then close the files or save the modified files to a new location.

To use the Batch command:

1. Click **File | Automate | Batch** to open the Batch dialog box, shown in Figure 10-3.

2. Open the **Set** drop-down list, and choose the action set.

3. Open the **Action** drop-down list, and choose the action.

4. Open the **Source** drop-down list, and choose the source for the batch process. You can choose:

   - **Folder**, a folder containing files and/or subfolders. Click **Choose** to open the Browse For Folder dialog box to select the folder.

   - **Import**, which displays the **From** drop-down list. Along with PDF Image, the other options will depend on what digital camera or scanner drivers you have installed on your system.

   - **Opened Files** executes the action on all the open files.

   - **File Browser** performs the action on the files selected in the File Browser.

5. With the Folder and File Browser options, you have a set of options, listed in Table 10-1, that you can select.

6. Open the **Destination** drop-down list, and choose one of these destination choices:

TABLE 10-1: *Folder and File Browser Options*

Option	Action
Override Action "Open" Commands	Applies Open commands in the action to the batch files, not the file names set in the action. The action must include an Open command, as the Batch command will not automatically open the source files. If the action is designed to apply to open files or if the action requires specific files to be opened, this option should not be selected.
Include All Subfolders	Processes all the files in any subfolders.
Suppress File Open Options Dialogs	Hides any File Open Options dialog boxes, which is useful when processing camera raw files. The default or previously selected settings in the dialog boxes will be used.
Suppress Color Profile Warnings	Hides any color policy messages.
Destination: None	Leaves the files open, unless the action includes a Save command.

TIP

With the Save And Close and Folder options, you can also select the Override Action "Save As" Commands check box. This saves files to the destination folder using the Save As commands in the action. The action you're using must include a Save As or Save command, or no files will be saved.

- **None** leaves the files open, unless the action includes a Save command.

- **Save And Close** saves the processed files in the same location, overwriting the original file.

- **Folder** saves the processed files to a new location. Click **Choose** to specify the new location.

7. If you selected Folder as the Destination, you choose the file naming convention using the **File Naming** drop-down lists. Type the starting number for the files in the **Starting Serial #** text box, and choose the operating system file naming compatibility in the **Compatibility** check boxes.

8. Open the **Errors** drop-down list, and choose a method for handling errors. Your choices are:

   - **Stop For Errors**, which stops the action if an error occurs

   - **Log Errors To File**, which continues the action when an error occurs and writes the error information to a log file

9. If you've chosen to use an error log file, click **Save As** to set the location for the error log. You can read the error log with a text editor, such as Notepad.

10. Click **OK**.

Create a Droplet from an Action

Droplets are icons that you can drag a file onto to execute an action. You first create the action using the steps described in the previous sections, and then create a droplet from the action. You can save the droplet to the desktop or another location on your computer. When you drag a file to the droplet, it will open the application needed to execute the action.

To create a droplet from an action:

1. Click **File | Automate | Create Droplet** to open the Create Droplet dialog box, shown in Figure 10-4. Many of the options are the same as in the Batch dialog box and behave the same way.

2. Click **Choose** to open the Save dialog box.

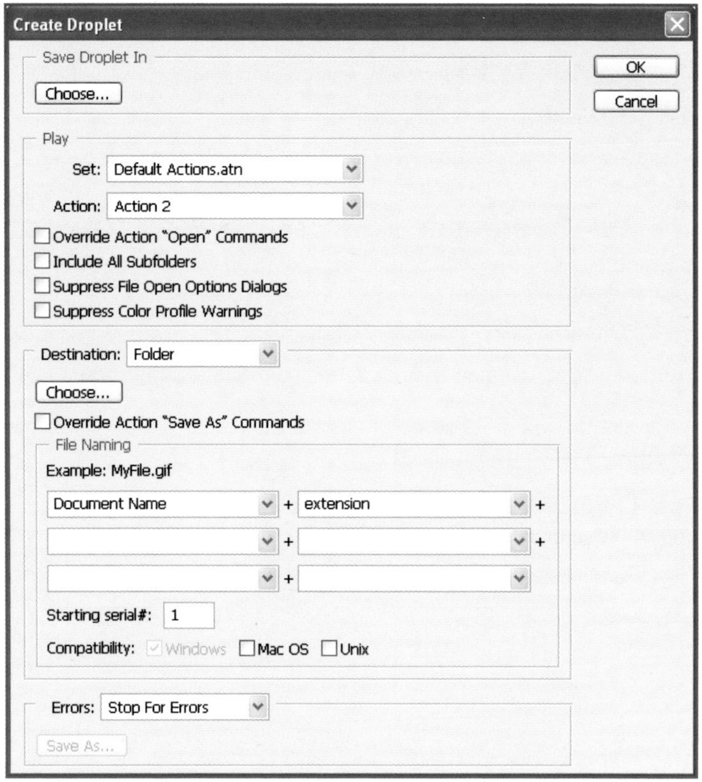

Figure 10-4: You use the Create Droplet dialog box to set the options for creating droplets.

3. In the Save dialog box, open the **Save In** drop-down list, and choose the location to save the droplet.

4. Type the name for the droplet in the **File Name** text box.

5. Leave the **Format** as it is.

6. Click **Save**.

7. Open the **Set** drop-down list, and choose the action set for the droplet.

8. Open the **Action** drop-down list, and choose the action for the droplet. The action options are explained in Table 10-1.

9. Open the **Destination** drop-down list, and choose one of the destination choices:

   ● **None** leaves the files open, unless the action includes a Save command.

   ● **Save And Close** saves the processed files in the same location, overwriting the original files.

   ● **Folder** saves the processed files to a new location. Click **Choose** to specify the new location.

10. If you selected Folder as the Destination, you choose the file naming convention using the **File Naming** drop-down lists. Type the starting number for the files in the **Starting Serial #** text box, and choose the operating system file naming compatibility in the **Compatibility** check boxes.

11. Open the **Errors** drop-down list, and choose a method for handling errors. Your choices are:

    ● **Stop For Errors** stops the action if an error occurs.

    ● **Log Errors To File** continues the action when an error occurs and writes the error information to a log file.

12. If you've chosen to use an error log file, click **Save As** to set the location for the error log. You can read the error log with a text editor, such as Notepad.

13. Click **OK**.

QUICKSTEPS

FITTING AN IMAGE

You can resize an image to a set image size using the Fit Image command. This resamples the image and resizes it to the selected size while retaining the aspect ratio. If you have an image that is 400 pixels high by 200 pixels wide and you resize it using the Fit Image command to 200 pixels by 200 pixels, the final image will be 200 pixels high by 100 pixels wide. The aspect ratio (2:1) remains the same, and the longer dimension (the height in this case) is reduced to the specified dimension (200 pixels), and the shorter dimension is reduced proportionally. You can also use Fit Image to enlarge an image.

To fit an image:

1. Open your image in Photoshop.
2. Click **File | Automate | Fit Image**. The Fit Image dialog box is displayed.

Fit Image
Constrain Within
Width: 300 pixels
Height: 200 pixels
OK
Cancel

3. Type the new values in the **Width** and **Height** text boxes.
4. Click **OK**.

TIP

For best results with the Crop And Straighten Photos tool, leave at least one-eighth of an inch between the photos, and have a uniform color behind the photos (usually the scanner cover). Crop And Straighten Photos works best with images with clearly delineated edges.

You can also create droplets in ImageReady, though there are fewer options available. To create a droplet in ImageReady:

● Drag the action from the Actions palette to the desktop.

–Or–

1. Select the action.
2. Open the **Actions** palette, and choose **Create Droplet**. This opens the Save This Action As A Droplet dialog box.
3. In the Save This Action As A Droplet dialog box, open the **Save In** drop-down list, and choose a location for the droplet.
4. Type a name for it in the File Name text box.
5. Click **OK**.

Crop and Straighten Photos

When you scan a group of photographs, it can be easier to scan several at once, rather than one at a time. This creates a single image file that you need to cut into separate images for each photo. Each photo will probably need to be straightened also, as it's difficult to have all the photos lined up evenly on the scanner bed. This is what the Crop And Straighten Photos tool does—crops the individual images, creating a separate file for each one, and straightens each one at the same time.

To use the Crop And Straighten Photo tool:

1. Open your scanned image.
2. Select the images to process: the entire image is the default, or you can draw a selection border around just the photos you want to crop and straighten.
3. Click **File | Automate | Crop And Straighten Photos**.
4. Save the individual images that are created.

Use Picture Package

When you print an image, you want to use the paper as efficiently as possible. You don't want to print one 4 × 5 inch picture on an 8.5 × 11 inch sheet of paper. You use Picture Package to place multiple copies of an image, or multiple images, in multiple sizes on a single sheet of paper. This is similar to the picture packages you would get from a portrait studio.

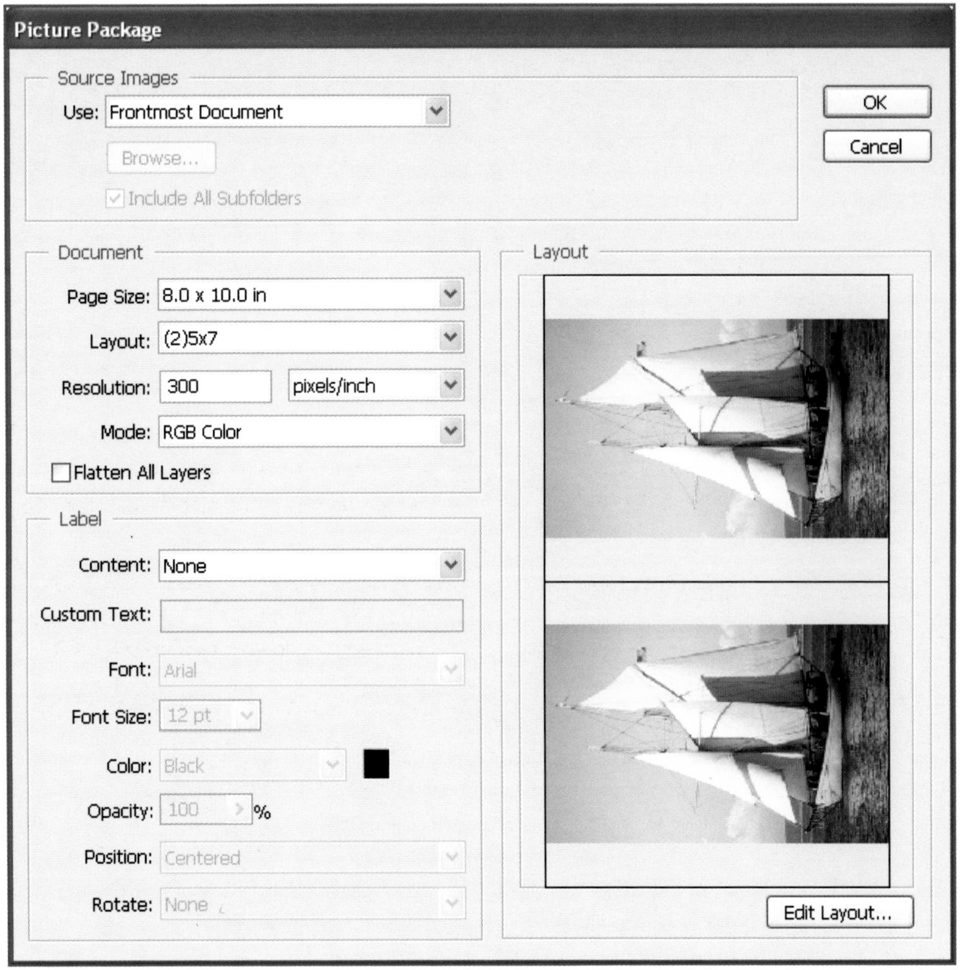

You use the Picture Package dialog box, shown in Figure 10-5, to create a picture package. To open the Picture Package dialog box:

1. Click **File | Automate | Picture Package**.

    –Or–

    Click **Windows | File Browser** to open the File Browser. In the File Browser, click **Automate | Picture Package**.

You now need to select the images to include in your picture package. You can use a single image or multiple images, and you can select your images from several sources. To select your images:

2. Open the **Use** drop-down list, and choose the source image or images for your picture package. Your options are:

    - **File** to use an image file that's not currently open

    - **Folder** to open a folder of images

    - **Frontmost Document** to use the active image open in Photoshop

    - **Selected Images From File Browser** to use the images you've selected in the File Browser (The File Browser must be open for this option to be available.)

Figure 10-5: You use the Picture Package dialog box to set the options for printing picture packages.

NOTE

If you choose Folder as your image source, you can also select the Include All Subfolders check box to include all the subfolders in the selected folder.

NOTE

Some standard larger photographic paper and print sizes are 5.0 × 7.0 inches, 8.0 × 10.0 inches, 11.0 × 14.0 inches, and 16.0 × 20.0 inches. Picture frames for these sizes are readily available.

3. If you chose File or Folder, the Browse button is active. Click **Browse** to open:

- The **Select An Image File** dialog box, if you chose File

- The **Browse For Folder** dialog box, if you chose Folder

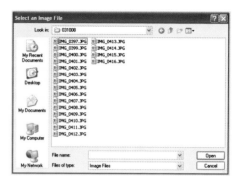

4. Your picture package will display the image you've chosen. You can add more images or change the image, but first you should set the properties of the picture package. To set the properties:

- Open the **Page Size** drop-down list, and choose the size of paper your printer will use. The choices are 8.0 × 10.0 inches, 10.0 × 16.0 inches, and 11.0 × 17.0 inches. These are a mix of standard photographic paper and office paper sizes. Choose the one closest to the size of paper your printer will use, but it must not be larger than your printer's paper size.

- Open the **Layout** dialog box, and choose the layout for your image or images on the page. The choices displayed will depend on the size of paper you chose from the Page Size drop-down list. The choices for the 8.0 × 10.0 page size are shown here.

5. Type the resolution for the printed image in the Resolution text box. This should be higher than for web use; 300 pixels/inch is a good choice.

(2)5x7
(1)5x7 (2)2.5x3.5 (4)2x2.5
(1)5x7 (2)3.5x5
(1)5x7 (8)2x2.5
(1)5x7 (4)2.5x3.25 (2)1.5x2
(1)5x7 (4)2.5x3.5
(4)4x5
(2)4x5 (2)2.5x3.5 (4)2x2.5
(2)4x5 (8)2x2.5
(2)4x5 (4)2.5x3.5
(4)3.5x5
(20)2x2
(16)2x2.5
(8)2.5x3.5
(4)2.5x3.5 (8)2x2.5
(9)2.5x3.25

NOTE

Images for use on the Web generally use a resolution of 72 pixels per inch, but printed images should use a higher resolution. If the resolution is too low, the image will suffer from *pixelation*. This gives a jagged look because each pixel is too large; it is particularly noticeable in curved lines. A resolution of 300 pixels per inch is better for printed images. If your original is at a lower resolution, it is resampled to the higher resolution. For the highest quality, your original should be at least as large as the largest image in your picture package and have a resolution of at least 300 pixels per inch.

NOTE

Unless you want a grayscale image, you should use RGB Color or CMYK color. You should run a test with your printer to see which works best for you.

6. Open the unit drop-down list, and choose **pixels/inch**.

7. Open the **Mode** drop-down list, and choose a color mode. Your choices are:

   • **Grayscale**, which will produce an image with only gray tones, including black and white

   • **RGB Color**, which is the system used by computer monitors

   • **CMYK Color**, which is the color system used by commercial printers but not photographic prints (CMYK stands for Cyan, Magenta, Yellow, and Black.)

   • **Lab Color**, which is a color mode used by Photoshop to convert between other color modes (Lab color images can be printed by PostScript Level 2 and 3 printers. If you don't have one of these printers you should use a different color mode.)

8. Select the **Flatten Image** check box if you want all the layers in your image merged. This doesn't affect the original image, only the picture package. This option is most meaningful if you have added a label to the image, which is described in the following steps. If you flatten the image, you will not be able to edit any labels in your saved picture package. If you don't flatten the image, you will be able to edit the labels, but your picture package file will be larger.

9. If you want a label to be printed with your image, open the **Content** drop-down list, and select the type of label. The label will be printed with each individual image. Your choices are:

   • **None** doesn't print a label.

   • **Custom Text** allows you to enter text, which will be printed with the image, in the Custom Text text box.

   • **Filename** prints the file name of the image.

   • **Copyright** prints the copyright information that is part of the image file.

   • **Description** prints the description information that is part of the image file.

   • **Credit** prints the credit information that is part of the image file.

   • **Title** prints the title information that is part of the image file.

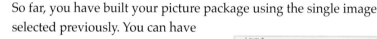

Alcyone01.psd

Description	Description
Camera Data 1	
Camera Data 2	
Categories	Document Title: Alcyone
History	Author: Erik Poulsen
Origin	Description: Alcyone under sail during the Wooden Boat Festival.
Advanced	

Description Writer: Erik Poulsen

Keywords: Alcyone; Wooden Boat Festival

ⓘ Commas can be used to separate keywords

Copyright Status: Copyrighted

Copyright Notice: Erik B. Poulsen - All Rights Reserved

Copyright Info URL:

Go To URL...

Powered By
xmp

Created: 1/14/2004
Modified: 1/17/2004

Application: Adobe Photoshop CS
Format: application/vnd.adobe.ph

OK   Cancel

Figure 10-6: You use the file information dialog box to save information about an image as part of the image.

TIP

You edit the file information that can be printed with your picture package in the dialog box shown in Figure 10-6. Click **File | File Info** to open the dialog box.

10. If you select Custom Text from the Content drop-down list, type the text in the Custom Text text box.

11. Open the **Font** drop-down list, and choose a font. Your choices are Courier, Arial, and Times New Roman.

12. Open the **Font Size** drop-down list, and choose the size of the font.

13. Open the **Color** drop-down list, and choose the color for the text. Your choices are Black, White, and Custom—chosen with the Color Picker dialog box.

14. Use the **Opacity** slider, and choose the opacity of the text. You can have any setting from 0 to 100 percent.

15. Open the **Position** drop-down list, and choose the location of the text in the image. Your choices are Centered, Top Left, Bottom Left, Top Right, and Bottom Right.

16. Open the **Rotate** drop-down list, and choose the rotation angle of the text. Your choices are None, 45 Degrees Right, 90 Degrees Right, 45 Degrees Left, and 90 Degrees Left.

ADD OR CHANGE IMAGES IN THE PICTURE PACKAGE

So far, you have built your picture package using the single image selected previously. You can have multiple images in your picture package also. To add or change the images in your picture package:

1. Click one of the placeholders in the Layout pane of the Picture Package dialog box. This opens the Select An Image File dialog box.

2. In the Select An Image File dialog box, click an image file to place in your picture package, then click **Open**. The image is placed in the space that you clicked to open the Select An Image File dialog box, as shown here. If you selected Folder as the source for your images, that folder is the default location for the Select An Image File dialog box, but you can change the location using the Look In drop-down list.

QUICKSTEPS

ADDING COPYRIGHT INFORMATION TO AN IMAGE

When an image is used on the Web, it's very simple for anyone to download the image and use it in their work. There's no way to prevent this, but you can embed your copyright information in the image file so that you can at least prove ownership of the image.

1. Open your image in Photoshop.

2. Click **File | File Info** to open the file information dialog box.

3. In the Copyright Status drop-down list, select the copyright status. Your choices are:

   - **Unknown**, which is used when the copyright status is not known.

   - **Copyrighted**, which is used when you own the copyright or know who the copyright holder is (this might be an organization you work for).

   - **Public Domain**, which is used when the image is in the public domain, that is, when there is no copyright holder.

4. If you selected Copyrighted, type the copyright text in the Copyright Notice text box. Alternately, you can select existing text (created for images previously copyrighted in Photoshop) by clicking the down arrow to the right of the Copyright Notice text box. The text should be something like your name followed by "All Rights Reserved." You could also include contact information such as your e-mail or mailing address and the year.

5. Type the URL of the web site that has detailed information about your terms of copyright in the Copyright Info URL text box. This site would display your terms of use, such as restrictions on using the image or credit for the image.

6. Click **OK**.

3. You can repeat the preceding steps until all the placeholders have an image. If you've selected a single image, all the placeholders will have that image. You can add images in any combination until your picture package is the way you want it.

4. Click **OK**. Photoshop creates a new image, which is your picture package. You can save this image or manipulate it just like any other Photoshop image.

5. If you want to save your picture package, click **File | Save**.

6. In the **Save As** dialog box, select the location to save the file, type the file name in the File Name text box, and open the **Format** drop-down list, and choose the file format. These are the same steps for saving any Photoshop image.

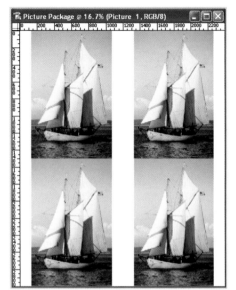

CREATE A CUSTOM PICTURE PACKAGE LAYOUT

You can also customize the Picture Package layout. To customize the layout:

1. Click the **Edit Layout** button in the Picture Package dialog box to open the Picture Package Edit Layout dialog box, shown in Figure 10-7.

2. Type a descriptive name for your custom layout in the Name text box.

3. Open the **Page Size** drop-down list, and choose a paper size. There are more choices here than in the Page Size dialog box that is accessed from the Picture Package dialog box, plus you can create a custom page size.

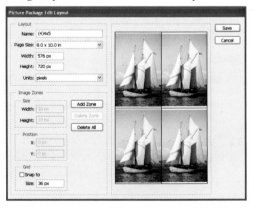

Figure 10-7: You use the Picture Package Edit Layout dialog box to create and save custom layouts for your picture packages.

ADDING DIGITAL WATERMARKS TO AN IMAGE

You can also embed digital watermarks in your images using Digimarc technology. To do this, you must first register with the Digimarc Corporation (http://www.digimarc.com) to get a unique Digimarc ID, which is embedded in your images. If your image is layered, flatten the layers before applying the watermark. If you don't do this, the watermark will only appear on the layer that was active when the watermark was applied. Once you have a Digimarc ID:

1. Click **Filter | Digimarc | Embed Watermark** to open the Embed Watermark dialog box.

2. Click **Personalize** to open the Personalize Digimarc ID dialog box.

3. Type your **Digimarc ID** in the Digimarc ID text box.

4. Type your **Digimarc PIN** in the PIN text box.

5. Click **OK**.

Continued...

4. If you've selected Custom from the Page Size drop-down list, open the **Units** drop-down list, and choose the measurement unit you want to use, then type the dimensions in the Width and Height text boxes.

Next, you set the size and position of the zones (the image areas in the layout). The defaults are the zones that are in the layout that was selected in the Layout drop-down list accessed from the Picture Package dialog box. You can add and delete zones and change the size of a zone. To change a zone's size or placement:

1. Click the zone you want to edit to select it.

2. Type the new width and height in the Width and Height text boxes.

3. Type the position using the X and Y text boxes. These start measuring from the upper-left corner. To place the image in the upper-left corner of the page, the position would be X = 0 and Y = 0. To place the image in the lower-right corner of the page, X would be the width of the page minus the width of the image zone, Y would be the height of the page minus the height of the image zone.

4. If you want the image zones to be aligned with a nonprinting grid on the page, select the **Snap To** check box, and type the grid spacing in the Size text box.

5. To create a new zone, you click the **Add Zone** button, and then enter the dimensions and placement as described above. You can also delete all the existing zones by clicking the **Delete All** button and creating new zones.

6. Click **Save**. The Enter The New Layout File Name dialog box is opened.

7. In this dialog box, type the name for your layout in the File Name text box. Leave the Save In folder as it is (this will save your layout with the existing layouts).

8. Click **Save**. Your new layout will now appear in the Layout drop-down list in the Picture Package dialog box where you can select it.

ADDING DIGITAL WATERMARKS TO AN IMAGE *(Continued)*

6. In the Embed Watermark dialog box, select the type of information to embed from the Image Information drop-down list. Your choices are:

- **Copyright Year**, which is the year you created the image
- **Image ID**, which is an ID you create for the image
- **Transaction ID**, which is an ID you create for the transaction the image is part of (This might indicate the client for whom you prepared the image so you can trace its use back to those to whom you gave permission to use it.)

7. After you've selected the information type to embed, type the specific information in the text box.

8. Select the image attributes you want applied to the image using the Image Attributes check boxes. Your choices are:

- **Restricted Use** if you are limiting the use of the image
- **Do Not Copy** if you do not want to allow copies of the image to be made
- **Adult Content** if the image is of an adult nature

9. From the Target Output drop-down list, select the medium where the image will be used. Your choices are Monitor, Web, and Print.

10. Set the durability of the watermark using the Watermark Durability text box or slider. The more durable the watermark is, the more visible it will be in the image. You can choose a value between 1 and 4.

11. Select the **Verify** check box to verify the watermark's durability after it's been installed.

12. Click **OK**.

To read the watermark after it's been installed, click

Filters | Digimarc | Read Watermark.

Use Web Photo Gallery

There are many reasons to put your photos on the Web. It's a great way to share photos with family and friends, or perhaps you have a portfolio of artwork you want online. This can be a fairly complicated project, involving images and HTML code, which the Photoshop Web Photo Gallery makes simple. Photoshop creates a home page with thumbnail images, each of which is a hyperlink to a page with the full-sized image. You have a set of style templates to choose from for the layout of the pages, plus you can customize an existing layout or create a new layout (both of which require knowledge of HTML programming).

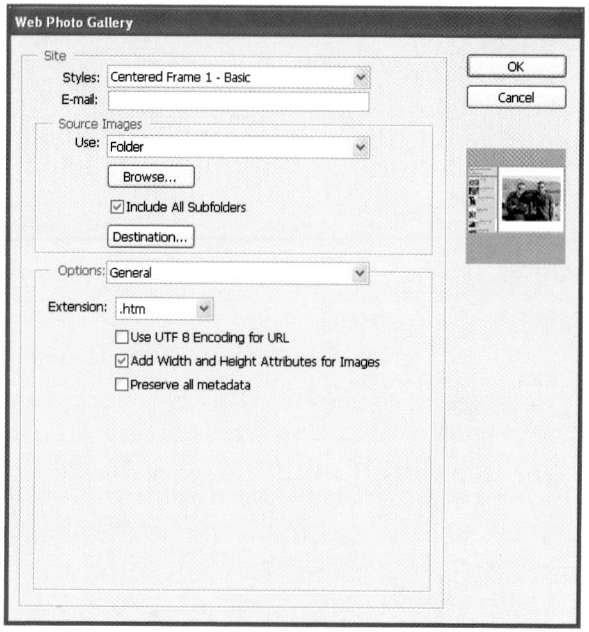

Figure 10-8: You use the Web Photo Gallery dialog box to create web pages to display your images on the Web.

To create a Web Photo Gallery:

1. Click **File | Automate | Web Photo Gallery** to open the Web Photo Gallery dialog box, shown in Figure 10-8.

2. Open the **Style** drop-down list, and choose a style for your Web Photo Gallery. When you select a style, a small preview is displayed in the dialog box.

The styles fall into three general categories:

- The thumbnail images are displayed vertically along the left side of the page, with the full-size image displayed in the center. These styles are Centered Frame 1 – Basic, Centered Frame 1 – Feedback, Centered Frame 1 – Info Only, and Centered Frame 2 – Feedback.

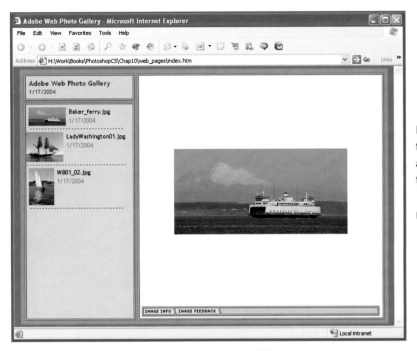

Figure 10-9: The Web Photo Gallery greatly simplifies creating web pages for your images.

- The thumbnail images are displayed horizontally along the bottom of the page, with the full-size image displayed in the center of the page. These styles are Horizontal – Feedback, Horizontal Gray, Horizontal Neutral, and Horizontal Slideshow.

- The home page shows all the thumbnails. To see a full-size image, you click one of the thumbnails. These styles are Simple, Table 1, and Table 2.

In addition to the basic layout, some of the styles include information about the image and the ability for the person viewing the page to enter feedback about the page. Such feedback can be e-mailed to you. Figure 10-9 shows the Centered Frame 1 Feedback style.

USE LINKS FOR IMAGE INFO AND IMAGE FEEDBACK

At the bottom of the web page are links for Image Info and Image Feedback.

- When you click the Image Info tab, the optional image information is displayed. You click the Close tab to close the information display.

- When you click the Image Feedback tab, a form is displayed where the viewer can enter feedback about the image. You can save the feedback, and it will be displayed in the feedback form; or you can e-mail it to the person who created the web page. You click Close to close the feedback form.

SELECT MORE WEB PHOTO GALLERY OPTIONS

1. Once you've selected a style for your Web Photo Gallery, you select the remaining options:

   - If you are using a style that includes feedback, type your e-mail address in the E-mail text box. This is the address to which e-mail from your Web Photo Gallery will be sent.

   - Open the **Use** drop-down list, and choose the location of your source image files. You can choose Folder or Selected Images From File Browser.

   - If you chose Folder from the Use drop-down list, click **Browse**. The Browse For Folder dialog box opens. Choose the folder with your images, and click **OK**. You can also select the Include All Subfolders check box to include all the subfolders in the folder you've selected.

   - Click the **Destination** button. This opens the Browse For Folder dialog box.

   - Browse to the folder where you want to save your completed Web Photo Gallery. Click the **Make New Folder** button to create a new folder for the Web Photo Gallery. Click **OK**.

   - Open the **Options** drop-down list, and choose the options for your Web Photo Gallery. These options are explained in the sections that follow.

2. Click **OK**. Photoshop will generate the thumbnails and other files required and save the pages in your destination folder. The home page will be in the folder you specified, and folders will be created for your full-size images, thumbnails, and web pages. Your default web browser will open to display your completed Web Photo Gallery.

3. You have a number of options to choose from the Options drop-down list. Each has its own set of options, which are displayed below the Options drop-down list. The options are:

   - **General**
   - **Banner**
   - **Large Images**
   - **Thumbnails**
   - **Custom Colors**
   - **Security**

TIP

Photoshop names the Web Photo Gallery home page "index" with the selected extension. If your web service provider requires a different name for the home page (such as "default"), you can change the file name using My Computer or Windows Explorer.

GENERAL

Your General options are:

- The Extension drop-down list sets the file extension (.htm or .html) for the generated web pages. This is a matter of personal preference.
- The **Use UTF 8 Encoding For URL** check box, if selected, conforms the URLs in your Web Photo Gallery to UTF-8 encoding.
- The **Add Width And Height Attributes For Image** check box, if selected, generates WIDTH and HEIGHT attributes for the HTML image tag (IMG).
- The **Preserve All Metadata** check box, if selected, preserves all the metadata with the image.

BANNER

The Banner information is displayed in the browser's title bar (the Site Name) and in the web pages. In Figure 10-9 this information (Adobe Web Photo Gallery and the date) is in the upper-left corner of the page. Your Banner options are:

- You type the name of your site in the Site Name text box. This appears in the browser's title bar and in the page banner.
- You type the name of the photographer(s) in the Photographer text box.
- You type your contact information in the Contact Info text box.
- You type the publication date (the date the gallery was created or updated) in the Date text box.

LARGE IMAGES

The Large Image options apply to the full-size images in your Web Photo Gallery. Your options are:

- The **Resize Images** check box, if selected, will resize your images to the size and options set in the Resize Images options.
- The **Resize Images** drop-down list lets you set the maximum dimension for your large images. The options are Small, Medium, Large, and Custom. The default values are displayed in the Pixels text box. If you select Custom, you type the dimension in the Pixels text box.

TIP

Specifying the width and height of an image is recommended. When these attributes aren't included, objects move around on a web page when it's loaded; the browser doesn't know the size of the images until they are loaded, so it doesn't know where to place objects around them. When the width and height are specified the browser reserves that space for the images and places the other content appropriately.

TIP

Search engines, such as Google and Yahoo!, index the site name. This text should briefly and clearly describe your web site.

- The **Constrain** drop-down list lets you set how the image will be resized. Your options are Width, Height, and Both. This is the dimension that will be constrained to the values you set in the Pixels text box.

- The **JPEG Quality** drop-down list lets you set the compression of the JPEG images. Your options are Low, Medium, High, and Maximum. The selected value is displayed in the text box next to the drop-down list box.

- The **File Size** slider allows you to select intermediate values between the values in the JPEG Quality drop-down list. The range is 0 to 12.

- The **Border Size** text box allows you to set a border around each image. You set the value in pixels.

- The **Titles Use** check boxes—Filename, Title, Description, Copyright, and Credits— determine the information that is displayed with each image on the web page and in the Image Info form.

THUMBNAILS

The Thumbnail options apply to the thumbnail images that Photoshop generates for your Web Photo Gallery. Your options are:

- The **Size** drop-down list lets you set the width of each thumbnail image. Your options are Small, Medium, Large, and Custom. If you select Custom, you type the value in the Pixel text box.

- If you're using a table layout, you can set the number of rows and columns of thumbnails that will be displayed.

- The **Border Size** text box lets you set a border, in pixels, around each thumbnail.

- The **Titles Use** check boxes—Filename, Title, Description, Copyright, and Credits— determine the information that is displayed with each thumbnail.

SECURITY

You can easily download images from any web page, so you may want some text to be placed on the images so it's clear who the owner is. The Security options allow you to easily do this. Your options are:

- The **Content** drop-down list displays the file information that can be displayed. Your options are None, Custom Text, Filename, Copyright, Description, Credits, and Title. If you choose Custom, you type the text in the Custom Text text box.

TIP

The Custom Colors options set the colors of the Background, Banner, Text, Active Link, Link, and Visited Link on the web pages. A link is *active* when the pointer is over it and *visited* after you have viewed the page it links to.

- You select the font for the text from the Font drop-down list. Your choices are Arial, Courier New, Helvetica, Times, and Times New Roman.
- You select the size of the font from the Font Size drop-down list.
- You select the color of the text from the Color drop-down list. Your choices are Black, White, and Custom. Custom opens the Color Picker dialog box, and you select a custom color. You can also click the color square next to the Color drop-down list to open the Color Picker dialog box.
- The **Position** drop-down list allows you to set where the text will be displayed. Your options are Centered, Top Left, Bottom Left, Top Right, and Bottom Right.
- You can rotate the text on the image using the **Rotate** drop-down list. Your options are None, 45 Degrees CW, 90 Degrees CW, 45 Degrees CCW, and 90 Degrees CCW.

NOTE

You can use the Security options in addition to the copyright metadata and watermarks covered in "Adding Copyright Information to an Image" and "Adding Digital Watermarks to an Image."

Create a Panorama with Photomerge

You have probably had an occasion when the view was spectacular, but your camera just couldn't get it all. With Photomerge, you can combine two or more images into a single panoramic image. To create a panorama:

1. Click **File | Automate | Photomerge**. The Photomerge dialog box opens.

2. In the Photomerge dialog box, choose the images you want merged by opening the **Use** drop-down list. You can choose Files, Folder, or Open Files. Open files uses the files that are open in Photoshop.

3. If you choose Files or Folder, click the **Browse** button. For Files, the Open dialog box opens; for Folder, the Browse For Folder dialog box opens.

4. If you are using Files or Folder, browse to the files you want to use in the appropriate dialog box. Your selected images are listed in the Photomerge dialog box list box.

5. When you have the images you want, click **OK**. The merged image is opened in the Photomerge dialog box, shown in Figure 10-10.

Select Image Tool is used to select one of the individual photos in the merged photo

Rotate Image Tool is used to rotate the individual images to make a better match

Set Vanishing Point Tool is used to set a vanishing point for the merged image

Zoom Tool zooms in or out on the images

Move View Tool is used to move images around the work area or to the lightbox

Lightbox stores images that are not part of the merged image

Navigator view shows what part of the image is displayed in the work area and allows you to zoom in or out

Work area displays the merged image

Status bar displays the name of the selected tool or view

Figure 10-10: You use the Photomerge dialog box to create and work with merged images.

6. When you have the merged image the way you want it, using the options described below, click **OK**. Photoshop opens a new image file of your panorama. You work with this image in the same way you would any other Photoshop image.

7. Click **File | Save** to save your merged image. This opens the Save As dialog box.

8. Open the **Save In** drop-down list, and choose the folder in which to save the image.

9. Type the name of the merged image in the File Name text box.

10. Open the Format drop-down list, and choose the file format for the merged image.

11. Click **Save**.

THE PHOTOMERGE DIALOG BOX

You work with your merged files in the Photomerge dialog box work area. You can change the order of the images by dragging them in the work area or to the lightbox to use later. Here is how you may work with the dialog box:

- Zoom in or out of the image using the Zoom Tool or the Navigator view tools.

- Under Settings, use **Perspective** to apply a perspective correction to the image. This is an effect you should use by trial and error—seeing if you like your image better with the Normal or with the Perspective option.

- Click the **Vanishing Point Tool** to set a vanishing point for the merged image. Each photo has its own vanishing point (the point to which parallel lines, like railroad tracks, appear to meet). The default is to use the vanishing point from the center image.

- Under Composition Settings, Cylindrical Mapping is applied to the image after you have the individual images placed where you want them. Cylindrical Mapping is only available when you have selected the Perspective option. It reduces the "bow-tie" effect that the Perspective option can create, as shown in the top image. Applying Cylindrical Mapping reduces this effect, as shown in the bottom image.

- Under Composition Settings, click **Advanced Blending** to reduce color inconsistencies in the image created by exposure differences. It is applied to individual images after they are placed as you want them. You should try to adjust the individual images to make them as close as possible before merging them, but this option is good for fine-tuning the image.

- Click **Preview** to see the effects of the Composition Settings options. This puts the Photomerge dialog box in Preview Mode where you can see the effects of your settings, but you cannot adjust any of the settings.

- Select the **Snap To Image** check box, to automatically align the images when Photoshop detects an overlapping area. For best results, your images should all have areas that overlap.

- Select the **Keep As Layers** check box to keep your individual images as separate layers in the merged image. This allows you to modify the individual images after you have created and saved the merged image.

A

actions, undoing, 20, 197
Acrobat interface, 173
Actions Palette, 136, 192, 193
Adobe Illustrator, 38
adjustment layer, 83-84
airbrush, 19, 96, 99
Algorithms, 166, 170
anchor points, 91
animation
    creating, 183-185
    exporting, 189-190
    frame delay, 184
    importing, 190
    optimizing, 186
    previewing, 185
    saving, 186-187
    SWF (Flash), 188-189
    tweening, 184-185
    viewing, 185
Animation Palette, 183, 184, 185, 186, 189, 190
Art History Brush, 104
Application Menus, 14
automate
    batch command, 198-199
    droplets, creating, 199-201
    editing, 195-197
    recording, 193-194
    play and undo, 194-195
    playback options, 195

B

Background
    anti-aliasing, 53-54
    color, selecting, 19, 62, 114, 115
    copy, 68
    deleting, 68
    definging, 55
    distance control, 77
    erasing, 60-61; 99-100
    Eyedropper tool, using, 115
    feathering, 53-54
    images, extracting from, 57-61
    layers, copying and deleting, 68
    restoring, 20; 56
    restrictions, 71, 72, 76, 83
    selecting, 8; 52; 96
    unlocking, 110

Web, placing on page, 175, 188
    within a gradient mask, 73
    See also images
Background Eraser Tool, 60-61
banners, 211
beveling 78; 147-149
Bit Depth, 29
Bitmaps, 25, 112, 90
blending modes, 80-83
blur, 131, 134; 135, 148, 149, 169
bounding boxes, 143-144, 154
Brush Library, 98
Brushes
    context menu, loading from, 19
    Healing, 132-133
    History, 21-22; 104; 135
    keyboard shortcuts, 14
    Liquify techniques, 107
    options, 18-19
    palette, opening, 19
    presets, 98
    stroke/fill, 93-94
    tips, changing, 18
Brush Tool options, 18-19, 73, 95-98

C

calibrating, 22-23, 24, 152
camera raw images (files), 43-45
canvas, 110, 111-114
Cascading Style Sheets, 172
Channels Palette, 124, 136
Character Palette, formatting with, 138-142
Clone Stamp Tool, 132
collages, creating, 84-87
    colorizing, 134-135
color
    algorithms, 166, 170
    anti-aliasing, 53-54
    automatic levels, changing, 120
    background, 19; 61, 62, 114
    balancing, 124
    Bit Depth, 29
    Bitmaps, 25, 112, 90
    borders, 113
    calibrating, 22-23
    Color Replacement Tool, 123-124
    Curves Command, 119
    defaults, restoring, 20
    definging, 55

desaturating, 21-22
erasing, 60-61
eyeballing, 117, 124
feathering, 53-54
filtering, 127
foreground, 19; 58, 61, 62, 114
highlight and fill, 59
histogram, analyzing with, 115-117
Hue, Saturation and Luminance, 23; 125-126
images, from a preset, 7-8
    indexed, 31
    grayscale, 134-135
Grow and Similar commands, 55
hexadecimal values, 172
Magic Wand Tool, 47-49
manage, while printing, 156-157
matching 128, 6:24-25
mattes, 169, 171
manually adjusting, 121-123
noise, reducing in digital photographs, 136
printing, management, 156-157
red-eye, curing, 123-124
Sampler Tool, 117, 121, 122
    selecting, 48-49; 51-52
    sepia tone, 85-86, 134, 136
    shortcuts, 118
    swatches, 11, 115
    text, 140, 141
    tonal range, 115-118
    touch-ups, 135
    transparencies, 166, 168, 169, 171, 186
    See also images
    See also text special effects
Color Picker, 96, 120,
compression, 27; 174; 169
contact sheets, 157-159
context menus, 11, 18, 19
contiguous and noncontiguous selections, 49
copyright, 162, 206
Crop Command, 114
cropping, 54, 55, 111-112, 153, 156
Crop Tool, 163, 166
cursor preferences, changing, 5
Curves Command, 119

D

defaults
  changing, 120-121
  cursor, changing preferences, 5
  History States, changing, 20
  images, 7
  keyboard shortcuts, 14
  Palette Well, changing, 13
  settings, documents, 57
  restoring, 20
defringing, 55
digital cameras, 42
digital photographs, 42, 136, 162
digital watermarks, 207-208
dimension, 27
documents, 57, 160, 162, 163
drawing
  with Freeform Pen Tool, 92
  freehand, 50-51
  with Magnetic Pen Tool, 92
  with Pen Tool, 63; 89-91
drop down boxes, 9
drop down controls, 10
drop down lists, 9
drop shadows, 76-77, 81, 146-147

E

edges
  anti-aliasing, 53-54
  defringing, 55
  Extract's Smart Highlighting brush, 59
  feathering, 53-54
  touching up, 58, 60
Edge Touchup Tool, 58, 60
edit
  16-bit mode, in, 129
  adjustment layers, using, 130
  colors, 118-120
  digital photographs, 123-126
  gradients, 101
  mode, 143
  presets, 105
  shapes, 95
  straightening, 110-111
  touch-ups, 131, 135
  See also text
  See also type
Elliptical Marquee Tool, 48, 49

embossing, 147-148
erasing, 60-61
errors, fixing, 132, 133
Eyedropper Tool, 19, 115, 117, 121-123, 126, 96, 99
extraction
  cleaning up, 60
  Edge Touchup Tool, 60
  erasing, 60-61
  images from background, 57-61
  filtering, 57, 58

F

feathering, 53-54
fields, See specific fields
File Browser
  Adobe Illustrator, locating files, 39
  camera raw files, 43-45
  customizing, 34-37
  files, arranging within, 33-34
  images, opening with, 7
  options, 199
  palettes, 35
  refreshing, 33
  using, 31-34
  workspace, 36
File Browser Palette, 35
files
  Adobe Illustrator, 39
  animations, 189-190
  arranging, with File Browser, 33-34; 37
  camera raw, 43-45
  copying, 36
  deleting, 36
  document, new, 57
  flagging, 33, 34
  information, saving, 162
  moving, 37
  multiple layers/transparency, 39
  naming, 37, 38
  opening, 6-7
  PDF, creating presentations, 163-164
  raster, 27
  saving, 38-39, 161
  searching for, 36
  vector, 27
  viewing, 34
  Web format, 39
  See also Adobe Illustrator
  See also File Browser

filters
  background extraction, 57, 58
  color, 127
  dust/scratches, 134
  gallery, 106
  Gaussian Blur, 131
  liquify tools, 107
  Motion Blur, 131
  photo, 127
  Unsharp, 130
fixed aspect ratio, 49
fixed size, 49
flagging, 33, 34
Flash player, See Macromedia® Flash™ SWF
Freeform Pen Tool, 92
Free Transform command, 110-111
fly-out menus, 10
foreground
  canvas, 114
  color, selecting, 19; 114, 115
  Eyedropper tool, using, 19; 115
  red-eye, curing 124
  restoring, 20
  selecting, 96
  Web, placing on page, 175, 188
  within a gradient mask, 73
formatting type, See type and text
frames, 77-79
freehand, sketching, 50-51

G

GIF (Graphic Interchange Format) 166-168
glowing, type effects, 148-149
gradients, 72-73, 100
graphics, printing, 165
grayscale, 29, 134-135

H

Hand tool, 8, 9, 10, 16
Healing brush, 132-133
Help, online 10
highlights, 115-120, 123, 124, 125, 129
histograms, 115-117, 129
Histogram Palette menu, 115, 118, 119
History brush, 21-22; 104; 135
History Palette, 20-21, 130
Horizontal Mask Type Tool, 150
Horizontal Mask Type Tool, 150
HTML, 172, 173, 174, 179, 185, 188

hue, 23
hyperlinks, 171
hyphenation, 141-142

I

ImageReady
  button, 9
  fly-out menus, 10
  maps, 171
  opening in, 18
  optimizing, 178
  output options, 173-176
  saving, 170
  slices, 176-177, 178
  values, typing in manually, 11
  Web content palette, 178
images
  analyze (with histogram), 115-117, 129
  animating, 183-190
  background elements, extracting from, 57-61
  Bit Depth, 29
  Bitmaps, 25, 39
  bluring, 131
  camera raw, 42-45
  CMYK, 30
  cleaning up, 41
  collages, 85
  color, correcting, 123-129
  colorizing, 134-135
  compression, 27, 174
  contact sheets, 167-169
  converting, 29-30; 134, 136
  creating, from a preset, 7
  cropping, 54, 55, 111-112, 153, 156
  defaults, 7
  digital photos, 42
  dimension/resolution, 27-28
  extracting from background, 57-61
  fitting, 201
  flattening, 71
  flipping, 110
  formats, 190
  freehand, 50
  grayscale, 29; 134-135
  histogram, analyzing with, 115-117,
  hue/saturation, 125-126
  indexed, 30-31
  information, adding, 172

large, 211-212
layers, matching, 128
maps, 171-172
marquee selection, 48
new document, copying to, 57
new layer, copying to, 57
opening, with File Browser, 7
optimizing, 169
PDF presentations, 173
Picture Package, 169-170, 202-207
presets, 8
previewing, 181-182
printing, 152-157
Quick Masks, 62
resampling, 162, 163
resizing, 27, 111-114; 153, 154
RGB, 29
resolution, 27, 28, 174
rotating, 110
retouch/repair, 132-136
saving, 160, 161, 162, 163, 170
scanners, 40
screen modes, viewing, 15
sepia tone, 85-86, 134, 136
sharpening, 113, 130, 131
smudging, 131
straightening, 110-111
tonal range, 115-118
thumbnails, 7
touch-ups, 135
trimming, 111-112, 114
types, 25-31
zooming, 8-9
See also automate
See also color
See also extraction
See also photos
See also ImageReady
See also selections
See also Web images
Image Map Palette, 171, 173
Image Maps, See images
Info Palette, 117, 121, 122

J

JPEG (Joint Photographic Experts Group), 129, 174, 166,
  168-169, 186, 188-189
justify text, 142

K

Keyboard, 3, 8, 14, 140

L

Lasso Tools, 50-51
layers
  adjustment, 84-84, 130
  backgrounds, 56, 68
  blank, 67
  blend modes, 81-82, 83
  collages, creating, 85-87
  copying, 57; 67, 68, 148
  deleting, 70
  defringing, 55
  dragging, 69
  editing, 72, 73
  effects, 76-80
  exporting, 182
  files, saving, 39; 151
  hiding, 67
  Image Maps, 171-172, 173
  levels, manually adjusting, 121-122
  linking/unlinking, 68
  masks, 72-75
  matching, 128
  merging, 68, 71
  multiple, selecting, 128
  new, 67
  opacity, 81-82
  order, rearranging, 69
  pasting, from another application, 69
  pasting, from another Photoshop document, 69
  Palette, 57, 66, 70, 121, 122, 130, 144, 146
  pixels, sampling, 132, 133
  renaming, 67
  restrictions, 68, 71, 83
  revealing, 67
  saving, 39
  sets, 70
  styles, 79-80;
  text, 143; 144, 146, 150
  tweening, 184-185
  viewing, 20
  See also masks
  See also modes
  See also special effects
Layers Palette, 121, 122, 130, 135, 146, 147, 148, 150
lighting, 79
line art, 41

liquify, 107
load, from Start menu, 2
luminance, 23, 127

M

Macromedia® Flash™ SWF, 183, 188-189
Magic Eraser Tool, 60; 100
Magnetic Lasso Tool, 51
Magnetic Pen Tool, 92
Magic Wand Tool, 48-49
margins, 162
Marquee Tool, 48
marquee selection, 48
masks
  applying, 75
  deleting, 75
  editing, 73
  gradients, 73-74
  hiding, 73
  off/on, 75
  painting, 72
  Quick Mask, 63, 72
  restrictions, 72
  selected area, 72
  selections, adding, 73
  text, 150
  See also layers
mattes, 167, 168, 169, 171, 175
Measure Tool, 111
menu bars, 4, 6, 7, 8, 11, 15, 16
menus, 2-4, 10, 11, 14, 15, 16
metadata, 162, 163, 175, 176
mid-tones, 115-120, 124, 125
modes
  blending, 81-82
  edit (in 16-bit), 129
  highlight/shadow, 79
  multiply, 83
  opacity and fill, 80-81
  screen, 15, 83
monitor, calibrating 24; 152, 155
Move Tool, 70

N

navigating. within document, 10
Navigator Palette, 8, 9

O

Online help, 11, 167, 171
opacity, 78, 79, 80-81
output settings 173-176

P

Paint Bucket Tool, 102
page breaks, specify no, 142
Page Setup Command, 152-153
Palette Options, loading brushes from, 19
Palettes
  Actions, 136
  Channels, 124, 136
  Character, formatting with, 138-142
  File Browser, 35
  Histogram menu, 115, 118, 119
  History, 20-21, 130
  Image Map, 171-172
  Info, 117, 121, 122
  Layers, 121, 122, 130, 135; 144, 146, 147, 148, 150
  Navigator, 8
  opening, 12
  Paragraph, 138-139
  Styles, 146
  Web content, 30, 33, 176, 177, 178, 180, 181, 183
  See also specific palettes
Palette well, 13
panes, resizing 34
Paragraph Palette, 141-142
pasting, from Adobe Illustrator, 38-39
Patch Tool, 133
paths, 38; 93-94
patterns, 102-103
Pattern Stamp Tool, 134
PDF, creating presentation, 163-164
photos
  camera raw images, 42-45
  colorizing and grayscale, 134-135
  cropping, 111-112, 201
  digital, importing, 42
  digital, reducing color noise in, 136
  panorama, 213-215
  picture package, 159-160, 202-207
  repairing, 134
  resizing, 27, 111-114; 153, 154
  scanning, 40-41
  straightening, 110-112, 201
  trimming, 114

Web photo gallery, 208-212
Photoshop, starting and closing, 2-4
picture package, 159-160, 202-207
PNG (Portable Network Graphic Specifications) 8 and 24,
  8, 166-168, 169-170
Polygonal Lasso Tool, 50
preferences
  cursor, changing, 5
  general, changing, 20
  setting, 4
presets, 8, 105
printing, 152-157

Q

Quick Mask, 62-63; 72
QuickTime, 183, 186, 187, 190

R

raster files, 27, 90, 94
Rectangular Marquee Tool, 49
red-eye, curing, 123-124
resolution, 27, 28; 112-113, 152, 153, 155, 158, 160, 164
reverting, 20, 22, 125, 126, 108
RFC (Request for Comments), 187
rollovers, 179-181
rules, 141-142

S

saturation, 23
Save As Command, 160-161
scanners, using, 40-41
screen modes, 15
searching, with keywords, 172
selecting
  color, 48-49; 51-52
  ellipses, 48, 49
  fixed-aspect ratio, 49
  fixed sizes, 49
  Magic Wand Tool, 47-49
  Lasso Tools, 50-51, 53-54
  rectangles, 48, 49
selection borders, 53-54, 55
selections
  adding, 53
  border, converting to a, 53
  cropping, 54
  deleting, 55

duplicating, 56
expanding/contracting, 54; 55
modifying, 52
moving, 56
multiple, 54
painting with Quick Masks, 62-63
saving/loading, 56
subtracting, 53
transforming, 52-53
sepia tone, 85, 134, 136
shadows, 115-120, 124, 125, 129
shape drawing tools, 50-51, 94-95
Shape Layer, pasting from Adobe Illustrator, 39
Sharpen Tool, 131
shortcuts
  drop down button, 14
  keyboard, 14
  layers, 69
  marquee tools, switching, 48
  Page Setup, 162
  start, 3
  tools, 14
Shutterfly, 157
sliders, 9, 43
Smudge Tool, 131
snapshot, 21
special effects, 146-150
spell checking, 142-143
start, from keyboard, 3
Start menu, 2
status bar, 6, 9
statistical information, viewing, 116-117
straight line drawing, 50
Styles Palette, 146
swatches, 11, 115

T

text
  collage, adding to, 87
  creating, 138-139
  edit on a path, 145
  find/replace, 143-144
  flipping, 144
  hyphenation, 141
  justifying, 142
  layers in drop shadows, 77, 81
  page break, specifying no, 142
  paragraph type, 139
  point type, 138-139

skewing, 144
special effects, 146-150
spell checking, 142-143
transforming, 143-144
warping, 144
See also type
text box, 9, 11, 14
thumbnails, 7; 35-36, 125, 168, 169, 212
tonal range, 115-118
toolbox, 16-19
Toolbox palette, 48, 50, 51, 53, 54, 60, 61, 62, 63
Tools
  Background Eraser, 60-61
  Blur, 131
  Brush, 18-19; 72, 73
  Cleanup, 60
  Color Replacement Tool, 123-124
  Clone Stamp Tool, 132
  Color Sampler, 117, 121, 122
  Crop, 54 –55, 63, 111-112, 163, 166
  defaults, 16
  Edge Touchup Tool, 60
  Elliptical Marquee Tool, 48, 49
  erasing, 41; 60-61, 99
  excluding, 52
  extracting, 57, 58
  Eyedropper, 19, 115, 117, 121-123, 126
  gradient, 73, 74, 100
  Hand, 8, 9, 10, 16
  Healing Brush, 132-133
  History Brush, 135
  Horizontal Mask Type Tool, 150
  Horizontal Type Tool, 138, 139, 142, 145
  Image Maps, 171, 172
  Lasso, 50-51
  list of, 16
  liquify, 107
  Magic Eraser, 60
  Magic Wand, 47-49
  Magnetic Lasso, 50
  Marquee, 47-48, 78
  Measure, 111
  Move, 70
  options, 18-19
  Patch, 133
  Pattern Stamp, 134
  Pen, 63
  Polygonal Lasso, 50,
  reconstruct, 108
  Rectangle Marquee Tool, 49; 77

shape, 94
Sharpen, 131
shortcuts, 14
Smudge, 131
stroke/fill, 93-94
touch-ups, 60, 131, 135
Vertical Type Tool, 138, 139, 142,145
zoom, 8
touch-ups, 60, 131, 135
transparency, 80-83
tutorials, accessing, 12
Tweening options, 184-185
type
  committing, 140
  editing/formatting, 140-142
  hyphenating, 141-142
  justifying, 142
  special effects, 146-150
  transforming, 143-144
  See also text

U

undoing changes, 20
URL, 171, 173

V

Variations Command, using to eyeball color corrections, 124-125
vector, files and graphic, 26, 27, 90, 155
Vertical Mask Type Tool, 150
Vertical Type Tool, 138, 139, 142,145
video, streaming, 187
viewing images, 15, 115

W

warp text, 144
Web Content Palette, 30, 33, 178
Web files, saving, 39
Web photo gallery, 208-212
Workspace
  customizing, 13
  File Browser, saving/loading, 36
  preparing/saving, 13
  restoring, 3, 12
  Status Bar, 6
  using, 5

International Contact Information

AUSTRALIA
McGraw-Hill Book Company Australia Pty. Ltd.
TEL +61-2-9900-1800
FAX +61-2-9878-8881
http://www.mcgraw-hill.com.au
books-it_sydney@mcgraw-hill.com

CANADA
McGraw-Hill Ryerson Ltd.
TEL +905-430-5000
FAX +905-430-5020
http://www.mcgraw-hill.ca

GREECE, MIDDLE EAST, & AFRICA
(Excluding South Africa)
McGraw-Hill Hellas
TEL +30-210-6560-990
TEL +30-210-6560-993
TEL +30-210-6560-994
FAX +30-210-6545-525

MEXICO (Also serving Latin America)
McGraw-Hill Interamericana Editores S.A. de C.V.
TEL +525-1500-5108
FAX +525-117-1589
http://www.mcgraw-hill.com.mx
carlos_ruiz@mcgraw-hill.com

SINGAPORE (Serving Asia)
McGraw-Hill Book Company
TEL +65-6863-1580
FAX +65-6862-3354
http://www.mcgraw-hill.com.sg
mghasia@mcgraw-hill.com

SOUTH AFRICA
McGraw-Hill South Africa
TEL +27-11-622-7512
FAX +27-11-622-9045
robyn_swanepoel@mcgraw-hill.com

SPAIN
McGraw-Hill/Interamericana de España, S.A.U.
TEL +34-91-180-3000
FAX +34-91-372-8513
http://www.mcgraw-hill.es
professional@mcgraw-hill.es

UNITED KINGDOM, NORTHERN, EASTERN, & CENTRAL EUROPE
McGraw-Hill Education Europe
TEL +44-1-628-502500
FAX +44-1-628-770224
http://www.mcgraw-hill.co.uk
emea_queries@mcgraw-hill.com

ALL OTHER INQUIRIES Contact:
McGraw-Hill/Osborne
TEL +1-510-420-7700
FAX +1-510-420-7703
http://www.osborne.com
omg_international@mcgraw-hill.com